**Do We Still Need Inspiration?**

# Judaism, Christianity, and Islam – Tension, Transmission, Transformation

Edited by
Patrice Brodeur, Alexandra Cuffel,
Assaad Elias Kattan, and Georges Tamer

# Volume 24

# Do We Still Need Inspiration?

Scriptures and Theology

Edited by
Matthieu Richelle, Camilla Recalcati,
and Martijn Beukenhorst

DE GRUYTER

ISBN 978-3-11-221542-5
e-ISBN (PDF) 978-3-11-129658-6
e-ISBN (EPUB) 978-3-11-129759-0
ISSN 2196-405X

**Library of Congress Control Number: 2023942761**

**Bibliographic information published by the Deutsche Nationalbibliothek**
The Deutsche Nationalbibliothek lists this publication in the Deutsche Nationalbibliografie;
detailed bibliographic data are available on the internet at http://dnb.dnb.de.

© 2025 Walter de Gruyter GmbH, Berlin/Boston
This volume is text- and page-identical with the hardback published in 2024.
Typesetting: Integra Software Services Pvt. Ltd.
Printing and binding: CPI books GmbH, Leck

www.degruyter.com

# Contents

Introduction —— 1

## Part I: **Inspired Writing?**

## Theology within Textual Plurality?

Emmanuel Durand
1    Biblical Plurality: An Ongoing Conversation Embodied in Scriptures —— 13

Konrad Schmid
2    Theologies in the Hebrew Bible and Theology of the Hebrew Bible: Some Methodological Considerations and Case Studies —— 25

## How to Deal with Textual Fluidity?

Matthieu Richelle
3    Textual Fluidity as a Challenge to Inspiration? A Biblical Scholar's Point of View —— 41

Benoît Bourgine
4    Textual Fluidity as a Challenge to Inspiration? A Systematic Theologian's Point of View —— 65

## Part II: **Inspired Reading?**

## Active Participation in Revelation?

Mark W. Elliott
5    Revelation's Activating: The Verbal as the Expression of the Personal Impression —— 83

Benjamin D. Sommer
6    Reception as Revelation: Correlational Theology in Jewish Tradition and Scripture —— 101

## Reception as Revelation?

Régis Burnet
7    New Testament Inspiration and Apocryphal Subtext: The Case of the Epistle of Jude —— 147

Mehdi Azaiez
8    Qur'ānic Inspiration: A Triple Rupture? Remarks on the Qur'ānic Process of Revelation —— 167

Alain Martial, Florence Draguet, Louis de Brouwer, Pedro Valinho Gomes
9    The Respiration of Scripture – Can there be Inspiration without Expiration? —— 183

**List of Abbreviations —— 199**

**List of Contributors —— 201**

**Index of Ancient and Modern Authors —— 203**

# Introduction

This volume is the result of a conference held in Louvain-la-Neuve (Belgium) on May 16-17, 2022, organized by the Scriptures & Theology research group of the Université Catholique de Louvain.[1] The purpose of this interdisciplinary and interreligious research group is to explore the interaction between the exegetical study of scriptural texts and theological reflection on the same texts. To that effect, the group is composed on the one hand of specialists of the Hebrew Bible / Old Testament, of the New Testament, and of the Qur'ān, and on the other hand of systematic theologians. It is the conviction of the members of this group that all can learn from a conversation between those who scrutinize the texts and those who try to think theologically on the basis of these texts within a religious tradition.[2]

Paradoxically, if there is one subject that exegetes and theologians rarely discuss together, it is the "inspiration" of the very texts that both of these kinds of scholars study according to the specificities of their field. In particular, the concept of inspiration is part and parcel of the theological tradition in several Christian confessions, but it has largely receded to the background, if not vanished altogether, in the discussions of biblical scholars. The question "Do we still need inspiration?" might well reflect the perplexity of many exegetes today. Systematic theologians, for their part, often further their own reflections on the subject independently of developments in the field of exegesis, with the risk of remaining purely theoretical.

There are reasons for this situation. On the one hand, academic biblical studies as we know them have been shaped by a move "from Scripture to text."[3] It is because the object of academic study is the text itself, not the text invested with its religious status, that it can be subjected to discussions by scholars of various religious persuasions or none. Moreover, a biblical scholar who also happens to be religious may well privately believe that the texts he or she is studying are inspired, but this does not change anything in his or her own academic work (although, of course, practitioners of exegesis are not immune to unconscious bias). As far as

---

[1] This research group is led by Benoît Bourgine, Régis Burnet, Mehdi Azaiez, and Matthieu Richelle. The conference was organized with the help of a team led by Camilla Recalcati and Martijn Beukenhorst, members of the committee of the research group.
[2] Benoît Bourgine already expressed a desire for this sort of dialogue between biblical scholars and systematic theologians in his book *Bible oblige. Essai sur la théologie biblique,* Cogitatio Fidei 308 (Paris: Cerf, 2019).
[3] To borrow an expression from Michael C. Legaspi, *The Death of Scripture and the Rise of Biblical Studies,* OSHT (New York: Oxford University Press, 2010).

exegesis is concerned, the Bible is studied academically just like any other text.[4] Belief in inspiration is a matter of faith; it is not empirically observable by means of exegesis. That being said, scholars have been so successful in practicing this methodological bracketing of inspiration in the last few centuries, that they have often forgotten inspiration altogether as a theological notion, and they do not know what to do with it anymore.

Moreover, exegetes may find it difficult to square the theoretical notion of inspiration with the practical complexity of the texts they study. Biblical research in the last decades has been marked by new insights about the nature of the biblical texts, stemming from the study of their inner plurality (insofar as they combine and sometimes intertwine conflicting theologies), of their "materiality" (the textual fluidity observed in the divergences between manuscripts), and of their reception (now regarded as an integral part of the "life" of the books). Can these new insights be integrated into a theological reflection on the notion of inspiration? These questions are often explicitly raised about the Jewish and Christian Scriptures, but they also prove increasingly relevant for qur'ānic studies. Furthermore, recent years have seen increasingly sophisticated discussions by theologians on the notion of revelation, and it remains to be seen how they can be connected to the concept of inspiration.

It is in order to discuss such questions and move beyond the current situation that the research group Scriptures & Theology convened a conference and invited specialists from various horizons (Emmanuel Durand, Konrad Schmid, Mark Elliott, and Benjamin Sommer) to provide their perpective on the discussion with professors and students of UCLouvain.

This collection of contributions is organized in two parts. The first part ("Inspired writing?") focuses on two aspects of biblical books that make them more complex and multifaceted than was acknowledged in the past. Thus, the two first contributions reflect on the phenomenon of *plurality* that is inherent to the Bible (whether the Hebrew Bible or the Christian Bible). Is it still possible to find some principle of unity beyond this multiplicity? Can we still speak of a theology of the Bible?

In his important book "Jusqu'où ouvrir le livre?" *Emmanuel Durand* has already addressed this problem from the perspective of both the authors and the interpreters of Scriptures, within the framework of Christian theology. Responding to the invitation of the conference organizers, he offers an updated discussion, partly based on sections of his book that have been translated and adapted, thus bringing to the

---

4 Konrad Schmid, *A Historical Theology of the Hebrew Bible*, (Grand Rapids, MI – Cambridge: Eerdmans, 2019), 113. Mention should nevertheless be made of attempts at a "theological exegesis," in which some exegetes take part, although this raises some problems (see Schmid, *A Historical Theology*, 113-15).

English-speaking world Durand's profound theological thinking.[5] By exploring the processes of kenosis, conversation and embodiment, he argues that we should not try to harmonize the textual pluralities of the biblical text, but that they are resolved in a "paradoxical synthesis" in the figure of Jesus Christ. Durand argues that the Bible exhibits a double kenosis: from divine word to human word and from oral to written tradition. Through the figure of Jesus Christ the Scriptures become reordered so that all point towards him. Thus the Scriptures should be understood as forming a system, an "organism" with an order and a limit. This is created through synergy between human action and the divine operator of inspiration via complex mediations. In the end, the plurality inherent to the biblical testimonies is a lesson of humility for believers; "the letter of Scripture should restrain interpreters and theologians from claiming the viewpoint of God."

Second, *Konrad Schmid* uses case studies to bring to light elements of micro- and macro-theology that can be found in the Hebrew Bible. He shows that Gen 18 is literarily dependent on Lev 2 and that Deut 34 likewise depends on Gen 6. Based on such instances of intertextuality between texts from different books, he argues that we cannot speak of a theology of the Hebrew Bible, but that we should instead speak of a diverse set of different theologies. These theologies exist alongside one another and the various readings they create do not pose a problem but create fruitful conversations, as he shows with a case study from Prov 26. Only at a later stage were attempts made to create a uniform theology of the Hebrew Bible, but this has not impacted the existence of multiple theologies side by side in the text.

The second pair of chapters tackle another factor of complexity that looms large in current biblical research: the notion of textual fluidity. The latter points to the malleability of texts, especially at the hand of scribes during the Second Temple period, the result being that each biblical text exists in many distinct instances, and sometimes in multiple literary editions. What does it mean to speak of an inspired text when the manuscript evidence reveals that it is fluid? In other words, is textual fluidity a challenge to the notion of inspiration? Two contributions aim to answer that question, from the point of view of a biblical scholar and from that of a systematic theologian, respectively.

On the one hand, *Matthieu Richelle* explains why biblical scholars who are still interested in the notion of inspiration may find that some realities are not fully represented in classical formulations of that doctrine. Although the focus of systematic discussions on inspiration has recently shifted from book to text, this actu-

---

[5] Emmanuel Durand, *Jusqu'où ouvrir le livre ? Brève théologie des Écritures*, Lire la Bible 198 (Paris: Cerf, 2021); the passages have been translated and adapted with permission from the Editions du Cerf.

ally raises new questions insofar as the text itself proves unstable or elusive, in the light of textual fluidity. Some books exist in several literary editions; passages and verses appear or disappear depending on the textual witness one considers. Are the "supplements" that appear in only some manuscripts inspired? Should we consider the successive editions of a particular book as all inspired? Do such questions even make sense? Richelle assesses a number of possible approaches to these issues, pointing out their strengths and their weaknesses. Finally, he suggests that recent research on the conceptualization of books in Antiquity could provide a way forward for rethinking our own conceptualization of inspiration. The notions of "vitality of Scriptures" (Hindy Najman) and of "literary projects" (Eva Mroczek) represent fresh metaphors to approach the multifaceted realities of biblical texts.

On the other hand, *Benoît Bourgine* proposes a solution to the "maximal tension" that exists between exegesis and theology. Theology demands unity and contemporary relevance, which exegesis does not provide. Thus, Bourgine remarks, theology often disregards exegesis, especially when it comes to the possible challenges posed by textual fluidity to the notion of divine inspiration. Yet Bourgine argues that the inspiration of Scripture and textual fluidity are two "rigorously heterogeneous realities." Moreover, he endeavors to solve the aforementioned tension by looking at exactly what inspiration means. He argues, with Karl Barth, that inspiration means that the text goes beyond its context and speaks to all generations. From this perspective, it is possible to observe an interplay between inspiration and textual fluidity: when later scribes rewrite the text, they do so with respect for the initial revelation preserved in it and under the guidance of divine inspiration. As a result, although the Scriptures retain a fully human character, the word of God is maintained. Bourgine concludes that textual fluidity is "less a challenge to inspiration than an invitation to a *practical collaboration* of exegete and theologian."

The second part of the book ("Inspired reading?") approaches the subject of the volume from a different angle. Whereas the biblical books have long been considered as "self-sufficient" writings, as if they were "self-contained" and complete reflections of the divine revelation recorded by faithful writers, two recent lines of research have undermined this model. These are the topic of two pairs of chapters.

The first line of enquiry starts from the idea of revelation itself. Far from considering the biblical writers and redactors as passive receptacles of divine revelation, recent research tries to reconsider this notion in all its dialogical complexity.

Thus, *Mark W. Elliott* proposes that the scriptural words encode a special religious experience that does more than just resonate with the readers' religious sense. Elliott states that the Scriptures radiate holiness in a way that interacts with our intuitions and human nature. He analyses revelation as dialectical and dialogical. Revelation is dialectical in its reception and dialogical in that the Scriptures encourage us to think of revelation as relational and personal. At the same time, he argues against the dangers of personalism in relation to revelation; prophetic revelation has nothing to do with the person of the prophet but entails the ability to see symbolically. Finally, Elliott focuses on the canon of Scriptures as the locus of revelation.

In his ground-breaking book *Authority & Revelation*,[6] Benjamin D. Sommer already defended an original approach based on the concept of "participative revelation." This important work, directly relevant to the topic of the conference, is perhaps less well known in Europe than in North America and other parts of the world, and the organizers of the conference invited Sommer to present a paper that would summarize his views. Sommer did more than that; while drawing on sections of his book, he updated his thinking and added new reflections in an effort to connect his book to the concerns of modern theology.[7] In his essay, he goes beyond the correlational theologies of revelation of Heschel and Rosenzweig to present his own *participatory theory of revelation* in which Jewish tradition is the result of a dialogue between God and Israel. First, to explain how the laws of the Torah are divinely inspired, Sommer points out five ambiguities in the description of the revelatory event and its reception by Moses and the Hebrews in Exod 19-20. These five ambiguities raise the question of the extent to which the persons present heard the divine voice at Sinai and participated in the revelation of the law. Second, Sommer deals with correlational theology in the book of Deuteronomy and its source (D) vis-à-vis Exod 19-20. Third and lastly, Sommer shows that the contrasts between the different sources (E, J, and D) in the Pentateuch convey a set of multiple and conflicting memories of the law-giving event. By doing so, the compiled Pentateuch is "forcing the reader to wonder about revelation and to contemplate its nature," and in that way, the reader is invited into the conversation.

The second line of inquiry that leads contemporary scholars to rethink the connection between revelation and inspiration is based on the notion of reception. In light of the developments in hermeneutics that occurred during the second half of the twentieth century, marked by the work of Hans-Georg Gadamer and others, reception is now often regarded as an integral part of the very nature of a book. Against this backdrop, should reception be taken as an integral part of revelation

---

[6] Benjamin David Sommer, *Revelation and Authority: Sinai in Jewish Scripture and Tradition* (AYBRL; New Haven, CT: Yale University Press, 2015).

[7] More precisely, the introduction and the first section of his contribution combine new material and material based on Sommer, *Revelation and Authority*; the second section is substantially similar to (though shorter than) part of chapter 2; the third section is new; the conclusion brings together material from chapter 2 with some new material. Permission was generously granted by Yale University Press.

and/or of the inspiration process? Two papers explore this issue, one in the New Testament, the other in the Qur'ān.

*Regis Burnet* uses the case of the Epistle of Jude to tackle the problem of inspiration in the New Testament in relation to a reference to an "apocryphal" text. Indeed, Jude quotes a verse from 1 Enoch, a writing from the Second Temple period that was not regarded as Scripture in Judaism, as if it contained an authentic prophecy by Enoch. This poses the problem of the canonicity and inspiration of a book that quotes a non-canonical work as a prophetic text. Examining both Jewish and Christian traditions and the history of the canon, Burnet concludes that the criteria used to justify the canonicity of Jude changed drastically throughout the centuries, especially when it came to the relationship of this issue to inspiration; in addition, he addresses the current situation. He also shows that by quoting Enoch, Jude offers an example of how inspiration and revelation can come from other – extracanonical – traditions.

*Mehdi Azaiez* studies the notion of inspiration in the Qur'ān by following a tripartite approach that reveals a triple rupture compared to earlier contexts. First, after discussing the semantics of the Arabic terms related to the notions of "inspiration" and "revelation," Azaiez proceeds to illustrate how the qur'ānic revelation and modality of revelation developed in a polemical way towards the pre-Islamic sacred world. Second, by analyzing a qur'ānic verse (Q al-Ma'ida 5:32), he shows how, surprisingly, an oral tradition known from the Talmud acquires the status of divine revelation in the Qur'ān. As a result, the qur'ānic conception of inspiration goes beyond the earlier, biblical conception on which it is based. Third, Azaiez examines Q. 26:192-227 in order to define the characteristics of qur'ānic revelation and prophetic inspiration; his philological analysis raises the question of the possibility of an active role for Muḥammad in the process of revelation.

Finally, a group of doctoral students from UCLouvain, consisting of *Alain Martial, Florence Draguet, Louis de Brouwer,* and *Pedro Valinho Gomes* offer their collective reflection on the limits of current formulations about inspiration, and propose a new model. In their view, the concept of inspiration, defined as "a collective reception of that which the community believes to be God's word, through the fragility and plurality of given testimonies," should be completed by the concept of *expiration*, by which they mean "the collective and finite testimony of that which the community believes to have received as God's word." The interplay and dynamics of inspiration and expiration create the *respiration* of Scriptures. Taking their cue from Karl Barth's view on the word of God, they argue that the Bible is a favored human testimony of revelation, and that it has its internal differences and politics. However, they argue that the Scriptures invite us to join the dynamic of respiration: an inspired interpretation that creates, in turn, expiration – it is this dynamic that underlies God's self-communication.

With the publication of the conference proceedings, this volume offers a unique contribution to discussions on inspiration of scripture. By bringing together scholars from different disciplines, the aim of the conference was to provide the conditions for a dialogue between two approaches that, at times, are seen as opposites: biblical exegesis and systematic theology. Furthermore, the variety of backgrounds of the invited scholars created an inspiring debate. Thanks to their contributions, the volume as a whole presents the reader with an overview of how inspiration – a central but often overlooked theme – is regarded by different disciplines, religions and, within Christianity, confessions. We hope that the variety of perspectives presented in this volume will both intrigue and inspire scholars in various different fields.

Part I: **Inspired Writing?**

# Theology within Textual Plurality?

Emmanuel Durand
# 1 Biblical Plurality: An Ongoing Conversation Embodied in Scriptures

In order to deal theologically with the textual plurality of the biblical testimonies, I will begin with an observation received from a colleague and friend, an exegete of the New Testament (1). I will then identify three movements or processes, which can be attributed not only to God but also to the authors and/or interpreters of the Scriptures: kenosis, conversation and embodiment (2). Finally, I will argue that the ambiguities and apparent contradictions of textual plurality should not be reduced too quickly and rationally: they find an intermediate resolution in a very real way, a paradoxical synthesis, in the figure of Christ (3). However, this point of convergence still awaits an ultimate resolution and, in the intervening time that is ours, engenders an additional theological plurality. In the end, I will suggest that such unmanageable plurality leads us to be appraised by God.

## 1 The astonishing loop of the biblical testimony to revelation

In the conclusion of his fine book entitled: *"Plus tard tu comprendras." La formation du Nouveau Testament*,[1] the Canadian exegete Michel Gourgues observes a singular phenomenon: in its biblical fabric, revelation assimilates human responses and these in turn become revelation.[2] This observable process seems to me both very simple and loaded with consequences. It is characteristic of a message that is addressed to people and leads to a richly layered form of writing. Very diverse human responses are integrated into biblical revelation.

---

**1** See Michel Gourgues, *"Plus tard tu comprendras": La formation du Nouveau Testament* (Paris: Cerf, 2019). The loop of biblical revelation is convergent with a participatory theory of biblical revelation as highlighted by Benjamin D. Sommer, *Revelation and Authority: Sinai in Jewish Scripture and Tradition*, AYBRL (New Haven, NY: Yale University Press, 2015).
**2** See Gourgues, *"Plus tard tu comprendras,"* 167–71.

---

**Note:** This article includes subsections which have been translated and adapted from Emmanuel Durand, *Jusqu'où ouvrir le livre ? Brève théologie des Écritures*, Lire la Bible 198 (Paris: Cerf, 2021), with kind permission from Editions du Cerf.

https://doi.org/10.1515/9783111296586-002

Correctness and dissonance thus both enter the biblical text. Revelation elicits diverse responses from its recipients: confession, praise, complaints, objections, evasion, refusal, putting God on trial, etc. All these responses are incorporated into the written testimonies to revelation. It is not surprising, therefore, that biblical revelation combines the gift with the very human refusals of that same gift, thus leaving room for imperfections, caricatures, dead ends and counter-testimonies. Revelation is not only pure illumination but also the unveiling of sin that distorts everything. Truth and its disfigurement confront each other within the biblical text, because God and the human being confront each other in the very process of revelation. Should not this lead us to a more integral understanding of the truth of the Scriptures, including the deformities that the light reveals and denounces?

If this is indeed the process of revelation, it must be recognized that not only the Old but also the New Testament are marked by strong tensions. The word of God receives from the Scriptures a unique and true testimony, but it is also possible to discern corrections, or even regressions, within the New Testament itself. This can be seen, for example, between the first Letter of John and the fourth Gospel on the characterization of sin against faith on the one hand and sin against love on the other; or even more so between the pastoral letters and the first Letter to the Corinthians on the role of women in the Christian assembly, with a progressive realignment with the codes of the Greek household.[3] How do we deal with possible corrections or unresolved tensions in listening to the many-voiced revelation of the fullness that has come about in Jesus Christ?

## 2 Three fundamental operations: Kenosis, conversation and embodiment

In this section, my priority is to trace a top-down movement, that of the kenosis of the word of God. Nevertheless, I will pay attention to human agencies and to contingent factors on this path from God to words, texts, and traditions. Moreover, conversation and embodiment call for a growing human involvement, including many contingencies, in the very process and the specific shape of biblical revelation.

---

[3] See Gourgues, *"Plus tard tu comprendras,"* 144–60; idem, *Ni homme ni femme: L'attitude du premier christianisme à l'égard de la femme. Évolutions et régressions* (Paris: Cerf, 2013).

## 2.1 The kenosis of the Word in the flesh and in the texts

The Word of God came in the flesh. It is possible to construct a certain analogy between letters or words and flesh. In the biblical sense, the flesh covers human frailty aggravated by the marks of sin. The Word did not assume a flesh free of this weight. Without sin, Christ nevertheless took on the flesh of sinners. Christ's flesh was passible, mortal, and susceptible to temptation. It was vulnerable and weak. Jesus bore and went through the "passions" of the flesh: hunger, thirst, fatigue, weariness, loneliness, tears, etc. The weaknesses of his flesh veiled the Word, so that recognizing the Son of God was anything but easy. Indeed, flesh and blood proved quite incapable of confessing the Messiah in Jesus – the Son in the flesh. When Peter confesses Christ in the man Jesus, or when the centurion glimpses the Son in the disfigured person of the Crucified One, it is God alone who allows them to pass through the veil of the flesh (cf. Matt 16:17; Mark 15:39).

While flesh may veil the Word and cause ambiguity, nonetheless it also constitutes its expression; and sometimes that expression is right. To recognize this implies describing the flesh not only through the fragility and weaknesses of the human condition, but also as the possibility of belonging to a common world. In the phenomenological sense, the flesh is the organ and the common medium of all the perceptions and emotions of life.[4] In the flesh is felt the immanence of life, that is to say of all that is experienced in "I": I am thirsty, I am hungry, I am in pain, I am sad, I get up, I listen to you, I love you, I breathe in the wind, etc. The flesh is that medium of life through which everything I feel acquires a resonance, an amplitude, and an extension. The flesh gives depth to perceptions and allows them to resonate with each other. Flesh is also the medium of human communications experienced through the perceptions of the senses. In the presence of others, I also perceive that I am perceived, because we belong to a common world through our flesh. This underlies affective and cognitive dispositions such as empathy, understood here in the sense that it gives the subject the ability to perceive how another is affected and to feel an emotion derived from what the other feels.[5]

From such a perspective, the flesh is not reducible to fragility or weakness. The vulnerability coextensive with the flesh is accompanied by a singular capacity for expression. This dimension is fully operative in the case of Jesus Christ. In the gospel accounts, he shows himself to be sensitive and very perceptive. He is also

---

[4] See Maurice Merleau-Ponty, *Le visible et l'invisible* (Paris: Gallimard, 1964), 172–204; Michel Henry, *Philosophie et phénoménologie du corps* (Paris: Presses Universitaires de France, 1965), 253–308.
[5] See Agata Zielinski, "Chair et empathie: Quelques éléments pour penser l'incarnation comme compassion," *Transversalités* 112 (2009): 187–99.

the subject of singular and revealing emotions.[6] Although he took on the flesh of sin, in the eyes of believers his humanity was sinless and he did not commit sin (2 Cor 5:21; 1 Pet 2:22; Heb 4:15). Therefore, Christ's flesh was even more expressive and communicative than ordinary flesh is, without being of a different nature.

Let us remember these characteristics of the flesh of the Word: it is fragile and "weak" like the flesh of sin; as such, it veils the divinity and is subject to the ambiguities of human judgment, especially for sinners; but as common flesh, it is also expressive and empathetic, all the more so because the humanity of Jesus proved holy in the eyes of the disciples and believers. Fragility, possible ambiguity, and expressiveness are also three characteristics of human speech, of letters and words, in which the word of God has lowered itself to become Scripture.

In order to become Scripture, the living word of God undergoes a double kenosis: that of the divine word to the human word; that of the internal or oral word to written traditions.

Let us consider the first stage of this double kenosis. Believers are aware of the effects of contraction or ambiguity that accompany such a lowering. However, they are justified in believing that prophecy and inspiration are the operators of a kenosis without betrayal. Through the mediation of prophecy and inspiration, the divine word gives rise to a just and true human expression, despite all the fragilities inherent in human speech. The human authors of this word are always situated in a particular time and thus limited; they are fallible and sinful; but they are inspired, at certain moments, to somehow pronounce the word of God in human words. In this way, a singular translation from the divine to the human takes place in a context of prophecy and inspiration.[7] This transfer links two immeasurable realities, the divine word and the human word, but the latter is fundamentally a creature of the former. As such, in spite of its inherent fragility and its possible ambiguities, human speech remains capable of being the vector of the divine word. It is true that the earthiness or ease of the prophet, the eloquence or woodenness of his speech, the complexity of the circumstances, or the blindness of any specific historical culture can veil the divine dimension of this word for its recipients. This is all the more frequent since the human authors themselves have to experience a struggle in order to receive the word of God in its novelty, its audacity, its sharpness and, very often, its capacity to turn everything upside down and inside out.

The second stage of the kenosis is more complex than the first. Between the internal word, the articulated word, the oral transmission, and the writing and dif-

---

[6] See Stephen Voorwinde, *Jesus' Emotions in the Gospels* (London: T&T Clark, 2011), 10–11; Emmanuel Durand, *Les émotions de Dieu, indices d'engagement* (Paris: Cerf, 2019), 239–69.
[7] See Adrian Schenker, "De la validité de l'exégèse croyante de la Bible," *RSPT* 97/4 (2013): 449–57.

fusion of the texts, there are several interfaces, with multiple possibilities of alteration, confusion and obscurity. However, the word of God follows the path of this kenosis to the end. The imperfections of a language, the complexities of grammar, the indecisions of punctuation, the approximations of translation, the multiplication of versions, the vagaries of human reproduction of texts, the variations of the canon of the received books. . . all these factors affect the divine word that has become the human word transmitted in writing. Here, complexity is not a late phenomenon, a form of degeneration. From the beginning, the word of God spans diverse languages, is subject to translations, adopts the plasticity of oral traditions, is probably copied in fragments, circulates by means of scrolls and not codices, etc. Hence the analogy, flexible and distant, between the weakness of the flesh assumed by the Word and the precariousness of the letters that compose the biblical texts.[8]

Moving from the living word to the text involves other major challenges. We recognize that prophets and sages, legislators and chroniclers, evangelists and other hagiographers are fundamentally human authors. With their abilities and limitations, they contribute to the translation of the divine word into the human word, and to the written determination of the latter. They *intend to express* the received word in various ways, and they *do express* it through discourses (in the broad sense, including narratives, prescriptions, prayers, etc.) and texts. The partial doubling of *intention* and *expression* applies not only to authors in the narrow sense, but also to the early editors of the biblical and gospel traditions. In an oral or written communication, the intention of the speaker is decisive, but what he actually expresses may partially fall short of that intention. We should not be too quick to conclude that the author's intention is no longer important or that it is completely inaccessible. It should, however, be recognized that the discourse or the text acquires a certain autonomy. It is open to a plurality of meanings and understandings. This is part of the precariousness of all human communication. This dimension is "absorbed" by the word through the words and letters of the texts of the Bible.

In addition to the objective precariousness of the mediations that intervene in the passage from the spoken word to the assembled text, another aspect of the precariousness of words and letters is their exposure to the subjectivity of listeners or readers. From the moment that God speaks in human languages, orally or in writing, he not only consents to the complexity of objective mediations, but he

---

**8** See Vatican Council II, *Dei Verbum*, §13; Emmanuel Durand, *Jusqu'où ouvrir le livre? Brève théologie des Écritures* (Paris: Cerf, 2021), 79–82. Between *Divino Afflante Spiritu* 37 and *Dei Verbum* 13, the differentiated use of the analogy of "incarnation" is instructive in its shift in emphasis: the similitude focuses first on the impeccability of Christ (*DAS* 37), then on the weaknesses of the flesh (*DV* 13).

also exposes himself to multiple subjective understandings (and deformations) as a result of the projections, diversions, and mental blockages of the reader/listener. This is part of the kenosis of the word. Therefore, in order to hear the salvific significance of the biblical word, it must be received through the Spirit who inspired it. The kenosis of the word of God in writing leads to a form of recovery through the proclamation of a living word within the believing community.

## 2.2 God's conversation with a sinful people

Revelation also adopts a "conversational" modality, including spoken words and human responses. However, conversation is not limited to dialogue. It also means the communication and sharing of life (cf. Bar 3:38). When God gives the law to his people, when wisdom is communicated to Israel, God engages in a long-term cohabitation with humanity. The Bible is a first-handwitness to this "conversation," in the double sense of dialogue and the sharing of a common life, with its tensions and conflicts.

Engaged in such a conversation with his people, the word of God is, conjointly, human words, gestures, and actions: shared life. The interlocutors and human partners in this conversation play a determining role in the events of the covenant as it is lived out in history. God's word is sovereign, to be sure, but when it becomes a word addressed to a people or an event requiring witnesses, human responses become co-determinants of the detours or delays of the life shared with God. As in the trial of Jesus, even the misunderstandings, caricatures and misappropriations of opponents are mysteriously assumed and become the paradoxical setting for divine revelation. The Bible traces the gift and the vagaries of the covenant as it is actually received, in faithfulness and in unfaithfulness. There is therefore room in the Bible for failed vocations, inconsistent responses, and collective wanderings. The conversation between God and his people sometimes requires fine discernment to know who is speaking, who is determining this or that, whose will is actually being revealed.

The motif of conversation allows us to move toward a fundamental theology of Scripture. The conversation of Christ Jesus with his contemporaries is the mediation and fulfillment of God's conversation with humanity. By his gestures and his preaching, by his sharing food with sinners, by his astonishment at the faith of some pagans, Christ facilitates access to God. Even more radically, he brings God closer to humanity in his person. Word of God in the flesh, Son of God among human beings, he expresses the divine offer of salvation and communion by his voice and his gaze, his gestures of mercy, his authority and his humility, his being in relationship and being close. Christ singularly brings God closer to humanity and offers humanity the most favorable conditions for a true knowledge of God.[9]

If the long conversation of God with his people, an invitation to all humanity, finds its maximum intensity and clearest expression in the person and life of Christ, the biblical accounts and testimonies of this conversation also find a first resolution in the gospels and other writings that bear witness to Christ the Savior. The ancient law is a code of fidelity for living the covenant, but it is also a prophecy of Christ, as the gospel according to Matthew points out (5:17; 11:13). The full intelligibility of the Torah thus lies beyond the Torah itself, in its fulfillment and its overcoming by Christ Jesus. The same is true for many of the stories of the Old Testament which find their resolution or their correction in the unique figure of Jesus Christ. Even though he is the high point and the key to the Scriptures that precede him, the singularity of Jesus is unprecedented and the synthesis he achieves could not have been anticipated.[10] It is only the figure of Christ, the event of his mission, the authority of his word, and the purity of his gestures that were able to reorder the whole of Scripture.

Following the logic of conversation, the Scriptures integrate the plurality of human responses to the divine word of salvation. Some of these responses, despite their imperfection, are constructive and mark stages of growth; other responses are slow, confused, distorted, caricatured, even hateful. In order to distinguish between a learning process and distortion, fidelity and infidelity, we must not forget that these responses are human and we must turn them over one by one to Christ who alone perfects or ultimately rectifies them.

## 2.3 Canonical embodiment as fields of intertextuality

The word of God communicated in its textual form is also an organic whole. This is the Hebrew Bible or the Christian Bible, which itself knows several canons and organizations: LXX, Vulgate, Orthodox, Ethiopian, Protestant.[11] In order to make this dimension of totality explicit, the analogy of embodiment completes, with

---

**9** See Thomas Aquinas, *De rationibus fidei*, ch. 5, in *The Leonine Collection*, vol. 40, ed. Hyacinthe François Dondaine (Rome: Ad Sanctae Sabinae, 1969), B 62, l. 101–23.
**10** See Hans Urs von Balthasar, *Convergences: To the Source of the Christian Mystery* (San Francisco, CA: Ignatius Press, 1983); Pontifical Biblical Commission, *The Jewish People and their Sacred Scriptures in the Christian Bible* (2001), §21.
**11** See Konrad Schmid, *A Historical Theology of the Hebrew Bible* (Grand Rapids, MI: Eerdmans, 2019), 62–7; Yves-Marie Blanchard, "Naissance du Nouveau Testament et Canon biblique," in *L'autorité de l'Écriture*, ed. Jean-Michel Poffet (Paris: Cerf, 2002), 23–50.

fittingness, that of kenosis and conversation.[12] The "body" of Scripture must then be understood as an animated organism with an internal system and an external limit.

The various books of the Bible form a whole, the canon; and within this whole, the textual units form a system. Apart from being a method of reading or analysis, intertextuality – that is to say, the significant play of borrowings, repetitions, echoes and recollections – is above all a reflection of the singular mode of writing the Bible. It forms a corpus of texts that maintain numerous relationships with one other. Ancient biblical literature often proceeds by successive rewritings, in a culture where transmission and interpretation are carried out by means of integration, adjustments and additions, without reduction. Hence the multiplication of narrative versions composed in successive layers and the repetition of stories through echoes.[13]

The biblical ensemble also has an order and a limit. The canonical order of the books, although it varies from denomination to denomination, plays an important role in interpretation. Thus, even though the primitive religion of ancient Israel probably consisted of exclusive worship of Yhwh in the land of Israel, before it became monotheism in the strict sense, the fact that the Bible begins with Gen 1:1, "In the beginning God created the heavens and the earth,"[14] places the believer within the explicit faith of a mature Israel. The editors of the Torah lead the believer somewhere. The great narrative of Israel, organized according to the internal succession of the Pentateuch and the historical books, forms a framework. The book of Exodus and Isaiah 40–55 respond to each other in a striking way by superimposing election and creation. Certainly, the experience of the exile may have historically influenced, like "a generative rupture," the writing or editing of the traditions of the Exodus. Nevertheless, the canonical order of the great biblical narrative, which is oriented towards a new exodus, presupposes reading the book of Exodus before Second-Isaiah. This is how Jewish eschatology takes shape.

Finally, like any organic body, the word of God in its biblical form has an external limit, although it varies according to the diverse Christian traditions or confessions (Catholic, Orthodox, Ethiopian, Armenian, Protestant). Some writings, as old as or more recent than other books of the Christian Bible, are not accepted as canonical. They can be relevant for getting to know the biblical milieu and for glimpsing how the traditions were spread. They bear witness to a cultural world

---

[12] See Henri de Lubac, *Histoire et Esprit: L'intelligence de l'Écriture d'après Origène* (Paris: Aubier-Montaigne, 1950), 93–4.
[13] See Jer 36:32. The practice of rewriting or "updating" is one of the driving forces of the Hebrew Bible; see Schmid, *A Historical Theology of the Hebrew Bible*, 3.
[14] All bible translations in this article come from the RSV.

and a surrounding literature. They may also have fed certain representations of the Christian imagination, and even the piety of the faithful, notably Marian devotion. However, these writings were not accepted as canonical by the ancient churches in communion or are not considered as such in particular Christian traditions.

Intertextuality, unity, order, and boundaries are found to varying degrees in other bodies of literature. However, for believers, the unity and integration of the biblical books is not merely a human enterprise of compilation and editing. In synergy with complex human mediations, the Spirit of God is the operator of the inspiration of the biblical books and, consequently, the principal artisan of the incorporation of the word into the Scriptures as an organic whole.[15]

The same Spirit who inspired the Law, the Prophets and the Writings for the servants of the covenant led Jesus all his life (Luke 1:35; 3:22; 4:1) and drove him in his mission of "Revelator" (10:21; 11:20). Once Jesus was exalted to the right hand of God (Acts 2:33), the same Spirit constituted, led and inspired the apostolic generation to spread the gospel, orally and in writing (5:32; 15:28). The link between the prophets and Christ and then between Christ and the apostles, always by the same and unique Spirit, underlies the organic unity of all the Scriptures. Because of the constitutive role of the Spirit, the Scriptures are indeed the word of God, in the full sense of the term, only when they are received, read and interpreted through the same Spirit that inspired them.[16] Otherwise, they remain venerable but dead letters.

It does not follow from the inspiration of the Scriptures by God that the Bible is materially a divine book or that it is deprived of a very complex human origin.

How are we then to elucidate controlling metaphors and key representations of biblical complexity and plurality? First of all, are we dealing primarily with oral traditions, texts, scrolls, books, scriptural vitality, and/or editorial projects? How do we connect unknown human origins and the divine transcendence of the Scriptures? Do we really have too serious a problem if we admit that, from the start, traditions, texts, and versions have multiple worldly origins which, to some extent, compete with one another? Within our historical framework of empirical investigation, multiplicity and diversity might be closer to the original than identified inspirations, to be acknowledged through inspired reception. Such a genetic

---

15 On the role of the Spirit in the constitution of a two-fold canon in Luke (Law and Prophets, Jesus and the apostles), see Denis Farkasfalvy, *A Theology of the Christian Bible* (Washington, D.C.: CUA Press, 2018), 159–64.
16 See Jerome, *Commentarii in epistulam Pauli apostoli ad Galatas*, CCSL 77A, ed. Giacomo Raspanti (Turnhout: Brepols, 2006), 189; Ignace de La Potterie, "L'interprétation de la sainte Écriture dans l'Esprit où elle a été écrite (*DV* 12,3)," in *Vatican II: Bilan et perspectives*, vol. 1, ed. René Latourelle (Montreal/Paris: Bellarmin/Cerf, 1988), 235–76.

complexity should not exclude God's inspiration as another level of action and intelligibility from the perspective of transcendence.

To connect the divine origin of the biblical text and the historical genesis of its constitution as a collection of traditions, an analogy might prove useful. The relationship between the divine inspiration and the historical embodiment of Scriptures is somewhat similar to the relationship between the divine creation and the genetic evolution of human beings. The emergence of human uniqueness can be described as a contingent process that took a very long time and has blurred historical origins, with diverse pre-human roots. Divine action cannot be observed here from a purely descriptive and empirical perspective. Nevertheless, the divine action and the historical genesis do not compete with one another. They are fully compatible, as divine causality never excludes worldly contingent processes. We might even press a little bit the analogy by stating that the complex development of biblical traditions works through theological selection and prophetic mutations, with some similarity to natural selection and genetic mutations highlighted in the standard theory of evolution. However, my main point is not to overstress this analogy, but to assert that the top-down perspective I have adopted while dealing with the kenosis of the word of God calls for a full recognition of the complex historical genesis of biblical traditions over a long period of time. Conversation and embodiment are both parts of this process.

## 3 Textual plurality leads us to be appraised by God

My central argument is that the Bible does not deliver a unilateral word from God, but involves us in God's conversation with his sinful, slowly converting people. God, however, retains the extended initiative in this conversation, not least through his gift of the Holy Spirit to the hearers and witnesses of the Word. All human responses to God remain partial here on earth, even when they are fully true. The resolution of tensions and paradoxes still eludes us, even though we identify Jesus Christ as the connecting point and integrating figure of the plural totality of Scripture.

Nevertheless, plurality and unity still alternate: the contraction of plurality into unity gives room to a new kind of plurality. To the original plurality of biblical testimonies (the OT's figures and theologies), condensed in the unique figure of Christ, responds the plurality of theologies (the NT's theologies and those issuing from the NT) which spell out the abundance of the figure of Christ. On both sides of the Christ event, plurality is the indication of both an incompleteness, with regard to God who gives himself up, and of an overabundance, with regard to our receptivity as creatures.

Until the end of the intermediate time between Pentecost and the parousia, the scriptural data resists our attempts at systematization. Attempts at dogmatic harmonization or literary coherence must always be brought back to the open plurality of scriptural testimonies, as an instance of otherness, overabundance, and judgment. At some point, by reading the text, we experience being appraised by God. Here, I mean that the believer is led to experience that the letter of the text should become a living word in order to be received in an existential way. This might occur through liturgy, prayer or worship. In these specific contexts, Scripture places the believer in a new posture of awe, love, and wonder towards God himself, beyond any human grasp or mastery.

The obscurities, contortions and incongruities of the text lead the reader to find himself in a posture analogous to that of a prophet who is exposed to the saturating phenomenon of his vision, in the manner of Ezekiel at the opening of his book (Ezek 1). The unmanageable nature of the text exerts an effect analogous to the unharmonizable nature of the vision.[17] As saturation by vision causes the seer to abdicate, saturation by text will cause readers to do so as well. The irreducible properties of the biblical text thus leave God outside the text, on his heavenly throne, and prevent the reader from believing that he has God's perspective. The biblical text cannot be tamed and thus witnesses that God always stands beyond the "firmament" of the text. The vision and the text transform both the seer and the reader; however, each remains in their own place. They are appraised by what they see and read. The letter of Scripture should restrain interpreters and theologians from claiming the viewpoint of God, or substituting necessarily limiting ideas for his. This cautionary note is consistent with the recurring challenge offered by several theologians who give real prominence to apophaticism in Catholic theology (e.g. Denys Turner, John Caputo, and Karen Kilby).

The excessive abundance of God's word then draws us to God himself. If it is still impossible today to resolve the complexity of the Scriptures by a simple linear theological message, it is ultimately because the purpose of a good use of the Scriptures is silence, union, desire, contrition and praise – all theological dimensions that momentarily put reason at a standstill.

---

[17] I rely here on the main insight spelled out by Baptiste Sauvage, *Le char des Chérubins: Exégèse littérale d'Ézéchiel 1* (Doctoral Dissertation, Fribourg: Faculté de théologie, Université de Fribourg, 08-04-2022).

# Bibliography

Aquinas, Thomas. *De rationibus fidei*, cap. 5. In *The Leonine Collection*, vol. 40, edited by Hyacinthe François Dondaine, B62,1. 101–23. Rome: Ad Sanctae Sabinae, 1969.

Blanchard, Yves-Marie. "Naissance du Nouveau Testament et Canon biblique." In *L'autorité de l'Écriture*, edited by Jean-Michel Poffet, 23–50. Paris: Cerf, 2002.

De La Potterie, Ignace. "L'interprétation de la sainte Écriture dans l'Esprit où elle a été écrite (*DV* 12, 3)." In *Vatican II: Bilan et perspectives*, vol. 1, edited by René Latourelle, 235–76. Montreal: Bellarmin, Paris: Cerf, 1988.

De Lubac, Henri. *Histoire et Esprit: L'intelligence de l'Écriture d'après Origène*. Paris: Aubier-Montaigne, 1950.

Durand, Emmanuel. *Les émotions de Dieu, indices d'engagement*. Paris: Cerf, 2019.

Durand, Emmanuel. *Jusqu'où ouvrir le livre? Brève théologie des Écritures*. Paris: Cerf, 2021.

Farkasfalvy, Denis. *A Theology of the Christian Bible*. Washington, D.C.: CUA Press, 2018.

Gourgues, Michel. *"Plus tard tu comprendras": La formation du Nouveau Testament*. Paris: Cerf, 2019.

Gourgues, Michel. *Ni homme ni femme: L'attitude du premier christianisme à l'égard de la femme. Évolutions et régressions*. Paris: Cerf, 2013.

Henry, Michel. *Philosophie et phénoménologie du corps*. Paris: Presses Universitaires de France, 1965.

Jerome. *Commentarii in epistulam Pauli apostoli ad Galatas*. CCSL 77A, edited by Giacomo Raspanti. Turnhout: Brepols, 2006.

Merleau-Ponty, Maurice. *Le visible et l'invisible*. Paris: Gallimard, 1964.

Pontifical Biblical Commission, *The Jewish People and their Sacred Scriptures in the Christian Bible* (2001), §21.

Sauvage, Baptiste. *Le char des Chérubins: Exégèse littérale d'Ézéchiel 1*. Doctoral Dissertation, Fribourg: Faculté de théologie, Université de Fribourg, 08-04-2022.

Schenker, Adrian. "De la validité de l'exégèse croyante de la Bible." *RSPT* 97/4 (2013): 449–57.

Schmid, Konrad. *A Historical Theology of the Hebrew Bible*. Grand Rapids, MI: Eerdmans, 2019.

Sommer, Benjamin. *Revelation and Authority: Sinai in Jewish Scripture and Tradition*. AYBRL. New Haven, NY: Yale University Press, 2015.

Von Balthasar, Hans Urs. *Convergences: To the Source of the Christian Mystery*. San Francisco, CA: Ignatius Press, 1983.

Voorwinde, Stephen. *Jesus' Emotions in the Gospels*. London: T&T Clark, 2011.

Zielinski, Agata. "Chair et empathie: Quelques éléments pour penser l'incarnation comme compassion." *Transversalités* 112 (2009): 187–99.

Konrad Schmid
# 2 Theologies in the Hebrew Bible and Theology of the Hebrew Bible: Some Methodological Considerations and Case Studies

## 1 Is There Theology in the Hebrew Bible?

To ask the question of "Theologies in the Hebrew Bible and Theology of the Hebrew Bible" presupposes at least an elementary idea of what "theology" might mean in such a context. The term has been very fluid in its 2500 years of history, and a quick consideration of how it will be used in what follows seems to be both appropriate and necessary.[1]

As is well known, θεολογία "theology" is not a biblical term. It never occurs in the Greek New Testament, nor does it occur in the Septuagint. It was first used by Plato[2] and Aristotle[3] and quite simply denotes what the Greek term actually says: "theology" is God talk, talking about God, i.e., myths, hymns, and so on.

This usage continued into late antiquity, including in the early church, where "theology" predominantly meant the praise of God. "John the theologian" as the title of the author of the fourth gospel in the Greek Orthodox Church does not mean that John was a scholar, but that he was lauding and praising God with his gospel.

Not until the eleventh and twelfth centuries was the term "theology" associated with scholarship and systematic inquiry, when the newly founded universities in Bologna, Paris, Oxford and elsewhere adopted the term "theology" in the designation *facultas theologica* for its faculties of theologies. And it seems that this usage of "theology" also prompted Thomas Aquinas to entitle his great work "summa theologica." Today, "theology" is primarily characterized as an academic discipline.

Rather surprisingly, in the Reformation period the term "theology" became quite prominent, but the Reformation also gave it a particular twist. For Martin Luther and others, theology was the result of life experience: *experientia facit the-*

---

[1] See in more detail Konrad Schmid, *Is There Theology in the Hebrew Bible?* (Winona Lake, IN: Eisenbrauns, 2015); idem, *A Historical Theology of the Hebrew Bible* (Grand Rapids, MI: Eerdmans, 2021), 15–60.
[2] Plato, *Respublica* 379A.
[3] Aristotle, *Metaphysica* 1026a, 18–19; 1064b, 1–3.

*ologum*. This is important for the use of the term in the twentieth century: today, it is possible to speak about the theology of Psalm 1, and this usually does not mean what kind of doctrinal theology can be extracted from Psalm 1, but what kind of religious experience can be detected behind Psalm 1.

Within Judaism, the term "theology" has a fairly young and somewhat mixed history. In the context of the "Wissenschaft des Judentums" movement in the nineteenth century, the term "theology" was first enthusiastically received and applied to the Jüdisch-theologisches Seminar in Breslau, which then founded a branch in the Jewish Theological Seminary in New York. For unfortunately obvious reasons, the seminary in Breslau was terminated in 1938. The "Wissenschaft des Judentums" aimed at establishing a historical and critical approach to Judaism in the past and the present and the concept of theology seemed to be an appropriate term for analyzing the Jewish religious heritage and tradition. Samuel S. Cohon, for instance, presents an understanding of theology that corresponds exactly in formal terms to that of Christianity, in that it relates to the organization of religion:

> Theology conceptualizes religious experience. It translates the life and faith of a religious community into ideas that are intelligible and communicable and gives coherent answers to the spiritual questions which press upon the mind. The function of Jewish theology is to render the nature and goals of Judaism understandable and to show Judaism's relevance for our times. [. . .] Religion, supplying the data of theological investigation, naturally precedes theology, even as flowers precede botany, or as health precedes hygiene or medicine.[4]

Later on, however, the notion of "theology" was met with much skepticism for being a primarily Christian enterprise and a reductive approach to the Bible's richness (Jon D. Levenson).[5] Only in the last 20 years has the term "theology" encountered a renaissance in Jewish biblical studies, particularly through the studies of Benjamin Sommer, Shimon Gesundheit, Michael Fishbane, Marvin Sweeney, Isaac Kalimi, and Dalit Rom-Shiloni.[6]

---

[4] Samuel S. Cohon, *Theology: A Historical and Systematic Interpretation of Judaism and its Foundations* (Assen: Van Gorcum, 1971), xv.

[5] Jon D. Levenson, "Why Jews Are Not Interested in Biblical Theology," in *Judaic Perspectives on Ancient Israel*, eds. J. Neusner, Baruch A. Levine, and Ernest S. Frerichs (Philadelphia, PA: Fortress, 1987): 281–307 (German translation by Rolf Rendtorff and Matthias Henze: Jon D. Levenson, "Warum Juden sich nicht für biblische Theologie interessieren?," *EvT* 51 [1991]: 402–430).

[6] Shimon Gesundheit, "Gibt es eine jüdische Theologie der Hebräischen Bibel?," in *Theologie und Exegese des Alten Testaments / der Hebräischen Bibel: Zwischenbilanz und Zukunftsperspektiven*, ed. Bernd Janowski, SBS 200 (Stuttgart: Katholishes Bibelwerk: 2005): 73–86; Benjamin D. Sommer, "Dialogical Biblical Theology: A Jewish Approach to Reading Scripture Theologically," in *Biblical Theology: Introduction and Conversation*, eds. Leo G. Perdue, Robert Morgan, and Benjamin D. Sommer, Library of Biblical Theology (Nashville, TN: Abingdon, 2009): 1–53; Isaac Kalimi, ed.,

Within Christian theology, particularly in biblical studies, "theology" had an ambiguous career in the twentieth century. While the famous opening statement of Ludwig Koehler's theology, "[o]ne can designate a book as theology of the Old Testament if it offers the opinions, thoughts, and concepts of the OT brought into the correct contextual configuration, justified by its content, which is or could be theologically significant"[7] is charming, it marks the beginning of a process of diluting the concept of "theology" in the twentieth century. This process found its culmination in Gerhard von Rad's *Theologie des Alten Testaments* (1957/1960) in which he viewed the retelling of the Hebrew Bible as the only legitimate option.[8] Theology thus lost the requirement of systematization, and this has become the standard of many post-von Rad approaches to a "Theology of the Old Testament." At the same time, the term "theology" has become applicable to a variety of religious texts of ancient cultures; scholars can deal with the "theology" of Gilgamesh, or the "theology" of the Egyptian "Book of the Dead" and so on.[9] In addition, it has become common to speak of "theologies" in the plural – both within and outside of the Hebrew Bible. There are even books named "Theologies in the Old Testament," for instance by Erhard Gerstenberger and Georg Fischer.[10] It is actually only in the wake of von Rad that this development becomes understandable: "theology" is no longer an exclusively scientific project; the term now covers a much broader

---

*Jewish Bible Theology: Perspectives and Case Studies* (Winona Lake, IN: Eisenbrauns, 2012); Benjamin D. Sommer, *Jewish Concepts of Scripture: A Comparative Introduction* (New York, NY: New York University Press, 2012); Marvin Alan Sweeney, *Tanak: A Theological and Critical Introduction to the Jewish Bible* (Minneapolis, MI: Fortress, 2012); Michael Fishbane, *Jewish Hermeneutical Theology* (Leiden: Brill, 2015); Dalit Rom-Shiloni, "Hebrew Bible Theology: A Jewish Descriptive Approach," *JR* 96 (2016): 165–84.
7 Ludwig Koehler, *Theologie des Alten Testaments*, 4th ed., Neue Theologische Grundrisse (Tübingen: Mohr Siebeck, 1966), v.
8 Gerhard von Rad, *Old Testament Theology*, trans. D. M. G. Stalker (Edinburgh: Oliver & Boyd, 1962/1965), vol. 1, 121. Original version: Gerhard von Rad, *Theologie des Alten Testaments*, 2 vols. (Munich: Kaiser 1957–1960).
9 Jan Assmann, *Ägypten: Theologie und Frömmigkeit einer frühen Hochkultur*, 2nd ed. (Stuttgart: Kohlhammer, 1991); for an English translation, see Jan Assmann, *The Search for God in Ancient Egypt*, trans. David Lorton (Ithaca, NY: Cornell University Press, 2001); Angelika Berlejung, "Theologie in Babylon? – Theologien in Babylonien!," in *Theologie in Israel und in den Nachbarkulturen: Beiträge des Symposiums "Das Alte Testament und die Kultur der Moderne" anlässlich des 100. Geburtstags Gerhard von Rads (1901–1971), Heidelberg, 18.–21. Oktober 2001*, eds. Manfred Oeming, Konrad Schmid, and Andreas Schüle, Altes Testament und Moderne 9 (Münster: Lit, 2004): 105–24; Esther Eidinow, Julia Kindt, Robin Osborne, eds., *Theologies of Ancient Greek Religion* (Cambridge: Cambridge University Press, 2016).
10 Erhard Gerstenberger, *Theologies in the Old Testament*, trans. John Bowden (London: Continuum, 2002); Georg Fischer, *Theologien des Alten Testaments*, NSKAT 31 (Stuttgart: Kohlhammer, 2012).

spectrum. How can we evaluate the astonishing career of the term "theology" that now seems, at least in part, to have returned to its origins in Greek philosophy and in the ancient church?

It is quite obvious that the Hebrew Bible *does not contain theology* in a strict, systematized sense. Nevertheless, at the same time, its contents are not nontheological. A helpful description of this quality came from Christoph Levin, who spoke of "the way of the Old Testament to its theology" – he was thinking of the long processes of inner-biblical exegesis that added more and more theology to the texts of the Old Testament during its literary growth.[11] While Rudolf Smend hesitated to use the term "theology" in relation to the Hebrew Bible in his seminal essay on "Theology in the Old Testament," he still found it appropriate to speak of the texts of the Hebrew Bible as having "at least a strong convergence with theology."[12]

Similarly, Nobert Lohfink wrote: "The text type 'theological treatise' first emerged later and in a different cultural context. The Old Testament texts do *not* belong to it in terms of genre. 'Theology' appears in them only implicitly, indirectly, or in a reduced way."[13] Indeed: the distinction between *implicit* and *explicit* theology appears quite helpful for the Hebrew Bible, even if one might retort that the expression "implicit theology" is an oxymoron. But this would only be the case for a very narrow conception of theology. The history of the term "theology" in fact allows for the paradoxical formulation that the Hebrew Bible *contains* but also *does not contain* theology. In the context of its ancient Near Eastern environment, the Hebrew Bible is a unique corpus of tradition whose singularity is observable in its scribal exegetical character: its scribes provide a reflective interpretation of preexisting religious texts. It thereby fulfills – at least for the texts containing reflective interpretations – a basic requirement of "theology," when understood as the reflective examination and interpretation of a religious phenomenon or statement. The Hebrew Bible includes implicit theologies, but they, to a certain degree, already find different levels of explicitation as well.

---

[11] Christoph Levin, "Das Alte Testament auf dem Weg zu seiner Theologie," *ZTK* 105 (2008): 125–45.
[12] Rudolf Smend, "Theologie im Alten Testament," in *Verifikationen: Festschrift für Gerhard Ebeling zum 70. Geburtstag*, eds. Eberhard Jüngel, Johannes Wallmann, and Wilfrid Werbeck (Tübingen: Mohr, 1982): 11–26, repr. as "Theologie im Alten Testament (1982)," in *Die Mitte des Alten Testaments: Exegetische Aufsätze* (Tübingen: Mohr Siebeck, 2002): 104–17.
[13] Norbert Lohfink, "Alttestamentliche Wissenschaft als Theologie? 44 Thesen," in *Wieviel Systematik erlaubt die Schrift? Auf der Suche nach einer gesamtbiblischen Theologie*, ed. F.-L. Hossfeld, QD 185 (Freiburg im Breisgau: Herder, 2001): 13–47 (here 15).

# 2 Micro-theology in the Hebrew Bible: The case of Gen 18:6

Genesis 18:1–16 tells the story of Abraham and Sarah being visited by three men who eventually turn out to be God himself. It is a traditional *theoxenia* story.[14] Ovid's *Baucis and Philemon* (in his *Metamorphoses*) is probably the best-known text of this genre: gods come to visit a pious couple, they are hosted generously, and as a result, the couple is awarded a divine gift. In the case of Genesis 18, God appears as three men – in Christian tradition often interpreted as a *vestigium trinitatis* –, Abraham and Sarah prepare a rich meal for them, and in the end, they receive the divine promise of finally having a son. The preparation of the flatbreads that will be served to the three visitors is described as follows:

> וַיְמַהֵר אַבְרָהָם הָאֹהֱלָה אֶל־שָׂרָה וַיֹּאמֶר מַהֲרִי שְׁלֹשׁ סְאִים קֶמַח סֹלֶת לוּשִׁי וַעֲשִׂי עֻגוֹת׃
>
> And Abraham hastened into the tent to Sarah, and said, "Make ready quickly three *se'ah* of flour (*qemaḥ*), fine flour (*solet*), knead it, and make flatbreads."[15] (Gen 18:6)

It is noteworthy that the flour to be used for the flatbread is described in a double way: As *qemaḥ*, which is regular flour, but then immediately also as *solet*, which denotes something different: a special fine flour. This expression "flour (*qemaḥ*), fine flour (*solet*)" is somewhat puzzling. Which is it that Sarah should use, flour or fine flour?

An answer could be provided by the observation that the specific term "fine flour" (*solet*) can be found in the description of grain offerings to God in the book of Leviticus. Here, the regulation demands that such offerings need to be of fine flour (*solet*):

> וְנֶפֶשׁ כִּי־תַקְרִיב קָרְבַּן מִנְחָה לַיהוָה סֹלֶת יִהְיֶה קָרְבָּנוֹ וְיָצַק עָלֶיהָ שֶׁמֶן וְנָתַן עָלֶיהָ לְבֹנָה׃
>
> When anyone presents a [vegetarian] offering to YHWH, his offering shall be of fine flour (*solet*) (Lev 2:1)

The best explanation, therefore, for the sequence "flour (*qemaḥ*), fine flour (*solet*)" in Gen 18:6 is based on the assumption that either the author himself or a later redactor who read the story in Gen 18:1–16 felt that Abraham and Sarah's dish for the divine visitors should be in accordance with the provision in Lev 2:1: the

---
**14** See Jean-Louis Ska, "Genesis 18:6 – Intertextuality and Interpretation – 'It All Makes Flour in the Good Mill'," in *The Exegesis of the Pentateuch: Exegetical Studies and Basic Questions*, FAT 66 (Tübingen: Mohr Siebeck, 2009): 89–96.
**15** In this article, the translations are based on the NRSV, but slightly adjusted by me.

flatbread has to be made of the correct kind of ingredients that are necessary for offerings. He therefore added "fine flour" (*solet*) after "flour" (*qemah*) in order to highlight Abraham's unconscious following of the Torah that was only later, under Moses, given to Israel. At the same time, this redactor did not feel comfortable with simply replacing "flour" (*qemah*) by "fine flour" (*solet*). It seems that the text as it stood already had some authority, so that the redactor was unwilling or even unable to rewrite it – he simply added to it.

What does this mean with regard to the theology of such a story? Apparently, the current formulation of Gen 18:6 seeks to include Abraham's unconscious observance of the regulation in Lev 2:1. This is not made explicit, but remains an implicit statement for readers who are aware of this intertextual link between Gen 18:6 and Lev 2:1. Given that authors and readers of the Torah, in biblical times, were probably one and the same group, this is not a difficult assumption.[16] This example, however, shows that theology in the Hebrew Bible is a phenomenon that its redactors were reluctant to pinpoint in a specific formulation. Rather, they seemed to find it more appropriate to just hint at an additional dimension of a text in an indirect, implicit way.

## 3 Macro-theology in the Hebrew Bible: Deuteronomy 34 and the death of Moses

The biblical book of Deuteronomy plays out on the final day of Moses's life. It includes his farewell speech to Israel, and in its final chapter, it describes the death and burial of Moses.

Deuteronomy 34:7 states that Moses died at the age of 120 and surprisingly adds that he was in perfect health at the time of his death ("his sight was unimpaired and his vigor had not abated").

This information is especially remarkable because it establishes a certain contradiction to the preceding context. Deut 31:1–2 states:

> ¹וַיֵּלֶךְ מֹשֶׁה וַיְדַבֵּר אֶת־הַדְּבָרִים הָאֵלֶּה אֶל־כָּל־יִשְׂרָאֵל: ²וַיֹּאמֶר אֲלֵהֶם בֶּן־מֵאָה וְעֶשְׂרִים שָׁנָה אָנֹכִי הַיּוֹם לֹא־אוּכַל עוֹד לָצֵאת וְלָבוֹא וַיהוָה אָמַר אֵלַי לֹא תַעֲבֹר אֶת־הַיַּרְדֵּן הַזֶּה:

> When Moses had finished speaking all these words to all Israel, he said to them: "I am now one hundred twenty years old. I am no longer able to go in and out."

---

**16** See Schmid, *A Historical Theology of the Hebrew Bible*, 10–14.

While Moses is also 120 years old in this text, his health is anything but perfect. He is no longer able "to go out or to go in" (לָצֵאת וְלָבוֹא, probably: "march out" and "return home") – that is, he is no longer fit for military leadership. Why, then, does Deut 34:7 emphasize Moses's sound health in contrast to this preceding narrative?

The answer can be found at the very beginning of the Pentateuch. The motif of "120 years" in Deut 34:7 apparently refers back to Gen 6:3:

וַיֹּאמֶר יְהֹוָה לֹא־יָדוֹן רוּחִי בָאָדָם לְעֹלָם בְּשַׁגַּם הוּא בָשָׂר וְהָיוּ יָמָיו מֵאָה וְעֶשְׂרִים שָׁנָה׃

> And Yhwh said, "My spirit shall not abide in mortals forever, for they are flesh; their lifespan shall be one hundred twenty years."

If we read Deut 34:7 in light of Gen 6:3, it becomes obvious that Moses dies in Deuteronomy 34 for the sole reason that his lifespan had reached the limit set by God in Gen 6:3.

Deuteronomy 34:7 and Gen 6:3 form the only literary *inclusio* that spans from the conclusion of the Torah in Deuteronomy 34 to a point prior to the patriarchal history, i.e., into the biblical primeval history. This framing draws a specific theological outline around the Torah as an interpretive point of view.[17]

However, the statement in Deut 34:7 that Moses must die for the simple reason that the span of his lifetime has come to an end and not from any kind of guilt counters Num 20:12 (which likely belongs to the ongoing expansion of the Priestly document in the book of Numbers) on the one hand and Deut 1:34–37; 3:25–27 on the other. Deuteronomy 34:7 instead offers a more neutral theological explanation for the reason behind the prohibition against Moses's crossing into the promised land.

The Priestly tradition in Num 20:12 assumes that Moses's sin was his disbelief that he could make water flow out of a rock by simply speaking to it ("Speak to the rock . . ." Num 20:8). Instead, Moses struck the rock twice with his rod, which was possibly motivated by the thought that he could not make water appear, although the text remains quite ambiguous here, probably out of respect for Moses. But since the Priestly tradition somehow needed to construe a reason for Moses's death prior to the entry into the promised land, the result of this project was the story in Numbers 20.

The Deuteronomistic tradition also needed an explanation for why Moses died outside of the land, but it formulates a different answer than the Priestly tradition. Deuteronomy 1 and 3 include Moses in the collective guilt of the people: "Even with me was Yhwh angry on your account (בִּגְלַלְכֶם Deut 1:34–37; 3:25–27)." Moses is guilty here as well, not for any individual failing, but simply due to his being a member of the people.

---

17 See Schmid, *A Historical Theology*, 142–50.

Both the Priestly and the Deuteronomistic explanations reckon with guilt on the part of Moses, whether it be – in Priestly thought – individual or – conceived in Deuteronomistic terms – of a collective nature. In contrast, Deut 34:7 embraces neither of these two explanations, offering instead a thoroughly idiosyncratic interpretation. Moses is barred from entering the promised land because his 120-year lifespan concluded the day before Israel crossed the Jordan. According to Deut 34:7, Moses's death in Transjordan did not rest on his guilt, but rather on fate – the divinely ordained limitation of the human lifespan.

It is also indicative that this theological characteristic of Deut 34:7 – that Moses's death had nothing to do with a transgression but with fate – agrees with the orientation of Gen 6:3 within the context of Gen 6:1–4 itself.[18] The report here of the heavenly authored assault by the sons of God on the daughters of humanity offers an independent explanation for the flood. Accordingly, the flood did not result from human guilt; it was rather the result of a heavenly downfall. Responsibility is not seen as laying solely in human transgression, but events that, like the flood, can be interpreted as punishment can also be traced back to coincidences of destiny.

This is of primary importance for the later reception-historical equivalency between Torah and "law," which especially took place in the Greek tradition (νόμος *nómos*). As a text complex with a considerable amount of legal material, the Torah neither largely nor exclusively takes a simple retributive approach. Nor is the divine theology of grace that the Priestly document inscribes in the Torah clearly dominant. The redaction that concluded and now constitutes the Torah formulates a third angle – from a wisdom perspective – one beyond punishment and grace as the divine regulator of world events. There are issues in the world that are simply the way they are because they were predetermined.

If we look at the reception of Deut 34 in Josephus, it is interesting that here it is the argument of the fulfillment of the 120 years as well, and not – or better, not explicitly – the notion of personal or collective guilt, that explains Moses's death before the entry into the land:

Παρορμήσας οὖν τὸν Ἰησοῦν ἐπὶ τοὺς Χαναναίους στρατιὰν ἐξάγειν, ὡς τοῦ θεοῦ συνεργοῦντος οἷς ἂν ἐπιχειρήσειε, καὶ πᾶσαν ἐπευφημήσας τὴν πληθύν, 'ἐπεί, φησί, πρὸς τοὺς ἡμετέρους ἄπειμι προγόνους καὶ θεὸς τήνδε μοι τὴν ἡμέραν τῆς πρὸς ἐκείνους ἀφίξεως ὥρισε,

Now when Moses had encouraged Joshua to lead out the army against the Canaanites, by telling him that God would assist him in all his undertakings, and had blessed the whole mul-

---

**18** See Manfred Oeming, "Sünde als Verhängnis: Gen 6,1–4 im Rahmen der Urgeschichte des Jahwisten," *TThSt* 102 (1993): 34–50. See also Walter Bührer, "Göttersöhne und Menschentöchter: Gen 6,1–4 als innerbiblische Schriftauslegung," *ZAW* 123 (2011): 495–515.

titude, he said, "Since I am going to my forefathers, and God has determined that this should be the day of my departure to them . . . ." (Josephus, *Ant.* 4,8,47–49)[19]

Nevertheless, all three explanations for Moses's death in the Pentateuch are still present and discernible for its readers. How should one deal with this spectrum of theological diversity in the Hebrew Bible?

# 4 The ambiguity of the Hebrew Bible's theologies and its significance for a theology of the Hebrew Bible

At this point, it is helpful to introduce an idea of Thomas Bauer, who is a scholar of Islamic studies at the University of Münster. He described the intellectual approach of premodern Islam to reality as "Die Kultur der Ambiguität" ("The Culture of Ambiguity").[20] In his view, ancient cultures did not necessarily strive to render any intellectual, social, or political ambiguity unequivocal in order to live with it. Rather, they tried to balance ambiguities, in order to maintain different, sometimes even contradicting, but nevertheless legitimate perspectives side by side. It was only by the process of the "Islamization of Islam" that this culture of ambiguity was challenged and in certain parts of the Islamic tradition finally lost. The ancient authors who composed their texts, however, strived rather to maintain various philosophical and theological dimensions of the text in the sense that Bauer described and this was at the expense of the overall coherence which, however, might not have been even lamented as a cost in their own view.

A good illustration of how to handle theological "ambiguity" is Prov 26:4–5:

[4] אַל־תַּעַן כְּסִיל כְּאִוַּלְתּוֹ פֶּן־תִּשְׁוֶה־לּוֹ גַם־אָתָּה׃
[5] עֲנֵה כְסִיל כְּאִוַּלְתּוֹ פֶּן־יִהְיֶה חָכָם בְּעֵינָיו׃

Do not answer a fool according to his folly, lest you become just like him.
Answer a fool according to his folly, lest he be wise in his own eyes.

These two verses seem to relate one to another like A to non-A: Someone longing for a clear answer would be unsatisfied when being told to answer a fool accord-

---

[19] Translation: Flavius Josephus, *The Works of Josephus: Complete and Unabridged – New Updated Edition*, trans. William Whiston (Peabody, MA: Hendrickson Publishers, 1987), 124.
[20] See Thomas Bauer, *Die Kultur der Ambiguität: Eine andere Geschichte des Islams*, 6th ed. (Frankfurt am Main: Verlag der Weltreligionen, 2019).

ing to his folly but at the same time being told not to do so. The Greek translation of these two verses solved the problem of the ambiguity of the sequence of the two sayings by introducing an ἀλλά, "but" before the second verse:

⁴ μὴ ἀποκρίνου ἄφρονι πρὸς τὴν ἐκείνου ἀφροσύνην ἵνα μὴ ὅμοιος γένῃ αὐτῷ
⁵ ἀλλὰ ἀποκρίνου ἄφρονι κατὰ τὴν ἀφροσύνην αὐτοῦ ἵνα μὴ φαίνηται σοφὸς παρ' ἑαυτῷ.

But this is of course a harmonization. The Hebrew original certainly has other things in mind than the simplification of this juxtaposition: despite the fact that these two sayings seem to be contradictory, the two verses definitely belong together. The reason why they are juxtaposed is obviously that there is no clear answer to the problem of how to answer a fool. So, is anyone at a loss when encountering a fool?[21]

The question is whether there is a *tertium* besides answering or not answering a fool according to his folly. Is it possible to answer a fool in ways *other* than according to or not according to his folly? What would be a third way to avoid a negative consequence when speaking to a fool?

Seen from this perspective, the two verses (Prov 26:4–5) *implicitly* seem to suggest that a fool shall not be perceived according to his folly *at all*. Or to put it another way, being a fool is *not an unchangeable quality* according to the ensemble of the two verses. A fool can be healed from his folly when not treated according to his folly. Of course, Prov 26:4–5 does not state this point explicitly, but the perspective evolves necessarily when a reader asks how to avoid the dilemma of negative consequences from each of the two stated approaches.

Following a suggestion of Benno Landsberger in his seminal essay on the "Eigenbegrifflichkeit" of Babylonia, one may call this way of the intentional production of meaning a "stereometric reading,"[22] i.e., a reading that transcends the understanding of the text and takes it into a new dimension.

---

[21] See the discussion in Michael V. Fox, *Proverbs 10–31: A New Translation with Commentary*, AB 18B (New Haven, CT; London: Yale University Press, 2009), 792–94. His own conclusion: "By virtue of their placement, v. 5 responds to v. 4 and has the last word. In the end, there may be no choice but to give the fool a tongue-lashing." (794). Arndt Meinhold, *Die Sprüche: Teil 2: Sprüche Kapitel 16–31*, ZBK AT 16/2 (Zürich: Theologischer Verlag, 1991), 438, holds a different opinion than Fox: "Eine wirkliche Gegensätzlichkeit entfällt, wenn beachtet wird, daß es in V. 4 um den Angesprochenen selbst, in V. 5 jedoch um den Selbstklugen geht." See also Konrad Schmid, "Beyond Normativity and Description: The Literary Shape of Ethical Instruction and Reflection in the Book of Proverbs," in *La Bible en face: Études textuelles et littéraires offertes en hommage à Adrian Schenker, à l'occasion de ses quatre-vingts ans*, eds. Innocent Himbaza and Clemens Locher, CahRB 95 (Leuven: Peeters, 2020): 223–32.
[22] Benno Landsberger, "Die Eigenbegrifflichkeit der babylonischen Welt," in *Die Eigenbegrifflichkeit der babylonischen Welt: Leistung und Grenze babylonischer Wissenschaft*, eds. Benno Lands-

This might be an option for handling the many theologies in the Hebrew Bible. We don't need to look for a unifying principle within the Hebrew Bible. The Hebrew Bible pushes its readers beyond its texts and urges them to read them stereometrically. The Hebrew Bible is not just a text, it is a text plus its commentary, it is a collection of various texts, and it is this plurality that probably was responsible for its immense success in Judaism and Christianity.

Of course, the Hebrew Bible and also the Christian arrangement of the Old Testament provide overarching canonical structures that suggest an overall theology of the whole collection.[23] In the Hebrew Bible, at least according to its standard arrangement, Deut 34:10–12 and Josh 1:7–13 seem to place the Torah and the Prophets into a certain hierarchy. The Torah represents Moses's prophecy that is more binding than the prophecy of the subsequent prophets, because Moses was the only prophet to whom God spoke face to face (Deut 34:10). Joshua, the first representative of post-Mosaic prophets, is told to hold on to the Torah of Moses for all his days, a statement that is also repeated at the very end of the Nevi'im, in Mal 3:22–24. The Ketuvim are also sub-ordinated in a comparable way to the Torah, as Psalm 1 demonstrates.

Christian Old Testaments also seem to correspond to a specific overall theology, as the ordering of their books in the large Greek codices of the fourth and fifth centuries particularly demonstrates.[24] In the *Codex Sinaiticus*, the book of Job is put at the end of the Old Testament, in order to highlight the topic of suffering as a theological bridge to the New Testament. The *Codex Alexandrinus* ends with the Psalms of Solomon that present one of the most prominent messianic expectations in biblical literature, thus the theme of the messiah seems to be considered as the main element connecting the Old and the New Testaments. Finally, the *Codex Vaticanus* ends with the book of Daniel, which deals with the "son of man" in chapter 7. Here it is this topic that links the two Testaments.

But all these endeavors to structure the Hebrew Bible and the Old Testament did not reduce the complexity and multiple perspectives of these textual bodies on all the theological topics that they deal with. It is a plurality, but a structured plurality of topics, that can be observed in the Hebrew Bible, and its final redac-

---

berger and Wolfram von Soden (Darmstadt: Wissenschaftliche Buchgesellschaft, 1965): 1–18, esp. 17 (= *Islamica* 2 [1926], 355–372, esp. 371). The term was later taken up by Gerhard von Rad, *Weisheit in Israel* (Neukirchen-Vluyn: Neukirchener, 1970), 42–53. Cf. also Andreas Wagner, "Der Parallelismus membrorum zwischen poetischer Form und Denkfigur," in *Parallelismus membrorum*, ed. Andreas Wagner OBO 224 (Fribourg: Universitätsverlag / Göttingen: Vandenhoeck & Ruprecht, 2007): 1–26, esp. 11–13.

**23** See Schmid, *A Historical Theology*, 61–93.
**24** See Schmid, *A Historical Theology*, 133–40.

tors shied away, and rightly so, from censoring or unifying its different theological positions.

To a certain extent, reading the Hebrew Bible with its many theologies can be compared to looking at an architectural work that also grew over centuries, for example, the Cathedral of Syracuse in Sicily (see figure 1):[25]

**Figure 1:** The Cathedral of Syracuse.

The Cathedral of Syracuse[26] was originally a Greek temple dedicated to the deity Athena and erected in the fifth century BCE. The pillars of the temple were reused and are still visible on the sides of the cathedral today. Starting in the seventh century, a basilica was constructed, reusing the previous building. In 878, the church was transformed into a mosque, but was converted back into a church in 1085. After an earthquake in 1693, the baroque façade was added to the church. The result is a very diverse building that bears witness to its history. Also, for a modern contemplator, it

---

25 Photo: Martijn Beukenhorst.
26 See Rosalia Giangreco, *Templum Majus: Il Duomo Simbolo di Siracusa* (Siracusa: Edessae, 2009).

is possible and even delightful to ascertain the architectural tensions and incoherencies of the building that are responsible for its beauty.

Reading the Hebrew Bible requires a similar openness to perceiving diversity, but as in the case of the Cathedral of Syracuse, it is an achievable and rewarding task to engage with this kind of complexity. In the case of the Hebrew Bible, it is probably fair to say that its multi-layered character is one of the most important reasons for its survival over centuries: the Hebrew Bible's density as a text and its inclusion of a variety of different perspectives made it interesting for a reception that has lasted for centuries. Without the constant process of being read, copied, and commented upon, the Hebrew Bible probably would have been forgotten and maybe then we would only know about it through the possible coincidence of an archaeological finding.

## Bibliography

Assmann, Jan. *Ägypten: Theologie und Frömmigkeit einer frühen Hochkultur*. Stuttgart: Kohlhammer, 1991.
Assmann, Jan. *The Search for God in Ancient Egypt*, trans. David Lorton. Ithaca, NY: Cornell University Press, 2001.
Bauer, Thomas. *Die Kultur der Ambiguität: Eine andere Geschichte des Islams*. 6th edition. Frankfurt am Main: Verlag der Weltreligionen, 2019.
Berlejung, Angelika. "Theologie in Babylon? – Theologien in Babylonien!" In *Theologie in Israel und in den Nachbarkulturen: Beiträge des Symposiums "Das Alte Testament und die Kultur der Moderne" anlässlich des 100. Geburtstags Gerhard von Rads (1901–1971), Heidelberg, 18.–21. Oktober 2001*, edited by Manfred Oeming Konrad Schmid, and Andreas Schüle, 105–24. Altes Testament und Moderne 9. Münster: Lit, 2004.
Bührer, Walter. "Göttersöhne und Menschentöchter: Gen 6,1–4 als innerbiblische Schriftauslegung." *ZAW* 123 (2011): 495–515.
Cohon, Samuel S. *Theology: A Historical and Systematic Interpretation of Judaism and its Foundations*. Assen: Van Gorcum, 1971.
Eidinow, Esther, Julia Kindt, and Robin Osborne, eds. *Theologies of Ancient Greek Religion*. Cambridge: Cambridge University Press, 2016.
Fischer, Georg. *Theologien des Alten Testaments*. NSKAT 31. Stuttgart: Kohlhammer, 2012.
Fishbane, Michael. *Jewish Hermeneutical Theology*. Leiden: Brill, 2015.
Fox, Michael V. *Proverbs 10–31: A New Translation with Commentary*. AB 18B. New Haven, CT; London: Yale University Press, 2009.
Gerstenberger, Erhard. *Theologies in the Old Testament*, trans. John Bowden. London: Continuum, 2002.
Gesundheit, Shimon. "Gibt es eine jüdische Theologie der Hebräischen Bibel?" In *Theologie und Exegese des Alten Testaments / der Hebräischen Bibel: Zwischenbilanz und Zukunftsperspektiven*, edited by Bernd Janowski, 73–86. SBS 200. Stuttgart: Katholishes Bibelwerk: 2005.
Giangreco, Rosalia. *Templum Majus: Il Duomo Simbolo di Siracusa*. Siracusa: Edessae, 2009.
Josephus, Flavius. *The Works of Josephus: Complete and Unabridged – New Updated Edition*, trans. William Whiston. Peabody, MA: Hendrickson Publishers, 1987.

Koehler, Ludwig. *Theologie des Alten Testaments*. 4th edition. Neue Theologische Grundrisse. Tübingen: Mohr Siebeck, 1966.

Landsberger, Benno. "Die Eigenbegrifflichkeit der babylonischen Welt." *Islamica* 2 (1926): 355–72. Repr. in "Die Eigenbegrifflichkeit der babylonischen Welt." In *Die Eigenbegrifflichkeit der babylonischen Welt: Leistung und Grenze babylonischer Wissenschaft*, edited by Benno Landsberger and Wolfram von Soden, 1–18. Darmstadt: Wissenschaftliche Buchgesellschaft, 1965.

Levenson, Jon D. "Why Jews Are Not Interested in Biblical Theology." In *Judaic Perspectives on Ancient Israel*, edited by J. Neusner, Baruch A. Levine, and Ernest S. Frerichs, 281–307. Philadelphia, PA: Fortress, 1987. German translation (by Rolf Rendtorff and Matthias Henze): "Warum Juden sich nicht für biblische Theologie interessieren?," *EvT* 51 (1991): 402–30.

Levin, Christoph. "Das Alte Testament auf dem Weg zu seiner Theologie." *ZTK 105* (2008): 125–145.

Lohfink, Norbert. "Alttestamentliche Wissenschaft als Theologie? 44 Thesen." In *Wieviel Systematik erlaubt die Schrift? Auf der Suche nach einer gesamtbiblischen Theologie*, edited by F.-L. Hossfeld, 13–47. QD 185. Freiburg im Breisgau: Herder, 2001.

Meinhold, Arndt. *Die Sprüche*, Teil 2: *Sprüche Kapitel 16–31*. ZBK AT 16/2. Zürich: Theologischer Verlag, 1991.

Oeming, Manfred. "Sünde als Verhängnis: Gen 6,1–4 im Rahmen der Urgeschichte des Jahwisten." *TThSt* 102 (1993): 34–50.

Rom-Shiloni, Dalit. "Hebrew Bible Theology: A Jewish Descriptive Approach." *JR* 96 (2016): 165–84.

Schmid, Konrad. *Is There Theology in the Hebrew Bible?* Winona Lake, IN: Eisenbrauns, 2015.

Schmid, Konrad "Beyond Normativity and Description: The Literary Shape of Ethical Instruction and Reflection in the Book of Proverbs." In *La Bible en face: Études textuelles et littéraires offertes en hommage à Adrian Schenker, à l'occasion de ses quatre-vingts ans*, edited by Innocent Himbaza and Clemens Locher, 223–32. CahRB 95. Leuven: Peeters, 2020.

Schmid, Konrad. *A Historical Theology of the Hebrew Bible*. Grand Rapids, MI: Eerdmans, 2021.

Ska, Jean-Louis. "Genesis 18:6 – Intertextuality and Interpretation – 'It All Makes Flour in the Good Mill'." In *The Exegesis of the Pentateuch: Exegetical Studies and Basic Questions*, 89–96. FAT 66. Tübingen: Mohr Siebeck, 2009.

Smend, Rudolf. "Theologie im Alten Testament (1982)." In *Die Mitte des Alten Testaments: Exegetische Aufsätze*, 104–117. Tübingen: Mohr Siebeck, 2002.

Smend, Rudolf. "Theologie im Alten Testament." In *Verifikationen: Festschrift für Gerhard Ebeling zum 70. Geburtstag*, edited by Eberhard Jüngel, Johannes Wallmann, and Wilfrid Werbeck, 11–26. Tübingen: Mohr, 1982.

Sommer, Benjamin David. "Dialogical Biblical Theology: A Jewish Approach to Reading Scripture Theologically." In *Biblical Theology: Introduction and Conversation*, edited by Leo G. Perdue, Robert Morgan, and Benjamin David Sommer, 1–53. Nashville, TN: Abingdon, 2009.

Sommer, Benjamin David. *Jewish Concepts of Scripture: A Comparative Introduction*. New York, NY: New York University Press, 2012.

Sweeney, Marvin Alan. *Tanak: A Theological and Critical Introduction to the Jewish Bible*. Minneapolis: Fortress, 2012.

Von Rad, Gerhard. *Old Testament Theology*, trans. D. M. G. Stalker. 2 vols. Edinburgh: Oliver & Boyd, 1962–1965. Orig. German edition: *Theologie des Alten Testaments*. 2 vols. Munich: Kaiser, 1957–1960.

Von Rad, Gerhard. *Weisheit in Israel*. Neukirchen-Vluyn: Neukirchener, 1970.

Wagner, Andreas "Der Parallelismus membrorum zwischen poetischer Form und Denkfigur." In *Parallelismus membrorum*, edited by Andreas Wagner, 1–28. OBO 224. Fribourg: Universitätsverlag; Göttingen: Vandenhoeck & Ruprecht, 2007.

# How to Deal with Textual Fluidity?

Matthieu Richelle
# 3 Textual Fluidity as a Challenge to Inspiration?
A Biblical Scholar's Point of View

## 1 Introduction

The starting point for this contribution is a double observation. On the one hand, biblical scholars often regard the text of the Hebrew Bible as so "messy" (to be blunt) that when they read systematic theologians discussing the inspiration of Scriptures, they tend to wonder if the latter are talking about other books, or books that do not exist in the universe we inhabit. This "messiness" manifests itself in various ways, including the amount of contradictory discourses contained in the Bible, the conflicting ideological drives that exegetes surmise behind many redactions of biblical books, and the fluidity of the text, which seems to randomly flow in many directions and makes the very object whose inspiration is claimed appear elusive; the latter is the subject of the discussion that follows. On the other hand, systematic theologians may be disappointed by the fact that today, many biblical scholars (even those who are religious) dismiss out of hand the notion that the texts they are studying are inspired; to these exegetes, this notion is simply irrelevant.

Part of the unease felt by biblical sholars is certainly due to the fact that a number of them still think about inspiration in terms that retain some "fundamentalistic" overtones, whereby inspiration implies some problematic idea of inerrancy or some idea of textual fixity, for instance. But we should not rule out too fast the possibility that a number of biblical scholars have ceased to consider inspiration as an operative concept for more serious reasons. I am under the impression that systematic theologians rarely devote much time to discussing the concrete complexity of the Bible which I have just designated by the term "messiness." These sophisticated thinkers are aware of, and easily accept, the fact that the biblical texts are the fruit of a complicated compositional history, and that the transmission history is complicated too. Yet this merely concerns the *making* of a corpus and its outline, they often argue; it does not change the fact that this corpus was inspired. To take an analogy, biblical scholars involved in synchronic studies, such as narrative criticism, generally don't deny the insights of diachronic studies; they just work on the text "in its final form." Likewise, systematic theologians rightly leave it to specialists of the historical-critical study of the Bible to discuss the technical details about the formation and transmission of the text; what really matters is that the corpus exists. Yet those specialists tend today to consider that the "messy" aspects of the texts do not merely belong to their formation; they tell us something of the very *nature* of the texts. Thus, the fact that systematic discussions about the inspiration of Scriptures often seem far removed from the concrete, "messy" reality of biblical texts, does not help those biblical scholars who would like to take the notion of inspiration seriously, or at least to "give it a chance."[1]

Overall, the current situation seems to me to be the following: biblical scholars often regard inspiration as an outdated category, while systematic theologians speak of the text in terms that are too abstract in the eyes of exegetes. Let me specify that I am having this conversation in the framework of Christian theology, not only because this is my own religious setting (as a Protestant), but also because the questions I will raise would not necessarily be pertinent, or be the same, in Judaism, where the Masoretic Text is clearly the canonical form of the Bible.[2] And yet my own thinking is mainly informed and stimulated by the admirable work of Jewish biblical scholars and historians, to whom I am deeply indebted. Within Christianity, I am dialoguing with Catholic systematic theologians in this contribution because strong efforts have been made and are still being made in Catholicism to articulate formulations of inspiration. The problems I raise would not necessarily be issues for a number of my Reformed or Lutheran colleagues and friends who do not always attach the same importance to the notion of inspiration, if any, or view it differently. As André Birmelé notes, inspiration has little importance in some modern Protestant systematic theologies.[3] By contrast, inspiration still looms large in contemporary Evangelical theology, but often (not always) with a tendency to retain a fundamentalistic approach to it.

I must add that in my view, biblical scholars should not claim to be able to forge or modify theological concepts; at best, they can help systematic theologians to have a better grasp of the *phenomena* of the text in the hope that it might help those theologians to refine their own discourse. It is in this spirit that I humbly propose the following thoughts, and I insist on the fact that they are purely exploratory. For the same reasons, I believe that part of my role here is to raise some material

---

[1] There are exceptions, of course, among which the document *Inspiration and Truth* published by the Pontifical Biblical Commission, which tackles the issue of the truth of "problematic" texts, and Emmanuel Durand, *Jusqu'où ouvrir le texte? Brève théologie des Ecritures* (Lire la Bible; Paris : Cerf, 2021).

[2] On this subject, see Norman Solomon, *Torah from Heaven: The Reconstruction of Faith* (London: The Littman Library of Jewish Civilization, 2012), 93–112.

[3] André Birmelé, "Les références en dogmatique: L'Ecriture sainte et les confessions de foi," in *Introduction à la théologie systématique*, eds. André Birmelé, Pierre Bühler, Jean-Daniel Causse, and Lucie Kaennel, Lieux théologique 39 (Genève : Labor et Fides, 2008): 57 fn. 29. In particular, he notes that the systematic theologies published by Ebeling and Pannenberg do not include a specific paragraph on the subject of inspiration.

and sometimes naïve questions prompted by the concrete interaction with textual fluidity and a concern for the use of the Bible, especially in a liturgical setting. I will first try to give examples of what is called textual fluidity, then explain in what sense biblical scholars may feel that this reality is not fully represented in classical formulations of inspiration in systematic theology; finally, I will briefly explore several analogies or metaphors used by scholars to grasp the "nature" of the text, in the hope that it may prove stimulating.

## 2 Textual fluidity and its representation in classical formulations of inspiration

### 2.1 Textual fluidity: A brief overview

Awareness of the differences between textual witnesses is far from being a recent discovery; to take but one famous example from Antiquity, the correspondence between Augustine and Jerome illustrates the kind of theological discussion that revolved around textual variants. Rather, what has been (re)discovered in recent times is the full extent of this phenomenon. Thanks to the deciphering of the Dead Sea scrolls and to the renewed study of the Septuagint, scholars have come to realize that the biblical text existed in various forms in Antiquity; moreover, they have now a better grasp of the variety of textual changes to which the texts were subjected.

Textual fluidity refers to the malleability of the text in the hand of ancient scribes. Its manifestations are numerous, and varied. They include the replacement of words and phrases by others, the addition or omission of segments of text that may range from a word to entire chapters; and the rearrangement of passages. In other words, alongside the small variants that many of us know thanks to the critical apparatus of editions like the *Biblia Hebraica Stuttgartensia* (now progressively replaced by the *Biblia Hebraica Quinta*) or the footnotes of study editions of the Bible, there are many large-scale differences.

A good example of a significant addition is found in Judg 6. While prophets are virtually absent from this book, a prophet suddenly makes an appearance in Judg 6:8–10:

> The Lord sent a prophet to the Israelites, and he said to them, "Thus says the Lord, the God of Israel: I led you up from Egypt and brought you out of the house of slavery, and I delivered you from the hand of the Egyptians and from the hand of all who oppressed you, and drove them out before you, and gave you their land, and I said to you, 'I am the Lord your God; you

shall not pay reverence to the gods of the Amorites in whose land you live.' But you have not given heed to my voice."[4]

Biblical scholars have long surmised that this is an interpolation made to the book by a late scribe, imitating the Deuteronomistic theology. Indeed, this brief passage interrupts the cyclical pattern of Judges, which comprises four stages: (1) the people do what displeases God (cf. v. 1a); (2) God is angry and delivers Israel into the hand of foreigners (vv. 1b–6a); (3) the people endure oppression and, often, call out to God (cf. 6b–7); (4) God sends a judge to deliver them (cf. vv. 11–16). The discovery of a DSS fragment confirms this hypothesis: in 4QJudges[a], there is no space for vv. 8–10, the fragment contains the words "the Israelites cried to the Lord" (cf. v. 7a), then there is a lacuna, and the next preserved words, on the next line, belong to v. 11.[5]

In a number of cases, what we observe is not haphazard variations of the same text, but distinct literary editions. The textbook example is Jeremiah, which existed in two editions:[6]

- a shorter edition, which is attested in Greek in the Septuagint, but was, in its main features, the faithful reflection of a short Hebrew model that already exhibited the same characteristics; we possess small parts of a Hebrew text close to this shorter edition in two Dead Sea scrolls fragments (4QJer[b] and 4 QJer[d]);
- a longer edition, represented by the MT; here also, a few Dead Sea scrolls fragments (2QJer, 4QJer[a], and 4QJer[c]) contain a text close to that edition.

Among the main differences between these two editions is the placement of the oracles against the nations (at the end in the MT but at the middle of the book in the LXX, right after 25:12) and many plusses (about 8000 Hebrew words) in the longer edition. The longest supplement is Jer 33:14–26.

In fact, this phenomenon is more widespread than many people think.[7] To varying degrees, it concerns Exodus, Deuteronomy, Joshua, Judges, Samuel, Kings,

---

4 Biblical quotations are from the NRSV.
5 See Eugene Ulrich, "Deuteronomistically Inspired Scribal Insertions into the Developing Biblical Texts: 4QJudg[a] and 4QJer[a]," in *Houses Full of All Good Things: Essays in Memory of Timo Veijola*, eds. Juha Pakkala and Martti Nissinen (Helsinki: Finnish Exegetical Society, 2008): 489–506.
6 For a *status quaestionis*, see Matthieu Richelle, "Jeremiah and Baruch," in *The Oxford Handbook of the Septuagint*, eds. T. Michael Law and Alison Salvesen (Oxford: Oxford University Press, 2021): 259–84.
7 For examples of recent discussions, see for instance Emanuel Tov, "The Nature of the Large-Scale Differences between the LXX and M S T V, Compared with Similar Evidence in Other Sources," in *The Earliest Text of the Hebrew Bible: The Relationship between the Masoretic Text and the Hebrew Base of the Septuagint Reconsidered*, ed. Adrian Schenker, SBL.SCS 52 (Atlanta: SBL, 2003): 121–144;

Ezekiel, Psalms, Song of Songs, etc. The Book of Esther seems to have existed in at least three distinct editions.

Another crucial point is that scholars do not regard it as possible anymore to draw a line between composition and transmission of the text. Scribes copying the text in the last few centuries BCE often, in practical terms, acted in the same way as redactors, freely adding to the text and rearranging it. When was Judg 6:8–10 added? Was it added by a redactor or by a scribe? It is impossible to tell, so much so that the distinction between redactor and scribe might lose its pertinence here.

## 2.2 Basic questions

Against this background, the practical questions that may spontaneously come to the mind of text critics who happen to be interested in the notion of inspiration are: how does this complicated evidence relate to the standard doctrinal formulations about the inspiration of the Scriptures? Is the addition in Judg 6:8–10 inspired? Are the two distinct editions of, say, Jeremiah, both inspired? Do they all constitute "canonical forms" of the same book? Above all, do these questions make sense?

Basically, these biblical scholars may well be under the impression that a number of realities they observe are not represented or mentioned in current systematic discussions on inspiration. These realities include the role played by the scribes/copyists, and the fact that the text existed in a great variety of forms. Textual fluidity may serve as an umbrella term to designate these realities.

Let us consider, by way of illustration, the relevant passage in the magisterial document *Dei Verbum*:

> 11. Those divinely revealed realities which are contained and presented in Sacred Scripture have been committed to writing under the inspiration of the Holy Spirit. For holy mother Church, relying on the belief of the Apostles (see John 20:31; 2 Tim. 3:16; 2 Peter 1:19–20, 3:15–16), holds that the books of both the Old and New Testaments in their entirety, with all their parts, are sacred and canonical because written under the inspiration of the Holy Spirit, they have God as their author and have been handed on as such to the Church herself.(1) In composing the sacred books, God chose men and while employed by Him (2) they made use of their powers and abilities, so that with Him acting in them and through them, (3) they, as true authors, consigned to writing everything and only those things which He wanted. (4)
>
> Therefore, since everything asserted by the inspired authors or sacred writers must be held to be asserted by the Holy Spirit, it follows that the books of Scripture must be acknowledged as teaching solidly, faithfully and without error that truth which God wanted put into sacred

---

Ville Mäkipelto, Timo Tekoniemi, and Miika Tucker, "Large-Scale Transposition as an Editorial Technique in the Textual History of the Hebrew Bible," *TC* 22 (2017): 1–16.

writings (5) for the sake of salvation. Therefore "all Scripture is divinely inspired and has its use for teaching the truth and refuting error, for reformation of manners and discipline in right living, so that the man who belongs to God may be efficient and equipped for good work of every kind" (2 Tim. 3:16–17, Greek text).

12. However, since God speaks in Sacred Scripture through men in human fashion, (6) the interpreter of Sacred Scripture, in order to see clearly what God wanted to communicate to us, should carefully investigate what meaning the sacred writers really intended, and what God wanted to manifest by means of their words.

13. In Sacred Scripture, therefore, while the truth and holiness of God always remains intact, the marvelous "condescension" of eternal wisdom is clearly shown, "that we may learn the gentle kindness of God, which words cannot express, and how far He has gone in adapting His language with thoughtful concern for our weak human nature." (11) For the words of God, expressed in human language, have been made like human discourse, just as the word of the eternal Father, when He took to Himself the flesh of human weakness, was in every way made like men.

This passage has been admirably well contextualized and commented by Emmanuel Durand.[8] I will certainly not try to emulate him but only make a few modest remarks on what this document does not say. It may be helpful to remember that the discussions in the middle of the twentieth century, and still today, have typically oscillated between two poles that come from old debates from the seventeenth-nineteenth centuries. On the one hand, some theologians still stick to some version of verbal inspiration: they believe that God was involved, even if very remotely, in the process that resulted in the actual wording of the Scriptures; nobody argues today that it happened by dictation, but some theologians envisage some kind of mysterious influence, causation, guidance or supervision. At the other end of the spectrum, other theologians believe that inspiration merely concerns a number of theological *ideas* that found their way in the texts, not their concrete verbal expression. Intermediate positions argue that God has providentially guided the creation of the biblical texts while leaving an important degree of freedom to the biblical redactors in their wording. This sketch merely scratches the surface of a complicated debate, of course.

Against this background, *Dei Verbum* carefully abstains from endorsing either verbal inspiration or the "contents" inspiration theory. Yet it seems to imply that the inspiration of Scriptures by the Holy Spirit involves God's agency in the making of the text throughout a *relatively* close supervision, especially in the following sentences:

---

**8** Emmanuel Durand, "Relire *Dei Verbum* 11-13 dans son histoire... pour surmonter une fausse division entre exégèse scientifique et théologie," *Transversalités* 145 (2018) : 39–63. See also idem, *Jusqu'où ouvrir le texte?*, 36–60.

- "in composing the sacred books, God....": here, God is the subject of the verb "to compose";
- the authors "consigned to writing everything *and only those things* which He wanted";
- "everything asserted by the inspired authors or sacred writers must be held to be asserted by the Holy Spirit" (grammatically the end of the apodosis in the same sentence, "for the sake of salvation," qualifies only the apodosis)
- "... what God wanted to manifest by means of their words."

*Dei Verbum* makes it clear that God's agency was involved in some way in the making of the inspired writings. It insists on the fact that the biblical books "with all their parts" are inspired. Yet apart from that, it leaves open the issue of the *extent*, so to speak, of God's supervision in the making of the actual shape of the text. The possibility that God's supervision influenced or even determined the shape of the text does not amount to a return to the theory of verbal inspiration. The latter theory, at least in its strictest version, postulated a fine-grained determination of the text by God, on the level of the words themselves. But it is also possible to imagine that God's influence operated on a wider scale, or at a higher level. God may have wanted such or such part of a book to be present in it (a pericope, even a sentence), even though he did not supervise its wording. My point is that ever since *Dei Verbum*, contemporary articulations of inspiration often carefully avoid taking a stance on the issue of the extent of God's supervision in the shaping of the text, considering this aspect to be beyond our grasp; it remains an open question.

What *has* often been suggested since *Dei Verbum* is that we should speak of "redactors" instead of authors, and also include the believing communities. In addition, a relatively recent shift must be noted. In a recent issue of the journal *Communio*, Olivier-Thomas Venard notes that the Catholic councils claimed the inspiration not only of the humans, but also of the *texts*, or rather the *books*, which exist in different forms.[9] In the same issue, Olivier Riaudel writes:

> That which is maintained from age to age is not, therefore, the meaning, it is the text, and a certain number of rules for reading. It is here that we can seek the meaning of biblical inspiration.[10]

This focus on the *text* seems to reflect a general tendency in recent discussions. As Durand writes:

---

[9] Olivier-Thomas Venard, "L'inspiration des Ecritures – esquisse d'une problématique à la lumière des travaux de François Martin," *Communio* 41.3 (2016): 70–71.
[10] Olivier Riaudel, "De l'écrivain inspiré à l'inspiration du texte," *Communio* 41.3 (2016): 57.

> The theology of inspiration developed according to three successive models: author, community, and text. It is no longer possible to assume only one human author for each corpus or literary unit of the Bible. We must extend the concept of authorship to biblical editors and to communities who bore the traditions that were written down. Ultimately, it is the canonical text that is inspired.[11]

Now if God's agency is postulated behind the formation of the text, even in a mysterious way, then we are doomed to encounter "practical" questions such as noted above. Was God somehow involved in the innumerable changes that appear in the manuscript evidence? Are we dealing with *changes to an inspired text* or with *inspired changes*? To put it another way, if a systematic theologian says: "the text is inspired," the biblical scholar might well reply: "which text? I have many texts in front of me, for the same book." Or did God cease to be involved at some point in the textual history of the book? Was or is such edition of a given book inspired? In the same way that theologians have broadened the scope of the human agents, from authors to redactors and communities, should they also include the work of *scribes* and *copyists*?

These may sound like naïve and idle or pointless questions, and of course the issue is not being able to answer them for any given passage. But this is the underlying principle that is interesting. Do we think that God's agency lies behind a part of the textual history, or behind its totality? And why? I would also argue that they are good questions, especially if they bother us by their concreteness. Concrete texts is all that we have, and this is what the believing communities deal with in liturgical settings. As Durand notes, "it is in the liturgical context that inspiration is best perceived and received by the believing community."[12] It is in this context that individual passages are publicly read, and these readings are often followed by responses like "(this is) the Word of the Lord" (at least in the Catholic and Anglican liturgies). So can we really regard it as indifferent whether individual passages are inspired or not?

Several solutions have been suggested or can be imagined. I will discuss some of them successively.[13]

---

**11** Durand, "Relire," 62; *Jusqu'où*, 60.
**12** Durand, "Relire," 62; *Jusqu'où*, 60.
**13** Part of the complexity of the debate may also be due to some equivocity in the way "inspiration" is used in many discussions. Thus, there are basically two different uses of the word "inspiration": (a) it can designate the process whereby God is involved in some way in the formation of the text (it *was* written under the inspiration of the Holy Spirit); (b) it can designate an enduring quality of the text (it *is* inspired). To make things even more complicated, systematic theologians sometimes consider that the inspiration of the text is fully "realized" only when this text is received through the Spirit by the reader or the listener.

## 2.3 Textual fluidity and inspiration as pertaining to ideas

The first conceivable solution would be to give up any concern for the form or shape of the text. As long as we focus on ideas contained in the books, especially in the theory of inspiration based on the contents only, textual fluidity does not seem to be a problem at all. It does not seem to matter much that there existed two editions of Jeremiah, three editions (at least) of Esther, or whether this or that plus in a textual witness is inspired or not. What really matters is the fact that the Bible contains some key ideas, some key message. As long as the changes made by scribes to the text do not remove these ideas from the text or alter them, then it's fine.

What is more, textual fluidity may provide an argument in favor of the notion that inspiration only concerns ideas. Indeed, if there is so much variation among the textual witnesses, then doesn't it show that the wording was deemed unimportant by the ancient scribes? If God himself decided to use such a fragile medium, with fluctuating limits, to communicate his message, then how could the wording be of crucial importance?

However, this view does not avoid raising a number of questions.[14] First, let me note that if the amount of variation among textual witnesses is indeed considerable, this does not mean that the biblical books were wholly transformed without care for the wording. Scholars today distinguish between the reuse and the rewriting a book,[15] and the more limited kind of textual fluidity we encounter in the transmission of many other books. If scribes often felt free to make changes in the text, they nevertheless tried to copy it, to transmit it. Additions made to laws of Deuteronomy in order to harmonize them with laws found in Exodus, for instance, may impress us in the freedom taken by scribes to supplement the text, but it also means that the same scribes preserved the text of Deuteronomy they inherited, rather than replacing it.

Second, when we take into account textual fluidity, another problem appears: it is the fact that some textual additions do contain ideas and sometimes introduce new ideas. Let us take Jer 33:14–26 as an illustration. This is the longest addition, present in the Masoretic text, made to the earlier edition of the book, attested by the Septuagint. This passage contains several interesting ideas, including that of an eternal covenant for the Levites, which is a novelty. What do we make of such an idea? Was it, and is it, inspired? Is this an idle question? Yet if we feel free to dis-

---

**14** Note that if only ideas really matter, it is difficult to see how the classical philological approach to the text, minutiously studying it in its original languages, could matter, as long as the main ideas are satisfactorily conveyed in modern translations.
**15** For these notions, see Molly M. Zahn, *Genres of Rewriting in Second Temple Judaism: Scribal Composition and Transmission* (Cambridge: Cambridge University Press, 2020).

count such a passage as unimportant because its contents have no bearing on our theological thinking, then I find it troubling, because there are many such passages in the Hebrew Bible.[16] The Hebrew Bible does not just contain a few overarching theological ideas such as, in some texts, a form of monotheism, or an overarching narrative arc: the texts also make many historical points (e.g. about the extent of David's kingdom or the historicity of Josiah's reform) and ideological or secondary religious points (e.g. about the respective roles of priests and Levites, or the centralization of the cult). If inspiration only concerns ideas, one may wonder which ideas exactly are inspired.

Furthermore, let us assume that what really matters for the inspiration of a book is only the presence of some key ideas, not the precise form of that book, represented by the list of pericopes and verses it contains. It follows that we could theoretically add a new brief passage containing a theological absurd idea without changing the fact that the book is inspired, since it would not alter the presence of the key ideas just mentioned. Yet it is easy to imagine how the added presence of a theological absurd idea could fit badly with the notion that the book is inspired.

There are other problems with the view that only ideas matter, such as the debatable dissociation between ideas and words, as noted by Venard,[17] but my point here is that taking into account textual fluidity troubles the situation even within the framework of that theory.

## 2.4 "Everything is inspired"

A second, diametrically opposed solution to the problem discussed here consists in saying that "everything is inspired." All the variants and variations among the textual witnesses could be regarded as part of Scriptures. This view of inspiration would "absorb," so to speak, all the textual multiplicity. Venard writes:

> Can we not try to conceive that "supplementation" is always possible, inherent to every word in its capacity as a word, by discovering, quite simply, the natural and anthropological base of a realistic conception of the inspiration of the Scriptures? That which the theorists of the 1960s and 1970s called the rustle [*bruissement*] of the text, transposed into the Scriptures — from the simple lacuna, to the most illogical passage, via all sorts of textual corruption, accidents, corrections or additions occurring in the transmission of the text — is this not, just as much as the intention of the first writer, the Word of God in its historical communication?[18]

---

[16] Note that Jer 33:14–16 is part of the Catholic liturgical calendar; it was read at mass on the first day of Advent in 2021.
[17] Venard, "L'inspiration," 66.
[18] Venard, "L'inspiration," 70.

This view may prove attractive to text critics, because they are interested in the entire manuscript evidence; even when they are trying to reconstruct the archetype of a book, they are interested in its entire textual history. They consider that variability pertains to the very nature of the biblical books.[19] And they don't have any criteria for selecting the variants that would be inspired or not, so this view sounds quite "realistic," as Venard writes. Their task is descriptive, not prescriptive. They often thrive to tell what the earliest reading in a particular verse was, but it does not follow that this should be regarded as the "inspired" form of the verse. More generally, the ideal goal of textual criticism is a comprehensive description of the many instantiations of a text throughout the centuries, and an explanation of its complicated development along various tracks. From a scientific point of view, every variant deserves consideration. A theological view of inspiration that would not privilege one particular form of the text over the others but embrace the entire manuscript evidence would align with this scientific interest in the entire textual multiplicity.[20]

Moreover, as noted above, biblical scholars have come to realize that it is not possible to draw a line between the composition of the books and their transmission. The same kind of changes that were made during the successive redactions of a book can also be detected in the textual fluidity as attested by manuscripts. Note, in passing, that such a view would therefore involve including scribes among the circle of human agents that have been considered in the theory of inspiration so far: redactors and believing communities.

All that being said, such a "generous" view raises some questions. First, what about scribal accidents? A large part of the textual fluidity we observe in the manuscript evidence is due to scribal mistakes that result in, notably, omissions of words or phrases, or repetitions. If we hold that inspiration included the providential

---

**19** Even during Medieval times, the biblical text was not entirely stable; there were slight variations in the Masoretic Text, and the versions were subjected to changes. Moreover, even in the printing age, and to this day, there exist differences between the various editions of the Hebrew text. They do not print exactly the same text (the Biblia Hebraica Stuttgartensia, for instance, is a diplomatic edition of the Leningrad Codex, whereas the Hebrew University Bible is a diplomatic edition of the Aleppo Codex). In addition, there are many typos in the Biblia Hebraica Stuttgartensia, which can, in a way, be compared to the scribal errors of the past. Overall, the text is not completely stable. Finally, it is well know that there are many differences between modern versions, and even between the successive editions of a given modern version.
**20** For a defense of the variance of the biblical text seen as its very essence, see Brennan Breed, *The Nomadic Text: A Theory of Biblical Reception History* (Bloomington: Indiana University Press, 2014). For a critical assessment, see Matthieu Richelle, "Uncertainty and Undecidability in Textual Criticism of the Hebrew Bible: Three Epistemic Issues," in *Congress Volume Zürich 2022*, ed. Konrad Schmid (VTSup; Brill: Leiden, forthcoming).

supervision of the transmission history, then, are we to consider that the God's agency was involved in these scribal blunders? Now the reason why this kind of question may sound ridiculous is the fact that it implicitly rests on the notion that inspiration entails a very close supervision of the work of human scribes, in a way that would be analogous to the one that is supposed with regard to authors in the strictest theory of verbal inspiration. Precisely. My point is that if we hold the view that inspiration embraces the whole of textual multiplicity, then we are concretely talking of many little "uninspiring" variants alongside more significant ones.[21] If we want to include the entire textual multiplicity in the inspired corpus, then we are theoretically including the work of a scribe who in, say, the first century CE, accidentally omitted a sentence in a chapter, another in a different chapter, and added a few words due to dittographies. If his work was done under the inspiration of God, then this is what we are concretely talking about. And if we say that God was involved in some supervision at such a micro-level (sentences and words), then we are dangerously close to the notion of verbal inspiration in its most "literal" version. In addition, when we focus on these tiny "contributions," we seem to be far from the connection between revelation and inspiration that a number of theologians postulate; to put it simply, it seems difficult to imagine that the scribe who accidentally skipped a few words did so because he (or she) was a witness to a revelatory event; we are simply dealing with the concrete work of copyists.

Another concern is that including everything in the inspired corpus would mean "validating" all that scribes did as a *fait accompli*. Just because a scribe did this or that at an early period, it would automatically be "canonized," so to speak. Would Christian theologians reason in the same way with regard to the "unorthodox" changes made to the text of the NT in the first centuries CE? And what would be the *terminus ad quem*, the date after which we would regard variants as not inspired? It seems that any line traced in the sand in this regard would be arbitrary. Then what about the famous variant of the so-called Wicked Bible, the edition of the King James Bible where the printer accidentally (or not?) omitted the negation in "You shall not commit adultery?"

---

[21] This should be nuanced, however, since accidental mistakes at the hands of scribe sometimes result in new, interesting forms of a passage, as I argue in Matthieu Richelle, "Towards a Variegated Approach to Textual Fluidity: Limited Variations, Deliberate Duplication and Creative Scribal Mistake in 2 Kings 10:15–31," *Henoch* 42/2 (2020): 92–114.

## 2.5 "Only a part of the textual multiplicity is inspired"

If we remain within the framework of a view that holds that God's "supervision" or "monotoring" was somehow involved in the shape of the text, the alternative to the previous view would be to assume that inspiration concerns only *some part* of the textual multiplicity. Hence the embarrassing question of the criteria according to which this or that variant was inspired.

An interesting possibility would be to consider those changes that belong to *theological projects*. The revised and updated edition of Jeremiah evidently stems from a well thought-out project. In a similar vein, Adrian Schenker thinks that the MT of Kings represents a new edition stemming out of an earlier Hebrew edition that served as the *Vorlage* for the LXX translator of that book. Schenker considers that this scriptural book exists in two different forms that are both canonical, even though both of them are marked by ideological, political and religious prejudices. It is precisely a "synoptic" appreciation of the book in its dual form that can prevent us to identify the Word of God and any imperfect textual instantiation of the book.[22]

The importance of theological projects is further underlined by what we understand of the emic perspective of scribes in the last centuries BCE. Recent research has pointed out that a number of Jewish scribes, especially in the Hellenistic period, regarded themselves as apt, by virtue of a sort of prophetical inspiration, to rewrite authoritative books and improve them.[23]

But a focus on ancient theological projects does not account for all the textual variants – far from it. As already mentioned, a huge proportion of textual fluidity is due to scribal mistakes. Moreover, the notion of theological project does not account for all the differences between successive editions of the same book, for instance between the LXX and the MT in Jeremiah. In the centuries after the main redaction which gave to the MT its overall shape, and which included a change in the sequence of the chapters (the relocation of the oracles against the nations from the middle to the end of the book), as well as many additions, a number of other changes and *Fortschreibungen* were made. They were not part of the same great project. Were they inspired? Generally speaking, many textual changes, in many books, were made without any concern for an overall theological project. In fact, should we regard any *intentional* change as inspired? Think, again, of the "unorthodox" variants in the NT text.

---

[22] Adrian Schenker, *Älteste Textgeschichte der Königsbücher: Die hebräische Vorlage der ursprünglichen Septuaginta als älteste Textform der Königsbücher*, OBO 199 (Fribourg – Göttingen, Academic Press – Vandenhoeck & Ruprecht, 2004), 190–2.
[23] Zahn, *Genres of Rewriting*, 211–22.

Yet another theory would postulate that only those changes that belong to forms of the text received in a significant part of the Jewish people or the Church are *de facto* canonical. As Durand notes, canonicity is presented as subordinated to inspiration in *DV* 11:

> For holy mother Church, relying on the belief of the Apostles (see John 20:31; 2 Tim. 3:16; 2 Peter 1:19–20, 3:15–16), holds that the books of both the Old and New Testaments in their entirety, with all their parts, are sacred and canonical *because* written under the inspiration of the Holy Spirit, they have God as their author and have been handed on as such to the Church herself.[24]

So if we regard the two editions of Jeremiah as canonical because both have been received in Christianity throughout the centuries, should we consider that they are both inspired? That would not necessarily be satisfactory, because even those textual traditions which were widely received subsist in a multiplicity of forms, with innumerable variants in the LXX manuscripts of Jeremiah, for instance. If we hold that both the MT and the LXX editions of Jeremiah are inspired, we are still facing the immense textual multiplicity of the manuscripts that attest these editions, and the problem has only shifted.

## 2.6 Another solution based on the distinction between the Bible and the Word of God?

Yet another attempt at a solution would be to consider that the shape of the text does not matter much, because a distinction is necessary between the text of the Bible and the Word of God. As Benoît Bourgine reminds us, a simple identification between them would lead to fundamentalism.[25] If we follow Barth, it is only when it is proclaimed that the biblical text can become the Word of God. In some recent formulations, the inspiration of the text is fully realized only when it is received by believing communities animated by the same Spirit who inspired the text in the first place. Maybe some could infer from this that asking questions about the inspiration of the text independently of this reception is "premature," so to speak?

However, Bourgine also reminds us that a complete disconnect between the letter and the Spirit is problematic. Theologians keep talking of the inspired text even when they do not have in view its reception; they do not argue that the text considered on its own is "partly inspired," or "inspired to an incomplete degree." And, of course, if a passage is absent from an edition of a book that is used in a

---

24 Durand, "Relire," 43; *Jusqu'où*, 40.
25 See his contribution to this volume.

particular tradition, nobody in this tradition will preach about this text. Conversely, if a passage is a plus in an edition, it may serve as a basis for preaching. Thus the shape of a book partly determines its use in the proclamation, and, therefore, its reception.

In the end, textual fluidity raises concrete questions that may lead us to take more seriously into account the question of the form of the text. And yet, as I have tried to show, easy solutions do not seem satisfactory. Thus, it remains to be seen if there are more than dead ends here. Perhaps the complexity highlighted by textual fluidity is just the final proof that any definition of inspiration must remain vague. Adding "scribes" to the list of human agents involved in the inspired creation of the text, alongside redactors or believing communities, might prove problematic. Whereas it is desirable to include the work of redactors, doing the same for the people involved in the transmission history of the book might be too broadly inclusive. The trouble, for biblical scholars, is, again, that it is not possible anymore to draw a line between the work of redactors and that of scribes.

One could also wonder whether it makes sense to ask if a particular passage, or a particular form of a text, is inspired. Traditionally, theologians speak of inspired *books*. As we have seen above, recent discussions have been characterized by a shift from *book* to *text*. Yet one may argue that when some theologians speak of the inspiration of the text, they are talking of the text (of a given literary work) considered *as a whole*, not as a set of inspired pericopes. Hence perhaps the possibility of approaching inspiration in a very general way, as an attribute pertaining to the book or text as a whole? One could, for instance, argue that the sole fact that a book mediates the Word of God, or some message, suffices to qualify it as "inspired." However, would that not entail reverting to the "contents" theory of inspiration, which has its own problems, as noted above?

A way forward might be to consider recent discussions on the conceptualization, or even the ontology, of "books," a topic to which I now turn.

## 3 Analogies and metaphors to help conceptualize inspiration

As we have seen, recent discussions by theologians focus on the *text* as the object of inspiration. Yet the fluidity of the text makes the conceptualization of its inspiration more difficult. Scholars often have recourse to analogies and metaphors to approach this problem. The question I would like to raise in this section is whether some recent discussions on the conceptualization of books in ancient Judaism could not help refine our conceptualization of their inspiration.

## 3.1 The Incarnation analogy

A common approach, at least since *Dei Verbum*, is the Incarnation analogy discussed and revisited by Durand.[26] I find analogy fruitful and helpful. One of its implications is that the "fragility" of the text is *to be expected*. It is not a "bad surprise" that would challenge the notion of inspiration in itself. Another implication is that this "fragility" is not a huge problem for theology. The fact that the text has fluctuating limits only affects it at its margins; it does not change the existence of an inspired text.

That being said, like every analogy, the Incarnation model also has limits; it does not claim to be able to capture the entirety of the phenomenon it sheds light on. For instance, it does not solve the question of the possible inspiration of the textual variants or of their canonical status. I can also imagine that the notion of a kenosis of the "divine word," that is translated into a "human word," might prompt questions such as: does this "divine word" exist independently of the human words we have?[27]

In addition, I find it interesting to note that textual fluidity is sometimes approached as a manifestation of the "precarity" or "fragility" of the inspired text (as in the Incarnation analogy), and sometimes as a fruit of positive theological activity, that is, of redactional activity motivated by theological reflection (in agreement with the conception that a number of ancient scribes had of their own work[28]). Admittedly, as Durand rightly notes, the "complexity" of the textual composition and transmission is not a "degeneration" of the human word; it is there from the start. Yet the language of "precarity" is striking. This raises the question of whether the fluidity of the text is regarded as an inevitable limit or flaw of the text as a medium of communication, a problem to be dealt with or to live with, or whether it should be envisaged as a sort of *positive* dimension of the text. Or perhaps both alternately, depending on the situation.

Be that as it may, what I would like to do in what follows is to explore other possible analogies or, perhaps, metaphors, which will have their own limits but which might shed some light on the problem I am discussing.

---

26 See his contribution to this volume.
27 Durand, *Jusqu'où*, 94–96.
28 See also Bourgine's contribution to this volume.

## 3.2 The vitality of Scriptures

Hindy Najman's approach, based on the notion of "vitality of Scriptures," might prove stimulating here.[29] Without abandoning the distinction between canonical and non-canonical works, she argues that in the Second Temple period, scriptural authority was understood in a way that went beyond these boundaries. Taking her cue from Walter Benjamin's discussion on the "life and continuing life of works of art," she argues that

> (some) texts have an excess of vitality that expresses itself in the fact that they provide the basis for new texts. For example, they give rise to emulations that purport to "say the same" as the original scripture although they are self-evidently different. Thus Jubilees and the Temple Scroll claim to "say the same" as various pentateuchal texts, speaking in the voice of Moses, or in the voice of the angel dictating to Moses, or even in the voice of God.
>
> Far from contradicting the authoritative status of scripture, texts such as Jubilees and the Temple Scroll—and the "apocryphal" texts of the Melitians—arise precisely from that authority. To acknowledge certain texts as scriptural is to recognize them as possessing an excess of vitality, more life than ordinary texts, and it is the nature of life to generate life, to sustain and reproduce itself. Insofar as scripture is authoritative, it is also generative.[30]

Maybe we could, in turn, take our cue from this discussion about the vitality of Scriptures that manifests itself in a sort of overflow beyond the canonical boundaries, to consider, by analogy, that textual fluidity is another manifestation of this vitality, within the boundaries. The vitality of the Scriptures did not only result in the production of new works that did not find their way into the canon; it also translated into an excess of vitality at their own margins. When I say "margins," this is of course to be understood as a figurative trope; in actuality, it does not only designate supplements at the beginning or the end of the works or their pericopes; the growth and variations within the text are also concerned; they also represent an excess that overflows the main "body" of the text; they are "marginal" unless they amount to a rewriting that results in a new work, like Jubilees.

Because the canonical works were regarded as authoritative, and because they were "generative," they prompted the scribes who copied them to "update" them and change them in various ways. On this view, textual fluidity is not an inevitable and negative aspect of the text, it is the manifestation of an intrinsic quality of the literary works in question: their vitality, their generativity. Fluidity is, so to speak, an organic aspect of the text. It is a feature of the text not a bug. Perhaps this could encourage us to think of the biblical books not merely as "discrete" entities and

---
[29] Hindy Najman, "The Vitality of Scripture Within and Beyond the 'Canon'," *JSJ* 43 (2012): 497–518.
[30] Najman, "Vitality," 516.

fixed objects, but as entities subjected to processes. It might be interesting to draw an analogy with the difference, stressed by François Jullien, between the ontology in Western thinking, based on the "being" and favorising a "static" approach, and the focus on "processual" realities in China.[31] I am merely suggesting here that our conceptualization of the biblical works as fixed books does not render justice to their "dynamic" dimension and their generative character.

Of course, the approach I am imagining here has limits. It mainly concerns variants that were intentional or at least spontaneous; it is hardly adequate for including scribal mistakes; it concerns additions, it is less clear whether it concerns omissions (whether accidental or intentional). But, in contrast to theories criticized above because of similar limits, this approach may cover more than just editorial projects or theological rewriting. It may also account for little fluctuations that arose spontaneously when the vitality of the text prompted its tradents to make adjustments and add supplements here and there.

Further, while the notion of vitality may help us understand that variability belonged to the very "essence" of the biblical works, it does not solve the problem of the possible inspiration of variants or their canonical status. Nevertheless, in a Christian perspective, I imagine that a connection might be drawn between this "life" and the action of the Holy Spirit. If so, should this lead us to consider the fruit of the vitality, including at least part of the textual variants, as inspired? Returning to Najman's discussion about the canon, it is interesting to note that recognizing that the vitality of Scriptures exceeds them to the point of leading to the creation of new works does not necessarily imply that these new works are canonical. Can we reason the same way with regard to textual fluidity? Are there variants that are due to the vitality of Scriptures (and perhaps to the Holy Spirit) but not inspired, and/or non-canonical? Or should we consider that another mode of inspiration pertains to them, the same way as various modes of inspiration are certainly relevant to different literary genres?[32] Or perhaps it is the question of a sort of "gray area" that is raised here.

Another point that would be worth discussing is the fact that there was a virtual end to the phenomenon of vitality, insofar as the text was largely frozen at some point – not entirely, since there are slight differences even within the medieval manuscripts of the Masoretic family, and there are still variations in the editions of the Hebrew Bible, or of the Old Testament, today.[33] Yet it seems clear that after the first century CE, the variations in the Hebrew text were very limited, and this is a striking phenomenon from the point of view of *longue durée*. Should we consider

---

**31** François Jullien, *La pensée chinoise: En vis-à-vis de la philosophie*, Folio essais (Paris : Gallimard, 2015), 21–4 ; see also his reflections on the notion of *évasif* (173–84).
**32** See John Goldingay, *Models for Scripture* (Toronto: Clements Publishing, 2004).
**33** See above, fn. 19.

that the vitality of Scriptures is then "taken up" by its reception (although reception was already at work within the biblical corpus)?

## 3.3 "Books" and other metaphors

It may possible to go further and to problematize the very notion of "book." In her important work entitled *The Literary Imagination in Jewish Antiquity*, Eva Mroczek notes that "book" is an anachronistic concept when it is applied to the work of Jewish scribes during the late Second Temple period. She takes as examples Psalms, Jubilees and Ben Sira. Psalms is attested in 11QPsalm$^a$, a long scroll from the first century CE, in a form that differs widely from the MT form we know, both with regard to the order of the psalms, and with the list of poems: ten psalms are not found in the MT. This is not an "eccentric" scroll; other Psalms scroll exhibit different sequences of psalms.[34]

In Mroczek's view,

> no book of Psalms as such exists in early Judaism. Instead, there are a variety of collections that preserve psalms and psalmlike compositions, in various lengths and arrangements, for pedagogical, exorcistic, interpretive, and liturgical purposes (...) psalms are not conceptualized as a "book" prior to the New Testament and rabbinic texts. Instead, they are imagined as an open genre, a heavenly archive that is only partially reflected in the extant texts.[35]

Mroczek rightly notes that textual fluidity is also a striking aspect of Ben Sira. Even in that case, where an (actual) author is clearly identified, it is impossible to reduce the textual fluidity to reconstruct an *Urtext*: the literary work exists in different editions with a complicated relationship between them. More than that, Mroczek shows that this textual multiformity is in line with Jesus Ben Sira's project; he compares himself, in his authorial work, to "a canal from a river:"

> As for me, I was like a canal from a river,
> like a water channel into a garden.
> I said, "I will water my garden
> and drench my flower-beds."
> And lo, my canal became a river,
> and my river a sea.
> I will again make instruction shine forth like the dawn,
> and I will make it clear from far away.

---

[34] See also Eva Mroczek, "The Hegemony of the Biblical in the Study of Second Temple Literature," *JAJ* 6 (2015): 35.
[35] Eva Mroczek, *The Literary Imagination in Jewish Antiquity* (New York: Oxford University Press, 2016), 15.

> I will again pour out teaching like prophecy,
> and leave it to all future generations.
> (Sir 28:30–33)

Mroczek argues that "Ben Sira does not understand his work as a 'book' in the sense of an original and final written composition, but as the malleable and necessarily incomplete continuation of a long tradition of revealed wisdom."[36]

At the same time, Mroczek's approach is much more subtle than a mere rejection of the concept of "book" as anachronistic. Instead, she notes that "book" can be used as one metaphor among others:

> Thus, to call ancient texts "books" is not to make a historically indefensible faux pas. It is to do the work of metaphor: to make them at home in our own imagination, and to ascribe to them the power, mystery, and anxiety that the "book" holds for us. But perhaps this metaphor's descriptive power has been exhausted, and now, rather than being satisfied with how it can help us speak about ancient texts, we are more conscious of and troubled by what it cannot help us describe.[37]

Thus, Mroczek considers a number of possible other metaphors: archives, database, projects... She suggest regarding the biblical works as "multigenerational projects that enabled their own expansion and were not necessarily intended or received as original or complete."[38] Her approach is fascinating, although one may wonder if it is relevant for all the works that comprise the Hebrew Bible. Whatever the case, she brings into the debate an aspect that must be integrated into our understanding of the scribal work in the Second Temple period.

When it comes to reflecting on the possible implications of these considerations for our present discussion, it might be objected that the latter considerations only concern early periods, prior to the canonization process and the fixation of the text. After all, the shift to books *did* happen at some point during the first millenium CE, and it is books that the Masoretes left us, or, more precisely, splendid codices. So while it is interesting to realize that in the late second Temple period, Jewish scribes did not regard the works they were writing and copying as books in the sense we give to this word, this does not change the fact that what we have now are books.

The problem, however, is that Mroczek's observations concern the period during which the works in question were "written under the inspiration of the Holy Spirit," according to a classical Christian formulation. To put it another way, the works in question were not conceptualized as books precisely during the period when the

---

**36** Mroczek, *Literary Imagination*, 93.
**37** Mroczek, *Literary Imagination*, 11.
**38** Mroczek, *Literary Imagination*, 13.

inspiration is supposed to have taken place,[39] whereas our conceptualization of their inspiration is largely based on their conceptualization as books. It seems that at least some works that *were* not inspired *as books* are now regarded as inspired as books (not to mention the fact that the books are gathered in a single corpus, the Bible). Accordingly, we are trying to conceptualize inspiration from within a paradigm that was not current at the time when the biblical works were written; our etic perspective differs from the emic perspective of ancient scribes. Hence a question: should this change something in the way we conceive and speak of the inspiration of Scriptures?

Perhaps this could confirm that the shift from *book* to *text* in recent discussions is a good move. That said, as I have tried to show, "text" is not an easy notion to manipulate. Moreover, it is not clear either that Jewish scribes conceived of their work as the production of a *text*. Text does not capture the dynamic highlighted by Mroczek.

I find it interesting to note what Mroczek herself writes about the metaphor of project:

> Perhaps we may also consider the concept of text as *project*, which brings human agency and a sense of ongoing development and use back into the production of texts. The presence of textual variants and diverse configurations of psalms is no longer a problem to be solved – no longer to be studied as deviations from a preexistent "book" to which we compare them. Instead, they are part of the very shape of early Jewish literary expectations before that "book" emerged as such.[40]

Like the Incarnation analogy, and like the approach based on the vitality of Scriptures, this approach shows that textual fluidity is *to be expected*. It does not answer the question of inspiration or the canonical status of the variants, though. However, like the "vitality" approach, Mroczek's perspective allows us to see that variability is an integral part of the work of ancient scribes. On this view, it may be more difficult to justify the exclusion of textual variants from the sphere of inspiration.

# 4 Conclusion

In this contribution, I have tried to show that current formulations of the doctrine of inspiration do not seem to integrate a number of dimensions of the biblical texts that exegetes, especially text critics, observe in their daily frequentation of these texts. Let me summarize the main points of my discussion:

---

[39] Here, of course, I am only talking of the inspiration of the texts insofar as it concerns their writing, I do not consider the notion of inspiration of their reception.
[40] Mroczek, *Literary Imagination*, 41.

(1) Recent formulations have seen some progress insofar as they now prefer to speak of "redactors" rather than "authors." Textual fluidity raises the question of whether we should expand this to scribes and copyists. The problem is all the more acute in that the frontier between redaction and transmission vanishes: these realities overlap and it is often difficult to say whether a textual change is the work of a redactor or of a scribe copying an already authoritative work. Likewise, the distinction between scribes and copyists is difficult to maintain for early periods.
For this reason, integrating "scribes" into the number of actors involved in the making of the inspired text seems desirable. On the other hand, however, it might lead to complications, as it seems to imply that every textual variant is inspired. Are textual variants merely changes made to an inspired text, or inspired changes? Should we consider that part of the variants are inspired, and if so, on what criteria? I have tried to show that these questions are worth asking but difficult to answer.

Another way to look at the same problem is to say that the realization of the amplitude of textual variation may raise anew the question of the "canonical form" of the biblical books, which has never been entirely settled in the Christian traditions.[41] The variety of textual forms is greater than previously known. Saying that both the MT and the LXX are inspired would not solve the problem, because each of them, but above all the LXX, is a label that designate texts that concretely exist in innumerable forms. In addition, we know, thanks to the Dead Sea scrolls, other textual forms of the texts.

Faced with the difficulties, it may be tempting to maintain some ambiguity and be content with saying that each "biblical book" is inspired *as a whole*. Yet I am in favor of pursuing the conversation and the exploration, be it only for liturgical concerns (arguably, it does matter to know whether a text read during a service is "inspired").

(2) Another relatively recent shift in discussions involves a focus on the text, rather than on the authors, redactors or books. As we have seen, text(s) is still an elusive notion. Analogies and metaphors are helpful to try and approximate the realities that we often designate by terms such as books or texts. The Incarnation model has proved its utility and remains helpful. Other approaches used by biblical scholars and historians may be worth exploring by theologians: I briefly explored that of "vitality" of Scriptures, and that of "project." The latter approach is part of a qualification of the usefulness of the category of "book" for the very period when the bib-

---

[41] On this notion and its relationship to textual criticism, see Matthieu Richelle, "Critique textuelle et 'forme canonique' du texte de l'Ancien Testament," in *La formation des canons bibliques*, A voix haute: Conférences de l'IPT (Lyon : Olivétan, 2021): 49–77.

lical works were written. Here again, I suggest that these are interesting directions to explore further in future discussions.

In the end, although textual fluidity is not necessarily a challenge to the *notion* of inspiration, it may serve as a stimulus to rethink *formulations* of this doctrine.

## Bibliography

Birmelé, André. "Les références en dogmatique: L'Ecriture sainte et les confessions de foi." In *Introduction à la théologie systématique*, edited by André Birmelé, Pierre Bühler, Jean-Daniel Causse, and Lucie Kaennel, 49–76. Lieux théologique 39. Genève: Labor et Fides, 2008.
Breed, Brennan. *The Nomadic Text: A Theory of Biblical Reception History*. Bloomington: Indiana University Press, 2014.
Durand, Emmanuel. *Jusqu'où ouvrir le texte? Brève théologie des Ecritures*. Lire la Bible. Paris : Cerf, 2021.
Durand, Emmanuel. "Relire *Dei Verbum* 11–13 dans son histoire. . . pour surmonter une fausse division entre exégèse scientifique et théologie." *Transversalités* 145 (2018) : 39–63.
Goldingay, John. *Models for Scripture* (Toronto: Clements Publishing, 2004).
Jullien, François. *La pensée chinoise: En vis-à-vis de la philosophie*. Folio essais. Paris: Gallimard, 2015.
Mäkipelto, Ville, Timo Tekoniemi, and Miika Tucker, "Large-Scale Transposition as an Editorial Technique in the Textual History of the Hebrew Bible." *TC* 22 (2017): 1–16.
Mroczek, Eva. *The Literary Imagination in Jewish Antiquity* (New York: Oxford University Press, 2016).
Mroczek, Eva. "The Hegemony of the Biblical in the Study of Second Temple Literature." *JAJ* 6 (2015): 2–35.
Najman, Hindy. "The Vitality of Scripture Within and Beyond the 'Canon'." *JSJ* 43 (2012): 497–518.
Riaudel, Olivier. "De l'écrivain inspiré à l'inspiration du texte." *Communio* 41.3 (2016): 52–61.
Richelle, Matthieu. "Towards a Variegated Approach to Textual Fluidity: Limited Variations, Deliberate Duplication and Creative Scribal Mistake in 2 Kings 10:15–31." *Henoch* 42/2 (2020): 92–114.
Richelle, Matthieu. "Jeremiah and Baruch." In *The Oxford Handbook of the Septuagint*, edited by T. Michael Law and Alison Salvesen, 259–284. Oxford: Oxford University Press, 2021.
Richelle, Matthieu. "Critique textuelle et 'forme canonique' du texte de l'Ancien Testament." In *La formation des canons bibliques*, 49–77. A voix haute: Conférences de l'IPT. Lyon: Olivétan, 2021.
Richelle, Matthieu. "Uncertainty and Undecidability in Textual Criticism of the Hebrew Bible: Three Epistemic Issues." In *Congress Volume Zürich 2022*, edited by Konrad Schmid. VTSup. Brill: Leiden, forthcoming.
Schenker, Adrian. *Älteste Textgeschichte der Königsbücher: Die hebräische Vorlage der ursprünglichen Septuaginta als älteste Textform der Königsbücher*. OBO 199. Fribourg – Göttingen, Academic Press – Vandenhoeck & Ruprecht, 2004.
Solomon, Norman. *Torah from Heaven: The Reconstruction of Faith*. London: The Littman Library of Jewish Civilization, 2012.
Tov, Emanuel. "The Nature of the Large-Scale Differences between the LXX and M S T V, Compared with Similar Evidence in Other Sources." In *The Earliest Text of the Hebrew Bible: The Relationship between the Masoretic Text and the Hebrew Base of the Septuagint Reconsidered*, edited by. Adrian Schenker, 121–144. SBL.SCS 52. Atlanta: SBL, 2003.

Ulrich, Eugene. "Deuteronomistically Inspired Scribal Insertions into the Developing Biblical Texts: 4QJudg$^a$ and 4QJer$^a$." In *Houses Full of All Good Things: Essays in Memory of Timo Veijola*, edited by Juha Pakkala and Martti Nissinen, 489–506. Helsinki: Finnish Exegetical Society, 2008.

Venard, Olivier-Thomas. "L'inspiration des Ecritures – esquisse d'une problématique à la lumière des travaux de François Martin." *Communio* 41.3 (2016): 70–71.

Zahn, Molly M. *Genres of Rewriting in Second Temple Judaism: Scribal Composition and Transmission*. Cambridge: Cambridge University Press, 2020.

Benoît Bourgine
# 4 Textual Fluidity as a Challenge to Inspiration? A Systematic Theologian's Point of View

## 1 Position of the problem

From a different angle than the question of plurality, textual fluidity in relation to the category of inspiration brings to the fore the tension between exegesis and systematic theology. The practice of exegesis places at the heart of its explanatory exercise the study of *the biblical text, starting with itself* and with everything that can elucidate it: its date and author, its milieu of origin and formation, its structure and content, its theme, and issues. Systematic theology, for its part, is certainly attached to the materiality of the text; for all that, its guiding preoccupation is *two poles which it will try to link* as far as possible: the pole of divine otherness from which the message of the text ultimately emanates and the pole of the contemporary recipient to whom this message is addressed today. Systematic theology considers the biblical text in its capacity as *inspired* by God and as *inspiring* for the religious life of individuals and communities today. The linking of these two poles, the ultimate origin of the text and its present-day recipient, confers the *theological* character on the proposed reading. While the exegete is inclined to value the contextual distinctiveness of the text in question, the incomparable singularity of its texture and the contingent historicity of its transmission, the systematic theologian is led, for his part, to relate the meaning of this text to the divine author, on the one hand, and to the possible relevance of the text for the present recipient, on the other. The fact of linking the contribution specific to the text in question with the already constituted entirety of the divine word, according to the contemporary realities that the life of faith encounters today, leads theology to a demand for *unity and relevance*, whereas exegesis is most often led at the end of its analysis to an observation of insurmountable *fragmentation and historicity*. This is why the tension between exegesis and theology is maximal.

It is perfectly possible to live with this tension without trying to resolve it; this corresponds to a large extent to the current state of biblical studies and systematic theology, which ignore each other completely. The exegete makes his way through the accumulation of knowledge or conjectures that attempt to account for the biblical text, and the systematic theologian is most often condemned to remain foreign to the contribution of the most recent exegetical research because of the unbridgeable gap between his centre of interest and the exegete's point of view. We might well consider that this situation is neither desirable nor tenable in the long run for exegesis or dogmatics.

The hypothesis of this contribution is that, while recognising the heterogeneity of the respective points of view and practices of the exegete and the systematic theologian, the biblical text carries within itself, by its very nature and characteristics, the conditions, and terms of a fruitful dialogue between exegesis and systematic theology.

It is necessary to begin by discarding the easy solution which would be ruinous for the integrity of the two disciplines; this consists in invoking inspiration as a *deus ex machina* to counteract textual fluidity. For the exegete faced with two editions of the same work, a topical case of textual fluidity, this would amount to invoking the category of inspiration to resolve the difficulty implied by the dual versions. We can take the example of the two editions of the book of Jeremiah. The exegete may ask the question: which text is authoritative? Such a question may be considered not to be within his remit, any more than it is within the remit of the systematic theologian. For my part, I record Pierre-Maurice Bogaert's answer to this question: "The answer is not to be sought first of all in theories on the scriptural canon, but within the Bible itself."[1] The exegete dismisses a harmonising reading as invalid from the exegetical point of view, for lack of a criterion capable of discriminating between these editions. This would be a misuse of the concept of inspiration by the adoption of a position of superiority over realities that are not under one's control.

I will follow the indication of the exegete quoted in order to pursue the solution that I consider ideal and the only practicable one: to start from the biblical text itself, considered in its globality and its internal dynamics, in order to discover within it the clues that signal the kinship between the phenomenon of textual fluidity and the properly theological preoccupation of inspiration. The problem is thus approached from the opposite angle: fluidity is less a challenge to inspiration than the bearer of the traces of an affinity with the concern that emerges in the doctrine of inspiration.

Inspiration is not a category to be applied from the outside to the present state of the biblical books; like the process of canonisation, inspiration, in its dual modality of provenance and destination – an inspired text from the life-giving God; an

---

[1] Pierre-Maurice Bogaert, "'Vie et Paroles de Jérémie selon Baruch': Le texte court du livre de Jérémie selon la LXX et son modèle hébreu avec un test : Le dossier épistolaire LXX 36 (TM 29)," in *Le livre de Jérémie en perspective: Les deux rédactions conservées et l'addition du supplément sous le nom de Baruch: Recueil des travaux de Pierre-Maurice Bogaert*, eds. Jean-Claude Haelewyck and Bastien Kindt, BETL 308 (Leuven: Peeters, 2002) : 461–501, quotation on p. 497. This contribution is cordially dedicated to Prof. Bogaert.

inspiring text intended to nourish life, "these are written so that you may come to believe [. . .] and that through believing you may have life in his name" (John 20:31)² – is a concern to which the biblical text bears witness. The fluidity of the biblical text is often the result of the theological concern that corresponds to the category of inspiration, i.e., the linking of the text to the divine author and to the contemporary listener.

Here are the three stages of the reflection. I clarify what is meant by the inspiration of Scripture and textual fluidity respectively, I note the verifiable affinity between textual fluidity and inspiration in the biblical text, and then I draw conclusions from the point of view of biblical theology as well as from the notion of the Word of God.

## 2 What is meant by the inspiration of Scripture and textual fluidity

A brief definition of these notions seems useful, in particular to underline the radical difference in the perspectives from which they derive and thus avoid the temptation of hastily resolving an exegetical perplexity, namely textual fluidity, with the theological notion of Scriptural inspiration.

What is the inspiration of Scripture? As the Second Vatican Council's constitution Dei Verbum soberly writes of the books of the two Testaments: "they are authored by God" (". . . *Deum habent auctorem*. . ." *DV* 11). The canonical writings are deemed to have been written "under the inspiration of the Holy Spirit (". . . *Spiritu Sancto afflante*. . . *Spiritu Sancto inspirante*. . ." *DV* 11). This is the fundamental meaning of the inspiration of the Scriptures: through the human composition and redaction of the biblical books, God speaks the language of men and addresses himself to them in order to instruct them in the truth useful for their salvation. The divine origin of the Scriptures guarantees their normativity: inspiration qualifies these writings to deliver authentic religious teaching. The notion of inspiration is part of the theological problem of the Word of God or revelation. The believing community is indeed the place where holy books emerge; yet by presenting them to the world, the religious community proclaims in them what comes from beyond itself. That which the writers record and to which they bear witness is of a completely different nature than that which humans can say to themselves; it is the very voice of God that is heard in the word carried by these writings.

---

2 Biblical quotations are from the NRSV.

Let us note that from the first attestations of this doctrine in Christianity with the verses of 2 Pet 1:20–21[3] and 2 Tim 3:14–17,[4] we mention the *transition from the oral* ("...men and women moved by the Holy Spirit spoke from God...") *to the written word and then from the written word to the oral word* ("...useful for teaching, for reproof, for correction, and for training in righteousness..."). The inspired text is the result of a prophetic word and leads to a word of instruction and argumentation. Obviously, it is by inheriting the God of the religion of Israel, his Scriptures and oral Torah, his conception of revelation, that Christianity encounters the problem of inspiration, which arises for the prophets speaking in his name, but also for the writings claiming the authority of being vectors of a word that comes from beyond the writers, a word that they did not speak to themselves, but that was given to them in order to address to recipients. God does not merely speak or command, he speaks and commands in writing, and this is where the actual question of the inspiration of the Scriptures comes in, when we move from *Deus dixit* to *Deus scripsit*.

To this primary meaning of the inspiration of the Scriptures, we must add the threefold hermeneutical modality that Christianity has attached to the implementation of this inspiration – taking care not to encroach on the canonical question, which would require many other developments.

First modality: the inspiration of the sacred text qualifies it to carry the divine word beyond the immediate recipients, to recipients in other times and places. Between the seventeenth and twentieth centuries, the development and success of historical criticism ended up intimidating theology to the point that it abandoned interpreting Scripture as a means to hear a Word from God *hic et nunc*. In the Protestant field at first, and then in the Christian theological world as a whole, the movement of dialectical theology initiated by Karl Barth corresponded at the beginning of the last century to the reconquest of this native condition of theology, which consists in the act of thinking with the interpretation of Scripture as the base. This is what he wrote in August 1918 at the beginning of the first edition of his *Römerbrief*:

---

[3] "First of all you must understand this, that no prophecy of scripture is a matter of one's own interpretation, because no prophecy ever came by human will, but men and women moved by the Holy Spirit spoke from God" (2 Pet 1:20–21).

[4] "But as for you, continue in what you have learned and firmly believed, knowing from whom you learned it, and how from childhood you have known the sacred writings that are able to instruct you for salvation through faith in Christ Jesus. All scripture is inspired by God and is useful for teaching, for reproof, for correction, and for training in righteousness, so that everyone who belongs to God may be proficient, equipped for every good work" (2 Tim 3:14–17).

Paul, as a child of his age, addressed his contemporaries. It is, however, *far more* important that, as Prophet and Apostle of the Kingdom of God, he veritably speaks to all men of every age. The differences between then and now, there and here, no doubt require careful investigation and consideration. But the purpose of such investigation can only be to demonstrate that these differences are, in fact, *purely trivial*. The historical critical method of Biblical investigation has its rightful place: it is concerned with the preparation of the intelligence-and this can never be superfluous. But were I driven to choose between it and the venerable doctrine of Inspiration, I should without hesitation adopt the latter, which has a broader, deeper, *more important* justification. The doctrine of Inspiration is concerned with the labour of apprehending, without which no technical equipment, however complete, is of any use whatever. Fortunately, I am not compelled to choose between the two. Nevertheless, my whole energy of interpreting has been expended in an endeavour to see through and beyond history *into* the spirit of the Bible, which is the Eternal Spirit.[5]

The power of inspiration enables Scripture to make God's voice heard "to all men of all times." Through the Scripture transmitted and interpreted, God speaks today to a community of faith with the same words that he once spoke to the recipients of the Pauline letters.

The second modality is that the Spirit who dwells in the text of Scripture can only be accessed through this text and this text alone. This rule, which has been the common property of Christian exegesis since the beginning, states the principle of an unbreakable unity between text and Spirit. It marks the difference between the Bible and the Word of God: if the Bible contains the divine Word, it cannot be identified with it, since it is the Spirit who through it is the object of the search and ultimately of obedient listening. To allow for this difference forbids any fundamentalist drift. Above all, this rule imposes an unconditional respect for the biblical text itself and signals its inviolable character against any theological diktat that might claim to inflect it. For our topic, such a rule obliges us to recognise the value, consistency, and autonomy of the biblical text in its materiality and contingency. It can be noted that this relationship between Scripture and the Word of God, which corresponds to the doctrine of inspiration, has taken on a double expression in the theological tradition, Christological and pneumatological. At least since Origen, an analogy of Scripture, text, and Spirit, has been established between the double nature, human and divine, of Christ. The dogmatic constitution of Vatican II on revelation takes it up:

> For the words of God, expressed in human language, have been made like human discourse, just as the word of the eternal Father, when He took to Himself the flesh of human weakness, was in every way made like men (*DV* 13).

---

5 Karl Barth, *The Epistle to the Romans*, trans. Edwin Hoskyns (Oxford: Oxford University Press, 1968), 1.

The text of the Bible relates to the Word it contains, as the human nature of Jesus Christ relates to his divine nature. Just as the invisible divinity of the Word is accessed through the tangible humanity of Jesus, so it is through the text of Scripture that the Word of God can be perceived. Scripture thus takes on a sacramental dimension. As for the pneumatological expression, it refers to the correlation between the text of Sacred Scripture and the life-giving Spirit (2 Cor 3:1–4:6).

Third modality: the interpretation of Scripture cannot be carried out without the grace of God, in accordance with the patristic adage that the Bible is interpreted in the Spirit who inspired it. Let us leave it at that since this aspect is the subject of other contributions in this volume.

Let us move on to an even more summary description (in proportion to my competence) of the phenomenon of textual fluidity: it designates that which in the state of biblical writings distances them from an entirely stabilised and perfectly circumscribed corpus. It is the multiplicity of textual variants established by critics in a variable proportion according to the biblical books, the existence of a plurality of translations and recensions of passages or books, sometimes even the diversity of final editions as in the case of Jeremiah. Manuscript discoveries and epigraphic research contribute to the evolution of the state of knowledge of the biblical text, which is always provisional. This fluidity is the result of the often long and complex process, insofar as it can be traced, of writing and rewriting, editing, and re-editing, translation, and correction in diverse and varied contexts.

Such fluidity renders the ideal of a universally received and established version of the biblical books perfectly fanciful. It creates an uncertainty that is far from being always about details. Above all, it gives an account of a history of interpretation and a long series of interventions that precede or follow the process of canonisation, as oral traditions are put into writing and as these writings are transmitted. Successive authors, translators or editors allow themselves a freedom of interpretation that is impressive.

Let us come to the conclusion of this point. The notion of the inspiration of the Scriptures, on the one hand, and the fluidity of the biblical texts, on the other hand, are therefore two rigorously heterogeneous realities. Inspiration is a theological doctrine that describes a corpus, out of a religious faith's tendency to promote the value of such a corpus; since it is of a metaphysical order, this point of view escapes any empirical verification. In Christian theology, inspiration is of the supernatural order and refers to the power of God that makes a set of books inspired and inspiring, which amounts to maintaining that the divine power, in accordance with this doctrine, makes a text the mediation of a word that it addresses yesterday, today, and tomorrow to such and such recipients. As for the fluidity of the biblical text, it corresponds to a set of realities that fall within the scope of literary and historical criticism in all the variety of resources that the latter can mobilise. In other words, the exegete and the historian move in realities that do not *a priori* have to resort in any way to the supernatural order of divine power or providence: the literary and historical work applied to the biblical text obey in all respects the work that is valid for any other comparable non-biblical literature. Expressed from a theological point of view, this reality amounts to saying that God takes as the textual mediation of his Word a corpus presenting all the characteristic features of human knowledge, in its expression and transmission: uncertainties, errors, accidents, contingencies, historicity, ambiguities, ambivalences.

The heterogeneity between scriptural inspiration and textual fluidity puts into perspective the challenge posed by the latter to the former. The theological notion of divine inspiration applies to the whole of a canonical *corpus* in the state in which the exegete discovers it. It is indeed from a text expressed in human language and transmitted within the conditions of human knowledge, therefore historical and linguistic, that the magisterium of divine inspiration claims to be exercised. What would in fact pose a problem of a theological nature would be to have to deal with a corpus that escapes the common historical conditions of conservation and transmission, a kind of ideal corpus perfectly circumscribed and in every way fixed, in spite of its antiquity and the vicissitudes of its transmission – such a corpus, let us admit it, features in the popular imagination of some believers with regard to the Bible. But then how could we justify, in the resulting logic of the incarnation of the Word of God, that God would speak in a language which would not be quite human insofar as it would be removed from the usual conditions of transmission involving errors, accidents, variants? For a textual ensemble of this nature, somewhere between earth and heaven, would one be authorised to apply the methods used for any other corpus?

## 3 Inspiration, a preoccupation inherent in the genesis of the biblical text and its fluidity

At this juncture, the exegete could be disappointed: the theologian has not pulled out of his hat a solution that would allow him to resolve his perplexity in the face of problematic variants and contradictory recensions of the biblical text. The observation of heterogeneity between the inspiration of the Scriptures and textual fluidity forbids that the challenge posed by the uncertainty of the received text or the plurality of competing editions be magically resolved. This, however, is not the last word. Rather, let us follow the advice of the exegete quoted above to return to the biblical text itself. In spite of the heterogeneity of the views on divine inspiration and textual fluidity respectively, it is useful to observe that these two realities inter-sect in the process of the writing and transmission of the biblical text. In addition to contingent events that account for the fluidity of the biblical text, such as an accidentally damaged manuscript, a copying error or the disappearance of recensions, there are other reasons that are not unrelated to the problem of the divine inspiration of the Scriptures. In fact, the exegetical literature has drawn attention to the phenomena of rewriting, correction, re-editing or recontextualization which are part of the double intention presiding over the theological category of inspiration: to accredit the divine origin of the biblical text or to link its understanding to the mindset of a new generation. It seems relevant in this perspective to evoke the numerous cases studied by the exegetical literature pointing, beyond the heterogeneity of points of view, towards an affinity, attested by the biblical text itself, between textual fluidity and the recognition of divine inspiration as an integral part of its writing process, from its genesis to its present state. As a systematist, I can only refer to a certain number of exegetical works, without going into the details of their philological and historical analysis, which point to examples of textual fluidity motivated by a recognition of divine inspiration or by a need for updating for a new context of reception; concern for authenticity, concern for relevance: the scribal revisions point in one or other of these directions, sometimes in both directions simultaneously, which are characteristic of the theological category of inspiration.

Bernard Levinson exposes the literary strategies by which scribes allow themselves to revise laws that are nevertheless clothed with the authority of revelation.[6] This is particularly the case for a provision set forth in the Ten Words, the centre of the Torah, which is closely linked to the Israelite conception of revelation, namely transgenerational responsibility. The prohibition against Israel's idolatry to other gods is accompanied by an imprecation extending to the third generation: "I the LORD your God am a jealous God, punishing children for the iniquity of parents, to the third and the fourth generation of those who reject me, but showing steadfast love to the thousandth generation of those who love me and keep my commandments" (Exod 20:5–6). Levinson notes that the symmetrical formula of "those who love me" versus "those who hate me" refers to a pattern used in Hittite, Akkadian or Aramaic international treaties of allegiance in which violation of codified laws results in a curse for three or four generations. Several centuries after the promulgation of this provision, as mentalities have evolved, people's sense of justice is affronted by such a transfer of guilt from forefathers to children, grandchildren and even great-grandchildren. In a dual concern for theodicy and adjustment to

---

6 Bernard M. Levinson, "The Human Voice in Divine Revelation: The Problem of Authority in Biblical Law," in *Innovation in Religious Traditions: Essays in the Interpretation of Religious Change*, eds. Michael Williams, Collett Cox, and Martin Jaffee, RelSoc 31 (Berlin – New York: Mouton de Gruyter, 1992): 35–71.

the sense of justice conveyed by prophetic preaching, the author of Lamentations expresses an implicit criticism of the transgenerational punishment that falls to the exiles for the faults of the Israelite generations now extinct: "Our ancestors sinned; they are no more, and we bear their iniquities!" (Lam 5:7). The words used clearly allude to the terms of the Decalogue and at the same time underline the injustice of making the descendants bear the burden of the faults of those who are no more. The jerky rhythm of the sentence underlines its distorted logic. Between the faults of the departed ancestors and their consequences for the Israelites living in exile, there is a gulf of incomprehension which the author is not afraid to remedy in the mode of a muted protest, despite the authority of the inspired text in question.

As the author writes: "For both clear theological and existential-historical reasons, therefore, we can expect biblical authors to struggle against the injustice of this doctrine from the Decalogue. The problematic of such a struggle . . . is that it involves the need to revise an authoritative statement ascribed to revelation."[7] The author of Lamentations rereads the terms of the Mosaic law in order to disarm an understandable accusation against divine justice but also to allow his contemporaries to appropriate for themselves the words of the complaint, a source of consolation.

Levinson similarly analyses the teaching of chapter 18 of Ezekiel's prophecy, which establishes the personal responsibility of the Israelites in the covenantal arrangement: each one is punished for his own sin, not that of his ascendant or descendant, knowing that this punishment is incurred only in the case of impenitence: even the unjust can be converted and escape punishment. This drastic change in the principle of transgenerational justice does not take place by the prophetic text's annulling the text of the Decalogue, but by its taking up a proverb of popular tradition: "The parents have eaten sour grapes, and the children's teeth are set on edge" (Ezek 18:2). Like a straw man, the proverb is censured. No one should become a victim of his or her own past, or worse, a victim of someone else's past; in this way, a path of hope is opened for the exiles. The author of the prophecy attacks a popular maxim of the secular order; he undermines the authority of a merely human tradition; in this way, he conceals the inversion of a provision stated by the Decalogue, clothed with divine authority. Thus, it is not the author of the Decalogue who is contradicted; rather, it is the level of authority of the provision concerned that has been downgraded. Even more spectacularly, the inversion of jurisprudence appears in Deuteronomy from the mouth of Moses himself through a new formulation of the rule of the Decalogue: the faithful God "repays in their own person those who reject him. He does not delay but repays in their own person

---

7 Levinson, "The Human Voice in Divine Revelation," 50.

those who reject him" (Deut 7:10). This is a clever reworking of a text with divine authority. The author of the revision claims the authority of the Decalogue but disguises the enormity of the change through a clever rewording. In a time when only individual responsibility can be sustained, correction is needed. Levinson observes that far from obeying the injunction of unconditional respect for the text attached to the canonical status of a book, the canon, closely linked to the idea of inspiration, is rather a "sponsor of innovation."[8] Instead of consecrating the fixity of the text, which is clothed with the anointing of tradition, the transmission of the text by the scribes gives rise to ingenuity and diverse techniques (pseudonymity, anonymity) so as to satisfy in a single operation the double preoccupation represented by inspiration: a recognition of the divine authority of the text received, which camouflages a revision that updates and often corrects it.

Other dimensions of textual fluidity, such as translations, editions, and other variants, could be the object of similar observations: the internal process of writing the Old Testament (inner-biblical exegesis) betrays a dynamic that is aware of the double preoccupation taken as a reference by the category of inspiration. Once again, the existence of a plurality of witnesses to the same text or of a plurality of editions of the same book may well be a matter of pure contingency, as it is with any textual transmission. In the case of biblical writing, the exegesis of recent decades makes it impossible to ignore the fact that textual fluidity is also the result of a constant process of rewriting, in which the recognition of the authority of the received text is combined with an astonishing freedom to adjust the meaning of the text to the new conditions of understanding. Norbert Lohfink for the Pentateuch and the Writings, Odil Steck for the prophets, Michael Fishbane, Konrad Schmid, and Bernard Levinson for the whole of the Old Testament have observed this process of innovation and theologisation which can rightly be linked to the category of inspiration[9].

Let us recall the steps taken. The observation of the heterogeneity of the two realities that are textual fluidity (an exegetical element) and the inspiration of the Scriptures (a theological element), prevents them from being linked as if from the outside, overhanging the biblical text. Here, an intimate resonance has been brought to light between textual fluidity and scriptural inspiration starting from the consideration of the genesis of the biblical text and the long process of editing giving rise to rereadings. It can be seen that, beyond their heterogeneity, textual fluidity and scriptural inspiration, considered from the genetic point of view of

---

[8] Bernard M. Levinson, "You Must Not Add Anything to What I Command You: Paradoxes of Canon and Authorship in Ancient Israel," *Numen* 50 (2003): 47.

[9] See the overview in Benoît Bourgine, *Bible oblige: Essai sur la théologie biblique*, Cogitatio Fidei 308 (Paris: Cerf, 2019), 210–22.

biblical writing and the process of canonisation, are far from being foreign to one another. What does this mean for interpretation and the status of inspiration?

## 4 Biblical theology, humanity of the word, and inspiration of Scripture

If the relationship between textual fluidity and Scriptural inspiration cannot be short-circuited by invoking divine inspiration in order to magically resolve the difficulty of textual fluidity, this does not mean that the perspectives of the exegete and the theologian are foreign to each other. The phenomenon of fluidity considered in the diversity of its manifestations corresponds in a notable part to the process analysed by several authors as a "theologisation" process. As Levinson writes, "revelation is not prior to or external to the text; revelation is in the text and of the text."[10] The literary care and ingenuity of successive editors, revisers, translators, and publishers, which are deployed not without reference to the problem of inspiration, to adjust the biblical text to new theological ideas and to new historical contexts, are such as to establish between exegetes and theologians a dialogue focused on the letter of the text, in its very fluidity. Apart from the case of purely contingent textual fluidity, the plurality of versions deserves all the exegete's attention as he works towards an explanation, no less than that of the theologian as he envisages an interpretation. Since such fluidity is a matter of literary art and theological concerns, the elucidation of the text requires simultaneously the competence of the exegete and the know-how of the theologian. Textual fluidity is thus less a challenge to inspiration than an invitation to a *practical collaboration* of exegete and theologian, which is what biblical theology consists of, with the study and interpretation of the Bible at its centre.

The object of this collaboration focused on the text of the Scriptures concerns the exegetical explanation and the theological interpretation of the biblical text in the density of its text. In the two New Testament reference quotations on the inspiration of the Scriptures, one can note the close link established between the divine origin of the scriptural text and the requirement of an interpretation useful to the recipients of this word, which refers to the theological concern as we have defined it and taken it into account here: "no prophecy (πᾶσα προφητεία) of Scripture is a matter of one's own interpretation" (2 Pet 1:20) and "All Scripture (πᾶσα

---

[10] Levinson, "You Must Not Add Anything," 47. See the larger picture in Bourgine, *Bible oblige*, 181–223.

γραφή) is inspired by God and is useful for teaching" (2 Tim 3:16). One will also note the requirement of attaching oneself to the biblical text in all its integrity with the recurrence of the adjective πᾶς. This amounts to stating, in this case, the requirement that nothing be neglected in the reception of the inspired text and that it be received in its entirety, that is to say, also in *all the aspects of its fluidity*.

The problem of the relationship between the inspiration of the Scriptures and textual fluidity has given rise to the exploration of different aspects of the *humanity* of the scriptural attestation of the *divine Word*. From a theological point of view, the fluidity of the biblical text shows the extent of the risk assumed by God as soon as he speaks the language of men and submits the transmission of his knowledge to the normal human channels. To take into account the difficulty that textual fluidity entails and to accept all that it implies in a coherent manner is in keeping with the logic of incarnation which Christianity cannot but obey: how can one be inhuman where God is at his most human? The humanity of the scriptural attestation has not only been considered from the fluid state of the text, but also in relation to the bold, constant, decisive hermeneutical intervention of authors, translators, revisers, and editors by which alone the history of the writing, canonisation and transmission of the sacred text can be accounted for. The Word of God has not only surrendered itself to the vagaries of historical knowledge; it has also entrusted itself to the theological activity of the biblical witnesses, rather than jealously claiming its rights as author. God submits to the laws of human knowledge determined by language and history; he entrusts himself to witnesses, authors, and interpreters, exposing himself to the risk of misunderstanding, misinterpretation, or misappropriation.

* * *

In the Platonic dialogue dedicated to the inspiration of the poet and named after the rhapsode it features, Ion, the phenomenon of inspiration is identified with a divine power, like a magnetic force which, as if by magnetized rings inserted into one other, is transmitted from the muse by the interpreter to the listeners of the performance.[11] The poet thus communicates the performativity of Homeric inspiration. For Plato, Ion is incomparable in his ability to praise Homer. But to what does Ion owe this ability? For the philosopher of the Academy, Ion is devoid of art (*technè*) and science (*épistémè*). In reality, Ion is a divine man, possessed by the muse that inspires Homer, and not a man of art. This is the reason why Ion excels in explaining and reciting it, better than all the other rhapsodes. He owes all his ability to his god, the only one to play his cards right, and Ion is thus deprived of any active contribution. Moreover, does the Homeric text, which situates its action

---

[11] Plato, "Ion," in *Œuvres complètes*, ed. Luc Brisson (Paris: Flammarion, 2008), 572–85.

in a transparent present, exposing the thoughts of the characters as in a continuous foreground, leave room for interpretation, which the biblical text irresistibly calls for by its imperious claim to truth, authority, and existential performativity?[12]

Three millennia after Homer, and twenty-seven centuries after his writing, one can hardly find a poet claiming the divinity of Homeric poetry. Why then, with the same time scale, does a significant part of humanity continue to find light and nourishment in the biblical scriptures? Could it be that the God who inspires them is the most human of gods?

## Bibliography

Auerbach, Erich. *Mimesis. The Representation of Reality in Western Literature*, trans. Willard Trask. Princeton, NJ: Princeton University Press, 1995.

Barth, Karl. *The Epistle to the Romans*, trans. Edwin Hoskyns. Oxford: Oxford University Press, 1968.

Bogaert, Pierre-Maurice. "'Vie et Paroles de Jérémie selon Baruch': Le texte court du livre de Jérémie selon la LXX et son modèle hébreu avec un test: Le dossier épistolaire LXX 36 (TM 29)." In *Le livre de Jérémie en perspective: Les deux rédactions conservées et l'addition du supplément sous le nom de Baruch: Recueil des travaux de Pierre-Maurice Bogaert*, edited by Jean-Claude Haelewyck and Bastien Kindt, 461–501. BETL 308. Leuven: Peeters, 2002.

Bourgine, Benoît. *Bible oblige: Essai sur la théologie biblique*. Cogitatio Fidei 308. Paris: Cerf, 2019.

Levinson, Bernard Malcolm. "The Human Voice in Divine Revelation: The Problem of Authority in Biblical Law." In *Innovation in Religious Traditions: Essays in the Interpretation of Religious Change*, edited by Michael Williams, Collett Cox, and Martin Jaffee, 35–71. RelSoc 31. Berlin – New York: Mouton de Gruyter, 1992.

Levinson, Bernard Malcolm. "You Must Not Add Anything to What I Command You: Paradoxes of Canon and Authorship in Ancient Israel." *Numen 50* (2003): 1–51.

Plato. "Ion." in *Œuvres complètes*, edited by Luc Brisson, 572–85. Paris: Flammarion, 2008.

---

[12] "[. . .] the Homeric poems conceal nothing, they contain no teaching and no secret second meaning. Homer can be analyzed, [. . .], but he cannot be interpreted.[. . .] The Bible's claim to truth is not only far more urgent than Homer's, it is tyrannical – it excludes all other claims. [. . .] If the text of the Bible narrative, then, is so greatly in need of interpretation on the basis of its own content, its claim to absolute authority forces it still further in the same direction [. . .]: we are to fit our own life into its world, fell ourselves to be elements in its structure of universal history." Erich Auerbach, *Mimesis. The Representation of Reality in Western Literature*, trans. Willard Trask (Princeton: Princeton University Press, 1995), 13–15.

## Part II: **Inspired Reading?**

## Active Participation in Revelation?

Mark W. Elliott

# 5 Revelation's Activating: The Verbal as the Expression of the Personal Impression

As the title might all too clearly imply, I am trying to suggest that the scriptural words encode something of a special religious experience, that does more than just resonate with our present-day religious sense (where "our" means the present reader, reading no doubt as part of a community and a tradition, even taking note of the reality of "intersectionality"), but actually serves to inspire, instruct and correct that religious sense. One might say that through this encoding and decoding of that experience, they operate causally in a sense of a formal and even efficient cause, although one might wish to employ those categories lightly. Although there is an element of *dialogue*, in that the poetics of the psalms and the rhetoric of the prophets and of the Gospels and Paul allow or even demand room for the category of persuasion along with the demand of the authoritative. As with the *Summa Theologiae* so too with the Psalms or Job or Paul: objections are constitutive of the message, even if not the first or the last word of that message.

**Holy Scripture and its radiating holiness**
Catholic biblical theologians have traditionally preferred the "the interpreted bible" (glossed by the church's interpreters) to "sola scriptura" as the primary locus of Revelation to the Church. Ecumenically minded Protestants might well agree, and so they affirm "prima scriptura" and even "sola scriptura" (the books of the canon alone as that locus) or "pura scriptura." However, there is no such thing as *pura scriptura,* any more than there is such a thing as *pura natura,* for the minute it is being read it is being interpreted. Catholic theology thus has a certain affinity with Jewish Torah-centred interpretation, e.g, when Jewish interpreters think that the gift of land as per Deut 34:10–12 is now something "eternal" or at least for the future from the point of view of Deuteronomy, and that the major prophets agree that it lies well in the future such that it lies "beyond the Tanakh." This Catholic-Jewish consensus on method continues to inspire protests from the German and Anglo-Saxon Protestant guild who want to fix the sense to the historical sense, the more its meaning can be held at a distance, the better it can be historicized and objectified. Then comes an analogical imagination whereby the promise of liberation of one style (intended by the Exilic writers and redactors) is given its analogate in present-day culture, possibly liberation of another style. Taking history

seriously enough, so the biblical guild from Helsinki to LA means sitting askance from allegedly anachronistic ideas of "canon," and indeed the task of biblical exegesis requires so-called extra-canonical writings as interwoven into the fabric of the biblical texts (e.g. Enoch 14, 4Q246).[1] The upshot is that ancient texts are political, instruments in power-plays, then and now, often then intended for ill, but perhaps now only for good.

In a volume titled *Beyond Biblical Theologies*, Philipp Stoellger inveighs against the emphasis on continuity (of tradition) in overly confessional (and Catholic) biblical scholars such as George Braulik and Norbert Lohfink, who claim to find Pauline "Rechtfertigungstheologie" in Deuteronomy (!), and who like to drop in apologetic and normative features to their writing.[2] Better to emphasise the historical discontinuity between the testaments and stop any danger of some theological "skimming stone" from OT to NT to "our theological task of today." Hence the work of Otfried Hofius encourages Stoellger here to assert that HB/OT priestly theology is *not* identical with NT *Sühnetheologie*. Tensions are the stuff of biblical theology from Cain and Abel to priest and prophet, and howsoever it resolves these, theology has to look *beyond* the bible to be theology. Hence "Systematik ist nicht einfach konsequente Exegese, Theologie daher auch als 'biblische' unterbestimmt. Die Exegese wirft Fragen auf, die über sie hinausführen."[3] In the mature systematic-theological task more process is needed than merely reporting the contents of the bible. Biblical exegesis is useful in that it throws up valuable questions, such that one can start with the origin of a *debate* in the bible, and keep that playing even in the "now." Sometimes it will be right to take sides, as when John Collins writing in the same volume is sure that *Sachkrititk* is a duty for the interpreter who needs to choose between the way of love and the way of holiness.

> I would therefore reformulate Francis Watson's statement, and say that the reasons for resisting parts of canonical scripture are found not only in Christian (and Jewish) but also in secular traditions. Whether we regulate our biblical theology toward love of neighbor or toward the preservation of holiness will depend ultimately not on whether we are Jewish or Christian but on our intuitions about human nature, righteousness and justice.[4]

---

[1] Stefan Beyerle, "'Beyond' – Grenzbeschreibungen zur Biblischen Theologie," in *Beyond Biblical Theologies*, eds. Heinrich Assel, Stefan Beyerle, and Christfried Böttrich (Tübingen: Mohr Siebeck, 2012): 19–51, 49. One should note the similarly titled work by Timo Eskola, *Beyond Biblical Theology: Sacralized Culturalism in Heikki Räisänen's Hermeneutics* (Leiden: Brill, 2013).
[2] Philipp Stoellger, "Biblische Theologie – bildtheoretischer Perspektive," in *Beyond Biblical Theologies*, eds. Assel, Beyerle, and Böttrich, 455–81, 463.
[3] Philipp Stoellger, "Biblische Theologie," 480.
[4] John J. Collins, "Biblical Theology Between Apologetics and Criticism," in *Beyond Biblical Theologies*, eds. Assel, Beyerle, and Böttrich, 224–41, 240.

However, to surrender the concept of Holiness when it comes to God and his ways in our biblical interpretation, is to surrender a lot, not least and not only the *mysterium tremendum et fascinans* aspect of "holiness." Moreover, can love really fill the gap and do all the work "holiness" used to do? One thing about holiness is that it reserves that unrevealed quality: the divine hand is not quite completely played. For Mark C. Murphy, there are no obvious reasons for God to act to protect the well-being of creatures,[5] and Aquinas did not think to classify the supremely free God as morally perfect;[6] neither did Scotus.[7] God is not bound to love all he has made: and to make is not to be in covenant per se. Necessarily speaking God loves only himself. God has reasons not to associate with creatures, and that makes his choice to love all the more remarkable or praiseworthy, since presence is enabled only through self-sacrifice, since he is in himself far from the realm of decay and any need for procreation. Here Murphy draws on the work of Jonathan Klawans and Jacob Milgrom.

> But these divine reasons for action cannot be requiring reasons, or else the motivation would be a necessary one (6.1). Rather, the reasons that would have to be invoked to explain contingent divine motivation must be *justifying* reasons, reasons that do not in any way necessitate divine action, but which nevertheless are such that God may freely and rationally act on them. Some such reasons may be aptly called "moral reasons" and (even more aptly) "reasons of love."[8]

The most that can be said about divine reasons for action is that God as agent "requires" that he do something. Plus, just what he does is provide an effortless holiness which then radiates to and through creatures. Jewish interpretations of the obedient Abraham challenge "sola-fideistic" ones deriving from Rom 4. Yet surely this is a false alternative. Abraham is responsive to a holiness of God that is not so much amoral as it is definitive and inspiring of an obedience of love that would otherwise remain buried and very far from fulfilling its potential. One cannot think of patriarchal narratival theophany and covenant in simply moral command and fulfilment, but one driven by holiness when human agents choose to come close to it.

One might think of the Bible in an analogous way, of some amount of Revelation having left its mark as a deposit throughout Scripture. This will result in graded holiness (think "unclean-hands making" of Pharisaic Judaism),[9] then it is not so hard to see why there might not be a radiated holiness that does not just stay

---

[5] Michael Murphy, *Divine Holiness and Divine Action* (Oxford: OUP, 2021), 95.
[6] Brian Davies, *Thomas Aquinas on God and Evil* (Oxford: Oxford University Press, 2011).
[7] Marilyn McCord Adams, "Duns Scotus on the Goodness of God," *Faith and Philosophy* 4 (1987): 486–505.
[8] Murphy, *Divine Holiness and Divine Action*, 133.
[9] Timothy H. Lim, "The Defilement of the Hands as a Principle determining the Holiness of Scriptures," *JTS* 61 (2010): 501–15.

within the texts but affect the reader. This could be at the level of the NT reading the OT with the "apostolic" mind in charge in trying to construe the fuller sense of the prophets (*intentio auctoris*) and where a certain amount of rationality can be maintained, rather than the "midrashic" approach beloved of James Kugel (*intentio operis*), where conscious intentions and understanding matter more. This implies that conscience, that location of intentional and moral response, is also the place of revelation. What is revealed to that conscience is will (Sinai/Horeb), what the Lutherans called "law." Sure, law is a gift, but it functions as demand and obligation. Yet what one finds in the last part of Exodus and in the "ritual decalogue" presupposes sin and the need for atonement which thereby too is revealed. "Revelation consists in . . . the substitution of the voice of a Lawgiver for the voice of conscience."[10] Or perhaps we could better say that conscience needs forming and informing, if it is going to function as conscience and that Revelation makes this happen and expects some difference to be made. As people of conscience the Scripture writers bore the impress of revelation. It was not simply response but also included giving form to the revelation, conveying the message, radiating or passing on the holiness even as they produced holy Scripture.

Moses seeing God's back means seeing God go by in his deeds which bring Israel into his own space, rather than giving humans a new quality.[11] God bathes the world with glory, but then this gets intensified at Sinai and with the Incarnation:

> the Synoptic Gospels begin by portraying the event of Jesus without using the concept of "glory" (in a present sense), by setting the beginning wholly afresh at the point – where God's act of making himself present had begun: with the *momentum* of the presence, of the subject that forces its way forward and makes its own impression and expression; they begin with his force and authority, which especially in Mark calls forth anew the elementary terror before God at the foot of Sinai. . ., a stupefied being beside oneself through terror: Mk 1.22; 6.2; 11.18.[12]

In Hans Urs von Balthasar's scheme, one moves beyond this impression real as it is (God has both tactile shapeliness and infinitude) to a deeper encounter where one participates in a way that is passively active in the *Theodrama* to glimpse ontology

---

[10] Johann S. Drey, *Brief Introduction to the Study of Theology: With Reference to the Scientific Standpoint and the Catholic System* (Notre Dame, IN: University of Notre Dame Press, 1994); Wayne L. Fehr, *The Birth of the Catholic Tübingen School : The Dogmatics of Johann Sebastian Drey* (Chico, CA : Scholars Press, 1981), 51. "The liturgy is the means of God's continued self-disclosure of himself to the world" (cited by Fehr, 86).

[11] Hans Urs von Balthasar, *The Glory of the Lord: A Theological Aesthetics*, vol. 6: *Theology: The Old Covenant*, trans. Brian McNeil C.R.V. and Erasmo Leiva-Merikakis (Edinburgh: T&T Clark, 1991), 27. But also see Brevard S. Childs, *Exodus* (London: SCM, 1974), 74.

[12] Hans Urs von Balthasar, *The Glory of the Lord: A Theological Aesthetics*, vol. 1: *Seeing the Form*, trans. Erasmo Leiva-Merikakis (Edinburgh: T&T Clark, 1982), 216.

behind the scenes as it were.[13] Form includes "real pointing beyond itself into the depths."[14]

It is by means of revelation that holiness ensues. Jonathan Jacobs is worth hearing at length on this:

> In that sense revelation is guidance for humans qua rational beings. It does not direct them away from, or apart from their intellects. Revelation is a source of rational wisdom. Saadia and Baḥya held that the way in which divine graciousness most fully reaches human beings is through Torah, which, in requiring study of the commandments, directs us toward the fullest, knowing appreciation of God, enabling us to be like God insofar as that is possible. That the commandments are to be studied and reflected upon, and that we are to strive for the fullest possible understanding of them, is itself among what is commanded. (See, for example, Deut. 4:6).... Humility and the reasons for humility are not at odds with holiness. We are to be deeply humble before the power and wisdom and benevolence of God but we can also understand what is required for leading lives of holiness and in that way, come closer to God. This view is quite different from the moral psychology in much ancient Greek thought, some of the most influential of it maintaining that the more excellent the agent, the more pride is merited. The contrast with Aristotle's conception of the virtuous agent's appropriate pride is striking. For the Jewish thinkers the core of humility is humility before God, which in turn, shapes our attitudes toward worldly things such as the honor bestowed by others and the way we see ourselves in relation to others.[15]

One might be able to say that about *divine* holiness that it acts without deliberation and the need to suppress its concomitant motivations, since God lacks these. It is an unselfconscious desire for the good even while it is fully intentional and willed. It demands and gets humility and sobriety.

For Christians the figure of Jesus Christ, the Holy One of God (Mark 1:24), operates like some pineal gland between heaven and earth, or better a mediator who is no third thing of middling status but one comprises both the divine and the human in himself, yet without allowing either to overlap the other, which would be too "Stoic." There is definite mediation of a will to save from sins as well as a revelation of divine demands to be "like God" somehow, as well as an announcement of divine plans and purposes. To understand Christ's role as a reflector or radiator of holiness would not be too amiss. Is there a similar way with Scripture?

Somewhat more romantically, as Paul Ricoeur mentions, Franz Rosenzweig viewed the eucharist, that moment of the crucified Christ's exaltation, as the sacrament of revelation, which is always needing renewed and that moves out from the

---

**13** As stressed by Aidan Nicholls, *Say It Is Pentecost: A Guide Through Balthasar's Logic* (Edinburgh: T&T Clark, 2001).
**14** Von Balthasar, *The Glory of the Lord*, vol. 1, 119.
**15** Jonathan Jacobs, "Gratitude, Humility, and Holiness in Medieval Jewish Philosophy," in *Holiness in Jewish Thought*, ed. Alan L. Mittleman (New York – Oxford: Oxford University Press, 2018): 88–89.

suffering of sacrifice with powerful consequence. This, in line with Rosenzweig's emphasis on Revelation as relationship in a more mystical way that a more instruction-focused concept of revelation would be. One might employ the motto: "revelation for the soul, redemption for the neighbour."[16] This puts a lot of pressure on the present believer-God relationship to turn "revelation" into "redemption." As Norbert Samuelson summarised, for Rosenzweig, "to know God is to encounter a presence so radically other from ourselves that the experience can have no humanly expressible content whatsoever. However, the intensity of the divine presence is such that a human response to it is inescapable, and that response gives revelation the content that it, in itself, necessarily lacks."[17] This means an understanding of revelation as a pure experience of the divine that in turn inspires human response which contributes to its content. The second, weaker sense of the term "revelation," as inspiration of what they say and write seems to follow, remembering that according to Exod 34 divine takeover and provision of remedy is emphasized, as is the case with the Incarnation. For Christians Jesus echoes Moses as *mesites*, particularly in terms of the task of communication and interpretation of the divine so that "on earth as it is in heaven." Again, one might think in terms of a cascading holiness, at least as metaphor. Writing things seems to come quite late in the sequence, yet although the holiness of Scripture is derived, it is transparent or radiant of that derived holiness.

### Dialetical and dialogical

As Benoît Bourgine has pointed out,[18] in Paul Ricoeur's scheme there is "l'herméneutique du témoignage,"[19] but that is of a multiple witness, one which requires a dialectical exercise in order to avoid over-valorising any one witness, since many somehow conveying or channelling something of the absolute. As for "the absolute" this is similar to what Thomas wrote at *Summa Theologiae* II-II, 1.1 : "If we would consider the formal reason of the object, it is nothing other than the first truth; for the faith of which we are speaking does not assent to anything other than what is revealed by God; hence faith rests on divine truth as a medium." Yet perhaps in Ricoeur there is that modern felt-need for intersubjectivity, since differ-

---

[16] Paul Ricoeur, "The 'Figure' in Rosenzweig's The Star of Redemption," in *Figuring the Sacred* (Minneapolis, MN: Augsburg-Fortress, 1995): 93–105.

[17] Norbert Samuelson, *Revelation and the God of Israel* (Cambridge: Cambridge University Press, 2002), 237.

[18] Benoît Bourgine, *Bible oblige. Essai sur la Théologie Biblique*, Cogitatio Fidei (Paris: Cerf, 2019), 114–5.

[19] Paul Ricoeur, "L'herméneutique du témoignage," in *Le témoignage*, ed. Enrico Castelli (Paris: Vrin, 1972): 35–62.

ence and disagreement is more the norm than uniformity and agreement. Are we perhaps liable to project that felt-need on to the original witnesses, stressing their differences rather than their complementarities?

A recent example of multiple and dialectical approach to revealed truth and truths can be seen in the Christology of Heinrich Assel. The digital form of Christology, as Assel coins it, is bound by discourse, because it takes the biblical text as the foundation of a theological decision-making between opposing positions. It is this he posits as an alternative to the "konsequente Exegese" of the poetic textual sense. Texts provide co-ordinates or lines of trace so as to see the place of Jesus, analogous to geographical co-ordinates. The unity of Jesus is that of the unified narrative subject and this is merely a visible or apparent unity, not a real one. Hence one moves from *sprachlichen* to *imaginären*, which one builds up from the overlapping of many texts. Hence there is a space both for the knowing Jesus of John 12:27–30 and the somewhat ignorant one of Mark 14:32–42, in spaces in between Jesus gets created from texts.[20]

Revelation might to some extent be dialectical in its reception (multiple different witnesses) but is it "dialogical" in its origin? Of course a dialogical account in which the Bible is a record of a conversation encourages is to thinking of Revelation as an aspect of the divine who is relational and thus personal. Wolfhart Pannenberg named Friedrich Schelling (1775–1854) as the scholar who introduced the expression 'self-revelation' (*Selbstoffenbarung*). For Schelling, the Incarnation added personality to that of God's divine nature that was in a sense existing outside his divine personhood. "To say that God is man means the divine has become man; not truly the divine, but much more the externally divine of the divine has become man."[21] God through becoming incarnate gains freedom albeit a second type, that of the

---

[20] Heinrich Assel, "Den Text der Menschwerdung lesen lernen: Das Fiktive und das Imaginäre in Joh 1 als Aufgabe der Inkarnationschristologie," in *Beyond Biblical Theologies*, eds. Assel, Beyerle, and Böttrich, 94: "Der analoge Form der Christologie ist eine Form dogmatischer Christologie, die als 'konsequente Exegese' des poetischen Textsinns auftritt, während die digitale Form der Christologie diskursbedingt ist, weil sie den Text als Grundlage einer theologischen Entscheidungsfindung zwischen opponierenden Positionen setzt. . ." Both aim for "das Sprachereignis des fleischgewordenen Wortes und die imaginäre Herrlichkeit des Menschgewordenen, schliesslich die imaginäre Zeitsymbolik Gottes in der 'textgewordenen Geschichte' Jesu hören/sehen zu lassen."
[21] Friedriech W.J. Schelling, *Werke 14: Vorlesungen über die Methode des academischen Studium; Philosophie und Religion und andere Texte (1803–1805)*, ed. Patrick Leistner and Alexander Schubach, F. W. J. Schelling historisch-kritische Ausgabe I-14 (Stuttgart-Bad Cannstatt: Frommann-Holzboog, 2021), 165 (my translation).

(perfect) creature.[22] Schelling could even speak of the unity of Scriptures[23] and insisted that "revelation is never identified with immanent processes of being"[24] but that revelation is something located in and through sacred texts and their instruction. Walter Kasper comments how the historical filled up the idea so as to give it content: "Daß die Spekulation nicht die Aufhebung des Geschichtlichen im Begriff bedeuten muß, sondern eher die Erfüllung des begrifflichen Begreifens mit der Geschichte, das hat die Spätphilosophie Schellings erwiesen."[25]

Can "dialogical" be thought of as "participatory"? Well, one can only agree with Benjamin Sommer's idea that the tradition helps not just to overcome the firewall between the ancient text and the modern person but also enhances, enriches, explains, emphasises messages in the sacred texts. "According to participatory theology, the Pentateuch not only conveys God's will, but also reflects Israel's interpretation of and response to that will."[26] It might be a little more accurate to add that the very "reditus"-like action of response begins more fully with the history of interpretation, given that those whose response to revelation contributes to scripture are what makes this revelation unique and for all times. Now the Catholic equivalent of Sommer's Jewish account often ramps this up to an ontology as Matthew Levering has done in his *Participatory Biblical Exegesis*.[27] In Sommer's version, it is not a question of mixing the creator with the creature, but of seeing little definite boundary between the inspired writers with those who followed, ourselves included. My reading of Brevard Childs is that he felt a canonical approach preserved all the voices and layers in a text, so that what Sommer implies, that it is a quick step from Childs to those biblical theologians seeking a thematic *Mitte*, seems unfair. When Sommer writes: "As a result, I cannot see why, from a Jewish point of view, the redactor of the Pentateuch should have a more important voice than the P authors or D authors who came before him, or than various commenta-

---

22 Schelling objected to the ignoring of the Old Testament in much theology and claimed: "(T)here is *a coherence in the divine revelations*, which cannot be comprehended in the middle, but only from the beginning." Quoted in Joris Geldhof, *Revelation, Reason and Reality: Theological Encounters with Jaspers, Schelling and Baader* (Leuven: Peeters, 2007), 98.
23 Friedriech W.J. Schelling, *Urfassung der Philosophie der Offenbarung*, ed. Walter E. Ehrhardt (Hamburg: Meiner, 2010), 438.
24 Geldhof, *Revelation*, 104.
25 Walter Kasper, *Das Absolute in der Geschichte: Philosophie und Theologie der Geschichte in der Spätphilosophie Schellings* (Mainz: Grunewald, 2010), 459.
26 Benjamin D. Sommer, *Revelation and Authority: Sinai in Jewish Scripture and Tradition*, AYRBL (New Haven, CT: Yale University Press, 2018), 2.
27 Matthew Levering, *Participatory Biblical Exegesis: A Theology of Biblical Interpretation* (Notre Dame, IN: Notre Dame Press, 2008).

tors on the Pentateuch who came after,"²⁸ Childs might well have agreed with the former and only disagree with the latter – the point is not to overcome (e.g.) the Gen 1 – Gen 2 difference, but actually to preserve it. He would also prefer a Jewish ontology of Scripture to many Catholic ones (or Protestant ones, for that matter. However, he would have wished to preserve the scripture – tradition distinction, while seeing a continuity between then and now for what the people of God are to learn, mediated by a tradition of interpretation continually refreshed by the biblical text, as his great Exodus commentary and his *Struggle to Understand Isaiah as Christian Scripture*²⁹ both demonstrate. Dialectical in reception, but dialogical only in the text's origins, such that readers do not participate in the text's human voices in dialogue with or response to God, but simply learn from it. Response is included in Scripture, but it is an authoritative response for those who follow.

**The dangers of personalism**

For the Catholic Tübinger such as Johannes von Kühn, in the spirit of Schelling, Revelation carries on into church history, and is personal and non-verbal in in origin.³⁰ In the early to mid-twentieth century Romano Guardini went further in claiming that what Jesus reveals is "man," which is the very point of the "fundamental-theological" nature of the topic of "Revelation."³¹ With an echo of Guardini, John Montag observed: "Thus we see that for Thomas, revelation has to do primarily with one's perspective on things in light of one's final end."³² This is about reversing the effects of sin on reason. The Light shows things up, it is not the thing: Light is not the sun. What is illuminated is the human condition.

This spiritual personalism is all very well but it misses that the light in the discourse of the Fourth Gospel demands Tabor-like contemplation, as John 1:8 has it: "He [John the Baptist] himself was not the light, but he came to testify to the light."³³ The Light does not serve simply to illuminate the human condition, but somehow it is to be looked at, pointed at and described as in the 21 chapters of John's gospel of Jesus. Light is also the Sun.

---

[28] Sommer, *Revelation and Authority*, 230.
[29] Brevard S. Childs, *The Struggle to Understand Isaiah as Christian Scripture* (Grand Rapids, MI – Cambridge, UK: Eerdmans, 2004).
[30] Thomas F. O'Meara, *Romantic Idealism und Roman Catholicism: Schelling and the Theologians* (Notre Dame, IN: Notre Dame University Press, 1982), 459.
[31] Romano Guardini, "Heilige Schrift und Glaubenswissenschaft," *Die Schildgenossen* 8 (1928): 24–57.
[32] John Montag, "The False Legacy of Suarez," in *Radical Orthodoxy*, eds. John Milbank, Catherine Pickstock, and Graham Ward (London: Routledge, 1998): 43.
[33] Translation from the NRSV.

The new version of revelation, reaching its apogee in *Nouvelle Théologie* and Vatican II is seen to have reacted against the post-Tridentine theology of revelation, perhaps most fully articulated by Francisco Suarez, who was responsible for presenting supernatural knowledge like an addition to natural knowledge, and in the form of facts, stuff. In a now-famous article Montag employs what might be called genealogy in service of purifying the tradition, going back to unravel it, getting back to Thomas Aquinas whose thinking was falsely represented in the early Modern era. Suarez "wrongly attributed to Aquinas the idea that God is the formal object of faith since he reveals or testifies to by means of faith the things to believed, since faith accepts the propositions of faith as revealed immediately and uses them as principles…as testifying and revealing them he is the formal object of faith." There is, as Jean-Louis Marion has observed, little need for faith in Suarez:[34] one assents with reason to various propositions about "natural realities" including the existing God as supreme Being received by the light of reason. And yet the propositions of the creed are not so much about believing in a God beyond Being as giving assent to credal realities as though that were as natural as breathing even at the expense of the mysteriousness, and of reducing the acts of Christ to propositions.[35] This is "revelation" according to *Nouvelle Théologie*.

Montag argued that this movement could receive encouragement even from Luther, who described *Offenbarung* in terms of self-giving as baring oneself "offen," yet this was arguably achieved at the cost of separation of word and thing, with experience filing the gap created by the loss of a knowledge God attained through truths. Yet that seems the very thing Montag complains about in Suarez, when he writes, "faith relates to the believability and knowability of an object"[36] and that revelation comes from outside to reinforce reason by the infusion of interior light. There is a place for revelation as infusion of faith, but that is secondary to the object unveiled to knowledge.[37] Ironically, subjective factors increased when convinced knowledge that could exclude other propositions became of the *esse* of the faith.[38] Natural knowledge got stamped with a spirit of certainty.

"For Thomas, things revealed led to faith, but for Suarez, faith confirms what is revealed."[39] Why should those two things be contradictory? For Thomas what is

---

[34] Jean-Luc Marion, *D'Ailleurs, la Révélation* (Paris: Grasset, 2021), 90.
[35] Marion, *D'Ailleurs*, 107.
[36] Montag, "The False Legacy," 55.
[37] Suarez, *De fide* III.3.7.
[38] Jean-Yves Lacoste, "Révélation," in *Dictionnaire de Théologie Critique*, ed. Jean-Yves Lacoste (Paris : Presses Universitaires de France, 2007): 1215–22.
[39] Tracey Rowland, *Benedict XVI: A Guide for the Perplexed* (London: T&T Clark International, 2010), 49.

revealed formally is *God* although what is revealed materially-the matter known by faith – is diverse. Suarez reified mediated propositions with God as the formal object of faith–*De fide* III.2.3. Perhaps the main difference is that Thomas was a pastoral theologian with the goal of an "existentialist-spiritual guidance" sort,[40] whereas Suarez was a polemical one who needed to argue for a particular doctrine. The inheritors of Romantic Catholicism (via Blondel and Congar) such as Ratzinger are more like Thomas in their desire that their hearers might all "see the form."

Propositionalist theology received its imprimatur in the mid-to-late nineteenth century.

> Logically Vatican I explained the act of faith as assent to truths (plural) or believing "the things" to be true that God has revealed (DzH 3008; ND 118)...Moreover, far from being a Catholic monopoly, the view was widely shared, even if not always named as a "propositional" view of revelation. Thus a Calvinist theologian, Archibald Alexander Hodge (1823–86), wrote in a work published in 1863, *Outlines of Theology*: (p. 5) "we define faith...to be the assent of the mind to truth, upon the testimony of God, conveying knowledge to us though supernatural channels...when we know what He [God] says, we believe it because he says it."[41]

Now the problem with the Romantic Catholic Tübingen reaction (and that of *Nouvelle Théologie*) to the Suarezian model beloved of Vatican I and Old Princetonians alike was to emphasise the historical development of speculative reflection on the possibility and content of Revelation, which means that the meaning of Revelation could change with the understanding of each generation.[42] Naturally a more conservative theologian like Joseph Kleutgen criticized this: the divine revelation cannot be perfected. Even if there is development this amounts neither to the progressive revelation or the history of humanity's education by divine *Erziehung* (Lessing) nor to the human dialogical manner of to make hitherto undiscovered things come to light (Günther). The Church could only clarify and fix what was unclear: that was all one could say was truly "development."

---

[40] As noted by Rowland (*Benedict XVI*, 60): "This principle is something which [Benedict] has taken from Guardini's *Das Christusbild der paulinischen und johanneischen Schriften* (Würzburg, 1961). He has stated that 'the reflections on method that Guardini develops on pages 7–15 are among the most important things that have ever been said on the problem of methodology in scriptural interpretation."

[41] Gerald O'Collins, *Retrieving Fundamental Theology: The Three Styles of Contemporary Theology* (Mahwah, NJ: Pauli Press, 1993), 3.

[42] Hans Waldenfels, *Offenbarung: Von der Reformation bis zur Gegenwart* (Handbuch der Dogmengeschichte I/1b, (Freiburg: Herder, 1977), 89: "Die sich daraus ergebende Entwicklung ist ein Vorgang der philosophischen Reflexion, in dem die Offenbarung durch das spekulative Wissen überholt wird. Damit ist zugleich festgestellt, daß die von der Kirche definierten Offenbarungswahrheiten sich je nach dem Stand der Wissenschaft in bezug auf ihr Verständnis, ja sogar bezüglich ihres Sinnes ändern können."

Less defensive were the voices of Giovanni Perrone and Johannes B. Franzelin: the objectivity and historicity of Revelation by speech and act works to make an impression in experience. The saving act gets interpreted and proclaimed by a word, which then acts to inspire the church in continuing as part of God's new *Offenbarung*.[43] Something similar can be viewed in Matthias Scheeben, for whom God did his revealing through history to the church (not "humanity"), according to a three-stage sequence of revelation of nature through nature (*revelatio naturae per naturam*) to the Patriarchs, a revelation of grace through faith (*revelatio gratiae per fidem*) to Moses and a revelation of glory (*revelatio gloriae*) in and through Christ. Here can be witnessed a real influence of biblical-historical thinking on the concept of Revelation, with an emphasis more on the intellectual content of experience with words as necessary vehicles for this, and an avoidance of any characterisation of Revelation as act of encounter. The mysteries lie behind the doctrinal declarations of the church which work as a kind of deposit.[44] The cumulative effect of the words of the tradition of interpretation together with the "fresh word from Scripture" in the present combine to ensure a continuity that is a living tradition open to correction from the preached word and not principally from the new context. This to my mind seems more ecumenically satisfying than the personalism and theology as spirituality to be found in the *Nouvelle Théologie*-informed *Dei Verbum*.

Thomas, as Montag relates, was clear that prophetic revelation had nothing to do with the person (or personal virtues or sanctity) of the prophet, but was a power of seeing symbolically. Likewise in more recent times. To hear Montag one more:

> Avery Dulles (*Models of Revelation*, 136–9) singles out four aspects of symbolic communication which parallel the use of the term "revelation" for Thomas: these are the participatory, transformative, motivational and supra-discursive properties of symbols, which invariably point beyond whatever is disclosed, toward mystery.[45]

Not much chance for clarity of what is to be believed, then. Further according to Gerald O'Collins, living faith through history worked as a catalyst for encounter in the minds of the biblical authors, but present-day encounter is that which in the same spirit receives along with divine self-revelation also a (propositional) deposit of faith as secondary.

> Thus the formulations of faith not only issue from such encounters but also provoke them. A narrative or other versions of prior revelatory events and "the things" disclosed through them can bring about fresh revelatory situations and initiate (or confirm) the faith of later

---

[43] Johannes B. Franzelin, *Tractatus de divina traditione et scriptura*, 4th edition (Rome: S. C. de Propaganda Fide, 1896), 640.
[44] Franzelin, *Tractatus*, 94.
[45] Franzelin, *Tractatus*, 49.

believers... Hence, pace Tracey Rowland, the Second Vatican Council did not endorse a "rejection" of the earlier propositional view of revelation advanced by Suárez, de Lugo, Franzelin, Garrigou-Lagrange, and others (including many non-Catholic Christians). Yes, the opening chapter of the Constitution on Divine Revelation, Dei Verbum, makes it abundantly clear that revelation means primarily God's personal self-revelation (DV 1–4). But that carries with it the conviction that, secondarily, the divine revelation discloses something about God and human beings. The pre-Vatican account of revelation is not rejected, as Rowland claims, but rather moved into second place. *Dei Verbum* (p. 14) accepts a propositional view of revelation, but only as coming after the primary, personal view.[46]

Here the (not unattractive) idea is of the act of personal revelation as having two actions or moments. This however can be primarily subjective with "objectivity" contained in the follow-through, such that the former is a hermeneutical principle for interpreting the latter.[47] This is apparent in O'Collins' later discussion:

> The Montreal report likewise described Tradition in global terms as "the Gospel itself, transmitted from generation to generation in and by the Church." The Montreal report leaned towards interpreting the essential *Traditum* (or what is handed on) as "Christ himself present in the life of the Church." It preferred to move beyond the *visible* human realities which make up the Christian life of faith and emphasize the (invisible) truth and reality of the risen Christ present among believers. That presence constitutes the heart of the Traditum: "what is transmitted in the process of tradition is the Christian faith, not only as a sum of tenets [equivalent to 'all that she [the Church] believes' of DV 8], but [also] as a living reality transmitted through the operation of the Holy Spirit. We can speak of the Christian Tradition (with a capital T), whose content is God's revelation and self-giving in Christ, present in the life of the Church."[48]

Tradition thus becomes the Holy Spirit at work. The invisible realities are present ones, not past, future or eternal and heavenly. Rightly, O'Collins hesitates to follow the Biblical Commission's *The Inspiration and Truth of Sacred Scripture* for comparing the Scriptures to a library of literary classics.

> The classics exemplify the deepest realities of human existence; in such books (and works of art), generations of readers have recognized "the truth of their own identity." But it is "the identity of Jesus" that is the basis for scriptural authority rather than the power of Scriptures to elicit from one generation to the next compelling truths about the human condition.[49]

Yet he replaces this with a "Jesus" who is very open to interpretation. One recalls what O'Collins previously said about the Risen Jesus and the Spirit as the content

---

**46** O'Collins, *Retrieving Fundamental Theology*, 14.
**47** Cf. Jared Wicks, "Vatican II on Revelation – From Behind the Scenes," *Theological Studies* 71 (2010): 637–50.
**48** Gerald O'Collins, *Rethinking Fundamental Theology: Toward a New Fundamental Theology* (Oxford: OUP, 2011), 204.
**49** O'Collins, *Retrieving Fundamental Theology*, 169.

of living tradition. Revelation is "the (invisible) truth and reality of the risen Christ present among believers... Tradition, whose content is God's revelation and self-giving in Christ, present in the life of the Church." Well here this is the written deposit of revelation considered as having a role that is no more than that of a catalyst or vehicle through which faith is occasioned rather than caused. Yet this seems quite close to the kind of thing being advocated here by O'Collins. One is saved by the personal encounter after logging into the presence of Christ that comes through the ages, with a bespoke relationship of each believer to his or her God. It seems that Scriptural content is left a long way behind.

**The Scriptural Canon: Locus and focus**
Amid all this intellectual and spiritual excitement the bible might seem rather dull and best left to historians and historical philologists. A canon of books that is Scripture witness to an experience after the manner of a fossil that is given shape by the life-form contained inside it still feels like something extinct or at least moribund, *ersterbend*. Balthasar used to insist that the *Novum Testamentum* was not a book so much as it was, well a what? Something to which a book witnesses, namely a covenant (*testamentum*) that was itself fully historical,[50] and one should be careful not to reduce this covenantal existence to an idea, when in fact covenant existed as a living natural movement towards God in seeking "our" own perfections (cf. Thomas Aquinas, *Summa Theologiae* I, q6, a1 ad2). The Israelite as "everyman" in mid-twentieth century existentialist forms of "biblical theology" plays a part here. There is no denying how essential the experiences of past Christians have been: but what they have left us with, and what present-day believers have to reckon with are articulations of what has been done and what that means for us: propositions.

The revenge of the Genre Critics can be seen in the preference of biblical scholars to cut across the canon and prefer to study for example "Apocalypses," that of John of Patmos with the Syriac Baruch, and the Animal Apocalypse. While exciting and extremely illuminating and worth a conference or six, it doesn't feel like these connect very well with what has stood the test of time as the content of the faith of the church. The canon is a family of different genres and personalities of which many pseudepigraphal works are imitations. Even if there are a few books in the New Testament that are possibly pseudonymous, it seems important that they were identified with an apostle, and the Four Gospels have names. Hebrews is not exception in that Origen knew some in doubt about the authorship of Hebrews: but the point is that it was important to have it attributed to Paul. Neither the *Shepherd of Hermas* nor the *Gospel of the Hebrews* makes the cut, in part due to their ano-

---

50 *Herrlichkeit III/1: Neues Bund.*

nymity. The literary genres of the NT are fairly unlike those of the OT, even if Luke borrows from Elijah-Elisha narratives in particular. We have Gospels, Letters, one History (acts) and one Apocalypse. Thomas Söding in his *Die Einheit der Heiligen Schrift*[51] makes something of this "balanced diet" of story, teaching, oracle, diatribe and argument, etc in the NT. So indeed there are voices and personalities in what goes to make up the NT. That is indeed personal, even if what ensues as revelation to be received is propositional.

One other thing: "Biblical theology" can sometimes seem to operate too much as a buffer between the biblical texts and systematic theology and just getting in the way (so, Stephen Fowl), who would prefer scripture to be received ethically, with the themes and topics of doctrine. Or even systematic theology can act like some sort of buffer, but a transparent one like the frame of a building that are the forms of Christian life. The Methodist theologian William Abraham preferred to see the deposit of traditional theology as part of revelation, in an analogous way to how Jewish interpreters saw the definition of Torah as including the interpretation of the Pentateuch. But unlike the Jewish tradition there is a tendency to talk about God in the same breath as the Scriptural text (e.g. "God subjects himself to scrutiny in historical criticism as in the Incarnation.")[52] Yet the idea in this Protestantism influenced by catholic "tradition" is that the church's interpretation gives back what historical criticism has taken away, or rescues the bible from death.

In the (Anglican) Reformed camp, John Webster, according to Levering, spoke of Scripture as simply belonging to the economy of the triune God, that is as an instrument God uses to save people and churches, not so much as a warrant for the rest of doctrine. Webster, Levering thinks, dislikes the notion of Scripture as a "means of grace" or medium, for the medium might then be seen as having agency. Scripture as "testimony" is better, especially "testimony as astonished indication". Yet that misunderstands Webster. For him, the church is not a channel of saving grace, but *Scripture* is. According to Webster's *Holy Scripture*, Scripture communicates self-revelation as instrument, as "an entity which embodies rather than serves the presence of God."[53] It could be a means of grace, an instrument, perhaps not an agent in its own right. It is still a channel or instrument of the God who comes close, not so much a witness: whereas the church *is* a witness for Webster. Meditation on the economy delivered in Scriptural terms leads one (eventually)

---

[51] *Einheit der Heiligen Schrift? Zur Theologie des biblischen Kanons* (Quaestiones disputatae 211; Freiburg – Basel – Wien: Herder, 2005).
[52] William J. Abraham, *Crossing the Threshold of Divine Revelation* (Grand Rapids: Eerdmans, 2006), 93.
[53] John Webster, *Holy Scripture: A Dogmatic Sketch*, Current Issues in Theology (Cambridge: Cambridge University Press, 2003), 33.

to the contemplation of the Trinity. But that happens by listening – along with the tradition – to Scripture.

Now, Levering seems to think Scripture can only be its true self when it is located liturgically, in the church being church. Ratzinger too has argued that the church mediates between the "results" of [a light form of] historical criticism and the present. "The People of God – the Church – is the living subject of Scripture; it is in the Church that the words of the Bible are always in the present."[54] Indeed, the people has "to receive itself from God, ultimately from the incarnate Christ... Revelation is indeed closed in terms of its material principle, but it is present, and remains present, in terms of its reality."[55] This is nicely put, but if the reality is something present, what does that have to say about the material principle of its presence, viz. Scripture? Is it first as having the privilege of setting the agenda, or is it a "long time ago" kind of "first," only to be heard of through the "Chinese whispers" of tradition and the chattering church of today? *Mē genoito!* "These things were written for our instruction." It is the heart of the fire of holiness, giving comfort, light and purity in dark times. This belief is not necessarily a Christian fideistic one, for the words of the bible and their personal yet propositional claims are in many ways more accessible and clear than those of ecclesiastical interpretations or academic models of inter-faith possible religion.

## Bibliography

Abraham, William J. *Crossing the Threshold of Divine Revelation*. Grand Rapids: Eerdmans, 2006.
Adams, Marilyn McCord. "Duns Scotus on the Goodness of God." *Faith and Philosophy* 4 (1987): 486–505.
Assel, Heinrich. "Den Text der Menschwerdung lesen lernen: Das Fiktive und das Imaginäre in Joh 1 als Aufgabe der Inkarnationschristologie." In *Beyond Biblical Theologies*, edited by Heinrich Assel, Stefan Beyerle, and Christfried Böttrich, 75–135. Tübingen: Mohr Siebeck, 2012.
Beyerle, Stefan. "'Beyond'—Grenzbeschreibungen zur Biblischen Theologie." In *Beyond Biblical Theologies*, edited by Heinrich Assel, Stefan Beyerle, and Christfried Böttrich, 19–51. Tübingen: Mohr Siebeck, 2012.
Bourgine, Benoît. *Bible oblige: Essai sur la Théologie Biblique*. Cogitatio Fidei. Paris: Cerf, 2019.
Childs, Brevard S. *Exodus*. London: SCM, 1974.

---

54 Joseph Ratzinger [Pope Benedict XVI], *Jesus of Nazareth Vol 1. Jesus of Nazareth: From the Baptism in the Jordan to the Transfiguration*, trans. Adrian J. Walker (New York, NY: Doubleday, 2007), xxi; idem, "The Question of the Concept of Tradition: A Provisional Response," in *God's Word: Scripture, Tradition, Office*, eds. Peter Hünermann and Thomas Söding, trans. Henry Taylor (San Francisco: Ignatius Press, 2008): 41–89, 86.
55 Ratzinger, "The Question of the Concept of Tradition."

Childs, Brevard S. *The Struggle to Understand Isaiah as Christian Scripture*. Grand Rapids, MI – Cambridge, UK: Eerdmans, 2004.

Collins, John J. "Biblical Theology Between Apologetics and Criticism." In *Beyond Biblical Theologies*, edited by Heinrich Assel, Stefan Beyerle, and Christfried Böttrich, 224–41. Tübingen: Mohr Siebeck, 2012.

Davies, Brian. *Thomas Aquinas on God and Evil*. Oxford: Oxford University Press, 2011.

Drey, Johann S. *Brief Introduction to the Study of Theology: With Reference to the Scientific Standpoint and the Catholic System*. Notre Dame: University of Notre Dame Press, 1994.

Eskola, Timo. *Beyond Biblical Theology: Sacralized Culturalism in Heikki Räisänen's Hermeneutics*. Leiden: Brill, 2013.

Fehr, Wayne L. *The Birth of the Catholic Tübingen School: The Dogmatics of Johann Sebastian Drey*. Chico, CA: Scholars Press, 1981.

Franzelin, Johannes B. *Tractatus de divina traditione et scriptura*. 4th edition. Rome: S. C. de Propaganda Fide, 1896.

Geldhof, Joris. *Revelation, Reason and Reality: Theological Encounters with Jaspers, Schelling and Baader*. Leuven: Peeters, 2007.

Guardini, Romano. "Heilige Schrift und Glaubenswissenschaft." *Die Schildgenossen* 8 (1928): 24–57.

Jacobs, Jonathan. "Gratitude, Humility, and Holiness in Medieval Jewish Philosophy." In *Holiness in Jewish Thought*, edited by Alan L. Mittleman, 88–111. New York – Oxford: Oxford University Press, 2018.

Kasper, Walter. *Das Absolute in der Geschichte: Philosophie und Theologie der Geschichte in der Spätphilosophie Schellings*. Mainz: Grunewald, 2010.

Lacoste, Jean-Yves. "Révélation." In *Dictionnaire de Théologie Critique*, edited by Jean-Yves Lacoste, 1215–22. Paris: Presses Universitaires de France, 2007.

Levering, Matthew. *Participatory Biblical Exegesis: A Theology of Biblical Interpretation*. Notre Dame, IN: Notre Dame Press, 2008.

Lim, Timothy H. "The Defilement of the Hands as a Principle determining the Holiness of Scriptures." *JTS* 61 (2010): 501–15.

Marion, Jean-Luc. *D'Ailleurs, la Révélation*. Paris: Grasset, 2021.

Montag, John. "The False Legacy of Suarez." In *Radical Orthodoxy*, edited by John Milbank, Catherine Pickstock, and Graham Ward, 38–63. London: Routledge, 1998.

Murphy, Michael. *Divine Holiness and Divine Action*. Oxford: OUP, 2021.

Nicholls, Aidan. *Say It Is Pentecost: A Guide Through Balthasar's Logic*. Edinburgh: T&T Clark, 2001.

O'Collins, Gerald. *Retrieving Fundamental Theology: The Three Styles of Contemporary Theology*. Mahwah, NJ: Pauli Press, 1993.

O'Collins, Gerald. *Rethinking Fundamental Theology: Toward a New Fundamental Theology*. Oxford: OUP, 2011.

O'Meara, Thomas F. *Romantic Idealism und Roman Catholicism: Schelling and the Theologians*. Notre Dame, IN: Notre Dame University Press, 1982.

Ratzinger, Joseph. "The Question of the Concept of Tradition: A Provisional Response." In *God's Word: Scripture, Tradition, Office*, edited by Peter Hünermann and Thomas Söding, trans. Henry Taylor, 41–89. San Francisco: Ignatius Press, 2008.

Ratzinger, Joseph [Pope Benedict XVI], *Jesus of Nazareth Vol 1: From the Baptism in the Jordan to the Transfiguration*. Translated by Adrian J. Walker. New York, NY: Doubleday, 2007.

Ricoeur, Paul. "The 'Figure' in Rosenzweig's The Star of Redemption." In *Figuring the Sacred*, 93–105. Minneapolis, MN: Augsburg-Fortress, 1995.

Ricoeur, Paul. "L'herméneutique du témoignage." In *Le témoignage*, edited by Enrico Castelli, 35–62. Paris: J. Vrin, 1972.

Rowland, Tracey. *Benedict XVI: A Guide for the Perplexed*. London: T&T Clark International, 2010.

Samuelson, Norbert. *Revelation and the God of Israel*. Cambridge: Cambridge University Press, 2002.

Schelling, Friedriech W.J. *Urfassung der Philosophie der Offenbarung*, ed. Walter E. Ehrhardt. Hamburg: Meiner, 2010.

Schelling, Friedriech W.J. *Werke 14: Vorlesungen über die Methode des academischen Studium; Philosophie und Religion und andere Texte (1803–1805)*, ed. Patrick Leistner and Alexander Schubach. F. W. J. Schelling historisch-kritische Ausgabe I-14. Stuttgart-Bad Cannstatt: Frommann-Holzboog, 2021.

Söding, Thomas. *Einheit der Heiligen Schrift? Zur Theologie des biblischen Kanons*. Quaestiones disputatae 211. Freiburg – Basel – Wien: Herder, 2005.

Sommer, Benjamin D. *Revelation and Authority: Sinai in Jewish Scripture and Tradition*. AYBRL. New Haven, CT: Yale University Press, 2018.

Stoellger, Philipp. "Biblische Theologie—bildtheoretischer Perspektive." In *Beyond Biblical Theologies*, edited by Heinrich Assel, Stefan Beyerle, and Christfried Böttrich, 455–81. Tübingen: Mohr Siebeck, 2012.

Von Balthasar, Hans Urs. *The Glory of the Lord: A Theological Aesthetics*, vol. 1: *Seeing the Form*, Translated by Erasmo Leiva-Merikakis. Edinburgh: T&T Clark, 1982.

Von Balthasar, Hans Urs. *The Glory of the Lord: A Theological Aesthetics*, vol. 6: *Theology: The Old Covenant*. Translated by Brian McNeil C.R.V. and Erasmo Leiva-Merikakis. Edinburgh: T&T Clark, 1991.

Waldenfels, Hans. *Offenbarung: Von der Reformation bis zur Gegenwart*. Handbuch der Dogmengeschichte I/1b. Freiburg: Herder, 1977.

Webster, John. *Holy Scripture: A Dogmatic Sketch*. Current Issues in Theology. Cambridge: Cambridge University Press, 2003.

Wicks, Jared. "Vatican II on Revelation—From Behind the Scenes." *Theological Studies* 71 (2010): 637–50.

Benjamin D. Sommer
# 6 Reception as Revelation: Correlational Theology in Jewish Tradition and Scripture

> Brothers, if you care for true piety, let us not feign agreement where diversity is evidently the plan and purpose of providence. (Moses Mendelssohn.)[1]

> Religious diversity reflects divine providence insofar as it helps assure proper representations of divine truth. In Mendelssohn's language, religious pluralism helps prevent idolatry. [...] Idolatry arises from regarding one's own metaphysical symbols as essential, adequate signs of the divine. Religious diversity helps impress on people that any signs used to represent God are arbitrary and inadequate. (Michah Gottlieb.)[2]

In an era that imposes black and white thinking upon us, I would like to devote a paper to shades of gray.[3]

During the twentieth century, many Christian and Jewish theologians developed what have been called *correlational* theologies. This term is famously associated with the Protestant theologian Paul Tillich, who used it to describe the way he links insights from revelation, scripture, and the history of Christian thought with questions prompted by the study of philosophy and psychology. As a correlational theologian, Tillich rejects both what he calls "supranaturalistic" and "naturalistic or humanistic" methods for understanding Christianity in favor of a middle way. The supranaturalistic method, Tillich explains, "takes the Christian message to be a sum of revealed truths which have fallen into the human situation like strange bodies from a strange world. No mediation to the human situation is possible. These truths themselves create a new situation before they can be received."[4] The naturalistic or humanistic method "derives the Christian message from man's natural state. It develops its answer out of human existence, unaware that the human existence itself is the question."[5] Tillich develops correlation theology to describe Christianity as something that cannot be explained without recourse to the supernatural but

---

1 Moses Mendelssohn, *Jerusalem, or, On Religious Power and Judaism*, trans. Allan Arkush, introduction and commentary by Alexander Altmann (Hanover: Published for Brandeis University Press by University Press of New England, 1983), 138.
2 Michah Gottlieb, "Mendelssohn's Metaphysical Defense of Religious Pluralism," *JR* 86 (2006): 219, 222.
3 In this contribution, I have reused (with modifications) some sections of my book: Benjamin David Sommer, *Revelation and Authority: Sinai in Jewish Scripture and Tradition*. AYBRL (New Haven, CT: Yale University Press, 2015), summarized others, and added new material.
4 Paul Tillich, *Systematic Theology* (Chicago, IL: University of Chicago Press, 1967), vol. 1, 64–65.
5 Tillich, *Systematic Theology*, vol. 1, 65. On pp. 65–66, Tillich also rejects a third type of theology, viz., natural theology. Like correlational theology, natural theology embraces elements of

that encompasses manifold elements of the human. The term "correlational theology" also appears in Jewish thought. Already the early twentieth-century Jewish philosopher Hermann Cohen spoke of revelation as stemming not only from heaven but from the heart of man, and especially (here recalling Maimonides) from man's verbal/rational capacity. For Cohen, duties are not simply imposed from above but embraced by humans who use a divine-like rational capacity to realize what duty should be. Cohen uses the term "correlation" to describe the aspect of revelation that stresses both humanity's duties and humanity's autonomy.[6] Because revealed duties become evident from the correlation between God and the human being, Cohen concludes, accepting duty does not impugn a person's autonomy.[7]

We can also recognize a correlational approach to revelation in the work of theologians and biblical scholars who, attempting to understand the phenomenon of prophecy, refuse to explain what the prophet experiences in wholly supernatural or exclusively human terms. A wholly supernaturalist theory of prophecy insists that God employed language of the sort normally used by humans to speak specific words to prophets; the prophets then repeated these words verbatim to the audience. The British theologian H. D. McDonald termed this approach to prophecy "dictation theory."[8] An exclusively humanist approach to prophecy as type of poetry appears in varied ways in authors as diverse as Baruch Spinoza, William Blake, and Friedrich Schleiermacher, for whom the divine element of prophecy involves the creation of persons with strong imaginative, rational, and moral faculties, but not particular moments of contact between God and the prophet. The Jewish theologian Abraham Joshua Heschel aptly describes this sort of theory as an attempt to "expand the notion of revelation in order to deny it."[9] Between these lies a correla-

---

both a supranatural and a natural or humanistic approach, but it lacks the existential focus of his correlational proposal.

6 E.g., Hermann Cohen, *Religion of Reason Out of the Sources of Judaism*, introductory essays for the second edition by Steven S. Schwarzschild and Kenneth Seeskin, translated with an introduction by Simon Kaplan, introductory essays by Leo Strauss, AARTTS 7 (Atlanta, GA: Scholars Press, 1995), 82, 98.

7 On the theme of correlations in Cohen, see Kenneth Seeskin, *Autonomy in Jewish Philosophy* (Cambridge—New York: Cambridge University Press, 2001), 162–69, and Robert Erlewine, "Reclaiming the Prophets: Cohen, Heschel, and Crossing the Theocentric/Neo-Humanist Divide," *Journal of Jewish Thought and Philosophy* 17 (2009): 205. For a further development of this theme in Jewish philosophy, see: Seeskin, *Autonomy in Jewish Philosophy*, 219–38.

8 For examples of attitudes (both positive and negative) toward what some Christian thinkers call the "dictation theory" among modern Christian (especially British) thinkers, see Hugh Dermot McDonald, *Theories of Revelation: An Historical Study 1860–1960* (London: George Allen and Unwin, 1963), 212–85, 307–11.

9 See Abraham Joshua Heschel, *The Prophets* (New York: Harper Collins, 2001), 524–29 (the phrase just quoted appears on 529, referring specifically to Spinoza), as well as the discussion of "illumina-

tional approach. Among Christians this approach appears among biblical scholars such as Samuel R. Driver, Gerhard von Rad, and Harold H. Rowley.[10] Related points of view appear among some Protestant theologians, such as Keith Ward and David Brown.[11] They are also known among Catholic thinkers,[12] including one prominent scholar of Christian theology who also found time to involve himself in practical issues of church governance.[13] According to this approach, prophets are bound by a divine commission to proclaim a message yet enjoy a degree of freedom in shaping their proclamation. Heschel introduces the apt terms of "vessel" (כלי) and "partner" (שותף) when he suggests that the prophet is not merely a vehicle God uses to convey a message but also a participant who helps to construct it.[14] Other thinkers suggest

---

tion" and "insight" theories and of Schleiermacher's influence, in McDonald, *Theories of Revelation*, e.g., 234, 237, 253, 256, 264. On the possibility that prophets are inspired in the manner that all great poets and artists are inspired, and the implications of that view, see the trenchant discussion in Heschel, *The Prophets*, 468–97, and cf. Stephen Geller, "Were the Prophets Poets?," *Prooftexts* 3 (1983): 211–21.

**10** For an especially clear articulation of this notion, see Samuel R. Driver, *Introduction to the Literature of the Old Testament* (New York: Meridian, 1956), viii-xi, and, at greater length, Harold H. Rowley, *The Relevance of the Bible* (London: James Clark, 1942), 21–51, esp. 24–28 and 35, where he affirms that the Bible contains "the record of man's growing experience of God, and progressive response to God"—a comment that strongly parallels Heschel's approach. See further the discussion of Rowley in McDonald, *Theories of Revelation*, 251–54. Gerhard von Rad, *Old Testament Theology*, trans. David M.G. Stalker (Edinburgh: Oliver and Boyd, 1962–1965), vol. 2, 50, speaks of the prophetic office as "consisting on the one hand of binding commitments and on the other of liberties and powers." See further his chapter, "The Prophet's Freedom," in *Old Testament Theology*, vol. 2, 70–79; on the interpretive nature of the prophet's task in moving from individual revelation to public proclamation, see especially *Old Testament Theology*, vol. 2, 72–73.

**11** See the discussion of "the ambiguity of revelation" in Keith Ward, *Religion and Revelation: A Theology of Revelation in the World's Religions* (Oxford: Clarendon, 1994), 21–25 and 343 (cf. 89–92 and 209–17), and the discussion of revelation as "interactive" in David Brown, *Tradition and Imagination: Revelation and Change* (Oxford: Oxford University Press, 1999), 106–35, esp. 107 and 129. For predecessors, see, in McDonald, *Theories of Revelation,* the discussions of figures such as W.H.G. Thomas, 192–223; G. D. Barry, 239–40; H. Wheeler Robinson, 244–47; William Lee, 261–63; Frederick Watson, 277–76; James Orr, 174–76 and 279–80; and McDonald's own statement, 286–87. A comparable, but less far-reaching, attempt appears in Peter Enns, *Inspiration and Incarnation: Evangelicals and the Problem of the Old Testament* (Grand Rapids, MI: Baker Academic, 2005), esp. 17–21 and 167–73.

**12** See especially Avery Dulles, *Models of Revelation* (New York: Doubleday, 1983), who lays out five models of revelation, all but the first of which describe the Bible as being at least in part a human response to revelation.

**13** Joseph Ratzinger, *Jesus of Nazareth: From the Baptism in the Jordan to the Transfiguration*, trans. Adrian J. Walker (New York: Doubleday, 2007), xix–xx.

**14** Abraham Joshua Heschel, *Torah min Hashamayim B'aspaqlarya shel Hadorot* [in Hebrew], 3 vols. (London and New York: Soncino and the Jewish Theological Seminary, 1965 and 1990), vol. 2, 264–98 (Abraham Joshua Heschel, *Torah min Hashamayim B'aspaqlarya shel Hadorot* [in Hebrew],

similar metaphors. Rowley says of Paul, "He was the ambassador, not the postman."[15] Already in 1854, William Lee argued that the writers of Scripture were "God's penmen, not His pens."[16] These thinkers are not identical to one another. Some deny that there is any verbal element in the original divine communication; others maintain that a verbal element is possible while still rejecting a dictation theory that would account for the precise wording of all prophetic texts. Some liberal Protestant and Jewish thinkers speak of the need to interpret God's activities in history; for them, historical events can act as symbols pointing towards the nature of God.[17]

Correlational theologies of revelation have played a strong role among modern Jewish theologians, who tend to emphasize not only prophets' interpretation of history, but their elucidation of the divine message vouchsafed specifically to them. This is especially the case in the stream of twentieth-century Jewish thought associated with Franz Rosenzweig and Abraham Joshua Heschel.[18] These thinkers

---

2 vols., ed. Dror Bondi [Jerusalem: Maggid Books, 2021], vol. 2, 269–714= Abraham Joshua Heschel, *Heavenly Torah as Refracted Through the Generations*, edited and translated by Gordon Tucker with Leonard Levin [New York: Continuum, 2005], 478–501).

15 Rowley, *The Relevance of the Bible*, 47.

16 Cited in McDonald, *Theories of Revelation*, 262.

17 See Wolfhart Pannenberg, ed., *Revelation as History*, trans. David Granskou (New York: Macmillan, 1969); Tillich, *Systematic Theology*, vol. 1, 120–22; the discussion of this model in Dulles, *Models of Revelation*, 53–67. Of course, this approach is also significant in Jewish (and especially biblical) thought; see Emil L. Fackenheim, *God's Presence in History: Jewish Affirmations and Philosophical Reflections* (New York: Harper Collins, 1972). On this notion in biblical and ancient Near Eastern thought including but not limited to Israelite literature, see Bertil Albrektson, *History and the Gods* (Lund: CWK Gleerup, 1967).

18 On the connections between the theme of correlation in Heschel and modern Christian theologians such as Tillich, see esp. Shai Held, *Abraham Joshua Heschel: The Call of Transcendence* (Bloomington, IN: Indiana University Press, 2013), 84–93 (and, for crucial differences among them, see 262–64 n. 80). Heschel and Hermann Cohen share an emphasis on partnership between heaven and earth, but we should not overlook differences between Cohen's demythologizing understanding of revelation and Heschel's view, which puts more emphasis on the personhood of God and the historicity of the Sinai event. On these differences, see Erlewine, "Reclaiming the Prophets," *passim*, esp. 185–86. In particular, Cohen, *Religion of Reason Out of the Sources of Judaism*, 86, contends that just as "spiritual succession was, in the course of political events, designated as an historical act in order that it might be considered a national one," so too in "proper, which is to say literary, history, criticism and correction appeared, which *transferred Sinai into the heart of man* [...] The eternal [...] is removed from all sense experience, therefore also from all historical experience." This attempt to spiritualize revelation while minimizing its particularism marks Cohen off from both Heschel and Rosenzweig. Cohen breaks decisively from the historicity, specificity, and content of the revealed law. He idealizes Sinai, removing its significance from the event itself; indeed, it matters little whether the event actually occurred, whereas for Heschel (and for the participatory theory I describe in what follows) it is crucial that an event occurred in which both God and Israel participated. Cohen sees the Sinai narrative not as historical event but as a symbolic rep-

maintain that the Bible, along with all of Jewish tradition, is a response to God's act of communication to Israel. The content we find in the Bible mixes divine and human elements, and perhaps divine and human words. Alternatively, God's act of revelation may not have conveyed content linguistically, so that all the words and laws we find in the Bible are human interpretations or paraphrases of the divine communications.[19] Heschel conveys ideas of this sort repeatedly, especially in *God in Search of Man: A Philosophy of Judaism*:

> Judaism is based upon a minimum of revelation and a maximum of interpretation, upon the will of God and upon the understanding of Israel [...] There is a partnership of God and Israel in regard to both the world and the Torah: He created the earth and we till the soil; He gave us the text and we refine and complete it.
>
> As a report about revelation the Bible itself is *a midrash*.
>
> The Bible contains not only words of the prophets, but also words that came from non-prophetic lips [...] There is in the Bible [...] not only God's disclosure but man's insight.[20]

In the first two quotes, Heschel seems to suggest that some of the Bible's language or specific laws may come directly from heaven; the third may intimate that the

---

resentation of a moral argument concerning the relationship between God and humanity. For an analogous rejection of a similar sort of idealization in Christian thought, see Ward, *Religion and Revelation*, 197–200.

We may further note that Heschel derives this correlational theme especially from kabbalistic and Hasidic sources. On correlation in kabbalistic literature as the reciprocal impact of God's and man's deeds on each other, see Moshe Idel, "On the Theologization of Kabbalah in Modern Scholarship," in *Religious Apologetics—Philosophical Argumentation*, eds. Yossef Schwartz and Volkhard Krech (Tübingen: Mohr Siebeck, 2004): 171. On the kabbalistic-Hasidic origin of this theme in Heschel, see Moshe Idel, "Abraham J. Heschel on Mysticism and Hasidism" [in Hebrew], *Modern Judaism* 29 (2009): 80–105, and Reuven Kimelman, "Abraham Joshua Heschel's Theology of Judaism and the Rewriting of Jewish Intellectual History," *Journal of Jewish Thought and Philosophy* 17 (2009): 219–38. The sense in which Idel uses the term correlation (viz., to relate to theurgy and divine dependence on humanity) is not as far afield from Tillich as one might assume. Tillich writes that one of the senses of correlation "qualifies the divine-human relationship within religious experience... [This] use of correlative thinking in theology has evoked the protest of theologians such as Karl Barth, who are afraid that any kind of divine-human correlation makes God partly dependent on man. But although God in his abysmal nature is in no way dependent on man, God in his self-manifestation to man is dependent on the way man receives his manifestation." (*Systematic Theology*, vol. 1, 61).

**19** On differences between Rosenzweig and Heschel in this regard, see Neil Gillman, *Sacred Fragments: Recovering Theology for the Modern Jew* (Philadelphia, PA: Jewish Publication Society, 1990), 24–25.

**20** Abraham Joshua Heschel, *God in Search of Man: A Philosophy of Judaism* (New York: Farrar Straus and Giroux, 1955), 274, 185, and 26 respectively.

Bible is entirely a human interpretation of the divine self-disclosure, in which case all the wording we find in the Bible is human.[21] Rosenzweig is more definitive in assigning all the Bible's words to the human interpreters:

> The primary content of revelation is revelation itself. "He came down"—this already concludes the revelation; "He spoke" is the beginning of interpretation, and certainly "I am."

> All that God ever reveals in revelation is—revelation. Or, to express it differently, he reveals nothing but himself to man. The relation of this accusative and dative to each other is the one and only content of revelation.[22]

Rosenzweig refers to the Bible as being, in this respect, "human throughout," even though it is possible, if only for a moment now and again, to sense "the divine in what is humanly written."[23] All the words, then, were authored by humans, but at crucial moments the reader rightly apprehends them to contain something divine. For Rosenzweig and Heschel the Bible remains holy as a response to God's self-manifestation, but its wording (or: most of its wording) is the product of human beings. This approach is also evident in the work of other modern Jewish thinkers, especially Louis Jacobs.[24]

---

[21] It is difficult to pin Heschel down on the question of whether the Bible contains any wording or even specific content uttered by God. Alexander Even-Chen, *A Voice from the Darkness: Abraham Joshua Heschel Between Phenomenology and Mysticism* [in Hebrew] (Tel Aviv: Am Oveid, 1999), 83, captures the duality and ambiguity well.

[22] The first quotation is from Franz Rosenzweig, *On Jewish Learning*, ed. Nahum N. Glatzer (New York: Schocken, 1965), 118 (in which he quotes Exod 19:20 and 20:1 respectively), and the second from Franz Rosenzweig, *Franz Rosenzweig: His Life and Thought*, ed. Nahum Norbert Glatzer (New York: Schocken, 1961), 285. Cf. Franz Rosenzweig, *The Star of Redemption*, trans. William W. Hallo (Boston: Beacon Press, 1972), 176–78 (= *The Star of Redemption*, trans. Barbara E. Galli, Modern Jewish Philosophy and Religion [Madison, WI: University of Wisconsin Press, 2005], 190–92). Nahum Glatzer expressed a kindred view of revelation, as Rosenzweig notes: Rosenzweig, *On Jewish Learning*, 119, also found in: Rosenzweig, *Franz Rosenzweig: His Life and Thought*, 242.

[23] Franz Rosenzweig, *Der Mensch und sein Werk: Gesammelte Schriften*, vol. 3: *Zweistromland: Kleinere Schriften zu Glauben und Denken*, eds. Reinhold Mayer and Annemarie Mayer (Dordrecht—Boston—Lancaster: Martinus Nijhoff, 1984), 761. The crucial sentence from which I quote here is missing from the English translation in Martin Buber and Franz Rosenzweig, *Scripture and Translation*, trans. Lawrence Rosenwald, ISBL (Bloomington: Indiana University Press, 1994), 59.

[24] From among Jacob's works, see esp. Louis Jacobs, *A Tree of Life: Diversity, Flexibility, and Creativity in Jewish Law*, Littman Library of Jewish Civilization (Oxford: Oxford University Press, 1984), and Louis Jacobs, *Beyond Reasonable Doubt* (London: Littman Library of Jewish Civilization, 1999), 106–31. For other presentations of this sort of approach, see Gillman, *Sacred Fragments*, esp. 39–62; Elliot Dorff and Arthur Rosett, *A Living Tree: The Roots and Growth of Jewish Law* (Albany: State University of New York Press, 1988); Elliot Dorff, *The Unfolding Tradition: Jewish Law After Sinai*, rev. edition (New York: Aviv Press, 2011).

Kindred but distinct correlational approaches appear both to the right and the left of Rosenzweig, Heschel, and Jacobs. Martin Buber understands scripture as a response to divine presence, but not a response to any divine command. For Buber, the law and even the command that underlies that law are entirely human in origin and therefore distinct from divine revelation itself.[25] Consequently, this law cannot be binding, and in this regard his approach to revelation breaks decisively with biblical and rabbinic Judaism.[26] Surprisingly enough, a correlational approach also appears among several modern thinkers not associated with liberal streams of Judaism: the nineteenth-century Ḥasidic master Ẓadok Hakohen, the early twentieth-century mystic and rabbi Abraham Isaac Kook, the mid-twentieth-century ultra-Orthodox leader Isaac Hutner, and the contemporary Orthodox feminist Tamar Ross.[27]

It will be useful to introduce two additional conceptualizations of what Tillich terms correlational and supranatural approaches. (As for the humanist approaches, they will not concern us for the remainder of this paper.) I use the term *participatory theory of revelation* to describe the conviction that the Pentateuch, and Jewish tradition generally result from a dialogue between God and Israel. The term "participatory" focuses our attention on the idea that the Pentateuch not only reflects God's will but conveys Israel's interpretation of and response to that will. Participatory theology puts a premium on human agency and gives witness to the grandeur of a God who accomplishes a providential task through the free will of human sub-

---

[25] See Alexander Even-Chen and Ephraim Meir, *Between Heschel and Buber: A Comparative Study*, Emunot: Jewish Philosophy and Kabbalah (Boston, MA: Academic Studies Press, 2012), esp. 159–204.
[26] On the preferability, from a Jewish point of view, of Rosenzweig's view of revelation over Buber's precisely because Buber's view does not lead to command, see Norbert M. Samuelson, *Revelation and the God of Israel* (New York: Cambridge University Press, 2002), 60, 74–75, and 111. Cf. Yehoyada Amir, *Reason Out of Faith: The Philosophy of Franz Rosenzweig* [in Hebrew], 'Aron Sefarim Yehudi (Tel Aviv: Am Oveid, 2004), 295.
[27] On these elements in Hutner's work, see David Bigman, "A Ladder Upon the Earth, Whose Top Reaches the Heavens," *Conversations: The Journal of the Institute for Jewish Ideas and Ideals* 11 (2011): 1–18. On their presence in Kook, see Tamar Ross, "R. Kook: A This-Worldly Mystic," in *The Cambridge Companion to Jewish Theology*, ed. Steven Kepnes (New York: Cambridge University Press, 2021): 200–4; as well as Tamar Ross, "The Cognitive Value of Religious Truth Claims: Rabbi A. I. Kook and Postmodernism," in *Hazon Nahum: Jubilee Volume in Honor of Norman Lamm*, eds. Yaakov Elman and Jeffrey Gurock (New York: Yeshiva University Press, 1997): 479–52. On Ross's own thought, with constant attention to R. Kook's theology, see Tamar Ross, *Expanding the Palace of Torah: Orthodoxy and Feminism* (Waltham, MA: Brandeis University Press, 2005), and, more briefly, Tamar Ross, "Orthodoxy and the Challenge of Biblical Criticism: Some Reflections on the Importance of Asking the Right Question," in *The Believer and the Modern Study of the Bible*, ed. Tovah Ganzel, Yehudah Brandes, and Chayuta Deutsch (Boston, MA: Academic Studies Press, 2019): 263–87.

jects under God's authority.²⁸ This approach contrasts with the more well-known view that I term *the stenographic theory of revelation*, according to which God dictated all the words of the Pentateuch to Moses, and Moses recorded God's words without altering them. In the stenographic theory, all the words of the Pentateuch are God's. In the participatory theory, the wording in the Pentateuch is a joint effort involving heavenly and earthly contributions; or the wording may be an entirely human response to God's real but non-verbal revelation. Some Jewish scholars use the metaphor of *translation* to describe the participatory approach, since it entails an act of rendering God's original, and perhaps non-verbal, communication into a human language.²⁹ Thus Shai Held identifies the core of Abraham Joshua Heschel's view of revelation at Sinai as the notion that "revelation conveys *divine content* in *human words* [. . .] The humanness of the words [found in the Bible] does not entail, for Heschel, the sheer humanness of the ideas conveyed."³⁰ Several other scholars use the metaphor of translation to describe this approach as well.³¹

---

28 My phrasing here borrows from my colleague Gary Anderson's summary of my approach.
29 On this term in relation to Heschel's own view of revelation, see Even-Chen, *A Voice from the Darkness*, 83 and 183; in relation to Buber, see Yehoyada Amir, *A Small Still Voice: Theological Critical Reflections* [in Hebrew] (Tel-Aviv: Yedi'ot Aḥaronot: Sifre Ḥemed, 2009), 179–80; on revelation as translation, or demanding translation, in Rosenzweig, see esp. Elliot R. Wolfson, "Light Does Not Talk but Shines: Apophasis and Vision in Rosenzweig's Theopoetic Temporality," in *New Directions in Jewish Philosophy*, eds. Aaron Hughes and Elliot R. Wolfson (Bloomington, IN: Indiana University Press, 2010): 102–07. See also Uriel Simon, *Seek Peace and Pursue It: Pressing Questions in Light of the Bible, and the Bible in Light of Pressing Questions* [in Hebrew] (Tel Aviv: Yedi'ot Aḥaronot: Sifrei Ḥemed, 2002), 284, who stresses that the Torah is truthful and eternal, but that "it is phrased in the language of human beings who lived at a certain time, which is to say that it results from an adaptation at the level of language and ideas, an adaptation to the (limited) ability of those who receive it to understand it, to internalize it, and to live by its light." This statement recalls the comment of Ernst Simon that "we must view the mitzvot as an echo of the Lord's words (כהד דברי הגבורה)," translated and quoted by Paul Mendes-Flohr, *Divided Passions: Jewish Intellectuals and the Experience of Modernity*, The Culture of Jewish Modernity (Detroit, MI: Wayne State University Press, 1990), 345. (On the connection between the last two views, see Proverbs 10:1a). For the analogous suggestion that the record of revelation relates to the revelation itself as phenomenon relates to noumenon, see Steven Kepnes, "Revelation as Torah: From an Existential to a Postliberal Judaism," *Journal of Jewish Thought and Philosophy* 10 (2000): 208–16.
30 Held, *Abraham Joshua Heschel*, 111–12.
31 Micah Goodman, *The Secrets of The Guide to the Perplexed* [in Hebrew] (Or Yehudah: Dvir, 2010), 169–87, argues that Maimonides regarded the Pentateuch as Moses' translation of divine wisdom into human terms: "Moses scrutinized nature, understood the depths of divine wisdom [it contains], and translated it into laws that shape the ideal society and ideal human beings [. . .] God created nature, and Moses wrote the Torah" (187). For the same view, argued on the basis of entirely different reasoning, see Alvin Reines, "Maimonides' Concept of Mosaic Prophecy," *HUCA* 40–41 (1969–1970): 325–61; Kalman Bland, "Moses and the Law According to Maimonides," in *Mystics,*

Participatory or correlational theories of revelation constitute a major stream of modern theology, but they do not begin in the nineteenth or twentieth century. In his masterpiece, *Torah Min Hashamayim Be'aspaqlaria Shel Hadorot*, Heschel contends that what I call a participatory approach appears already in some classical Jewish literature of the rabbinic and medieval periods.[32] Yochanan Silman refines and extends Heschel's thesis in his book, *Qol Gadol Velo Yasaf: Torat Yisrael Bein Shleimut Lehishtalmut*.[33] Similar arguments are found in work by others.[34] In what

---

*Philosophers and Politicians: Essays in Jewish Intellectual History in Honor of Alexander Altman*, eds. Jehuda Reinharz, Daniel Swetschinski and Kalman Bland (Durham, NC: Duke University Press, 1982): 49–66; and Lawrence Kaplan, "'I Sleep, but My Heart Waketh': Maimonides' Conception of Human Perfection," in *The Thought of Moses Maimonides: Philosophical and Legal Studies*, eds. Ira Robinson, Lawrence Kaplan, and Julien Bauer, Studies in the History of Philosophy (Lewiston: E. Mellen Press, 1990): 130–66 and note esp. the extraordinary conclusion Kaplan intimates (but dares not state explicitly) in 161 n. 50, to wit, that from the point of view of Maimonides' "Thirteen Principles," Maimonides' *Guide* is a heretical work. For a different perspective, see Menachem M. Kellner, *Dogma in Medieval Jewish Thought: From Maimonides to Abravanel*, The Littman Library of Jewish Civilization (Oxford: Oxford University Press, 1986): 229 n. 93.

**32** See note 14 above for bibliographic information. This work was recently republished as Heschel, *Torah min Hashamayim B'aspaqlarya shel Hadorot*, second edition, which contains Bondi's excellent notes and introductions as well as correction of many citations. An English translation is also available: Heschel, *Heavenly Torah as Refracted Through the Generations*; even scholars who can read the original will find Tucker's brief but rich comments enormously useful. The Hebrew title Heschel gave this book (תורה מן השמים באספקלריה של הדורות) reflects his masterful and always careful use of language. It can be understood as a phrase, in which case it defines the book's subject as a descriptive study: "Torah from Heaven in the Lens of the Generations," or, less literally, "The notion of revelation as viewed in Jewish tradition." But the title can also be translated as a sentence that makes a constructive theological claim: "Revelation occurs through the lens of the generations"—that is, "Torah comes to us through the medium of tradition itself." No doubt Heschel intends both senses.

**33** Yochanan Silman, *The Voice Heard at Sinai: Once or Ongoing?* [in Hebrew] (Jerusalem: Magnes, 1999).

**34** For the argument that a participatory view of revelation is far more loyal to the traditions of medieval Jewish philosophy than most scholars have realized, see Samuelson, *Revelation and the God of Israel*, chapters 2 and 7, esp. 173–75. For the claim that Heschel's philosophy of revelation has deep roots in classical rabbinic literature, see Lawrence Perlman, *Abraham Heschel's Idea of Revelation*, BJS 171 (Atlanta, GA.: Scholars Press, 1989), 119–33; Even-Chen, *A Voice from the Darkness*, 160–79. In a series of studies, Eran Viezel has argued that some pre-Maimonidean medieval exegetes of the Bible asserted that Moses composed significant sections of the Pentateuch (rather than writing them stenographically on the basis of God's dictation). Viezel further maintains that what I call the stenographic theory of revelation is less common among the Talmudic rabbis than is generally assumed, and that it became the standard in Jewish thought only starting in the thirteenth century CE. See Eran Viezel, "The Divine Content and the Words of Moses: R. Abraham Ibn Ezra on Moses' Role in Writing the Torah" [in Hebrew], *Tarbiz* 80 (2012): 387–407; Eran Viezel, "Rashbam on Moses' Role in Writing the Torah" [in Hebrew], *Shnaton: An Annual for Biblical and*

follows, I extend the search for precursors back to the biblical text itself. In so doing, I will suggest that this stream is far more ancient than has been recognized by many thinkers, including some of the modern correlational theologians themselves.

# 1 Participatory theology in the Bible

Rosenzweig and Heschel view revelation as an actual event and reject the idea accepted by some correlation thinkers (such as Hermann Cohen and Tamar Ross) that the revelation at Sinai was a metaphor or a mythological prototype. Moreover, Rosenzweig and Heschel understand this event as authoritative—in other words, as an event in which God gave binding instructions to the people of Israel. In other words, both these thinkers are traditionalist Jewish theologians in their commitment to the centrality of the rabbinic idea of חיוב or legal obligation.[35] Nonetheless, both raise doubts about the precise nature of the event at Sinai and argue that it is impossible to know exactly what happened there, or to what extent the specific commandments in the Torah are of divine origin. In their opinion, the text of the Torah is a human reaction to, or interpretation of, an event in which the divine will was expressed by supralinguistic means. Thus, Rosenzweig and Heschel encourage us to accept the Torah as legally or halakhically authoritative, but they

---

*Ancient Near Eastern Studies* 22 (2013): 167–88; Eran Viezel, "Moses' Literary License in Writing the Torah: Joseph Hayyun's Response to Isaac Abrabanel" [in Hebrew], in *Zer Rimonim: Studies in Biblical Literature and Jewish Exegesis Presented to Prof. Rimon Kasher*, eds. Michael Avioz, Elie Assis, and Yael Shemesh, SBL/IVBS (Atlanta: Society of Biblical Literature, 2013): 603–19.

**35** For my defense of the view that Rosenzweig viewed covenantal obligations as binding, see Sommer, *Revelation and Authority*, 128–32. See further Isaac Heinemann, *Ta'amei Hamitzvot Besifrut Yisrael* [in Hebrew], 2 vols. (Jerusalem: Jewish Agency and Horeb, 1996 and 1993), vol. 2, 195–237 (who, at vol. 2, 233, even locates Rosenzweig as in some respects to the right of Zechariah Frankel on this issue); Nahum N. Glatzer, "Introduction to *OJL*," in Franz Rosenzweig, *On Jewish Learning*, ed. Nahum Norbert Glatzer (New York: Schocken, 1965): 19–21; Samuelson, *Revelation and the God of Israel*, 74–75 and 96; Kepnes, "Revelation as Torah," 231–32. Rosenzweig regards revelation as corresponding to the imperative in human speech and thus as essentially commanding (while creation corresponds to the indicative and redemption to the cohortative); see Leora Batnitzky, *Idolatry and Representation: The Philosophy of Franz Rosenzweig Reconsidered* (Princeton, N.J.: Princeton University Press, 2000), 50, 112. In taking this position regarding Rosenzweig, I argue against others who maintain that Rosenzweig did not affirm the notion of legal obligation for modern Jews. For that view, see Zvi Kurzweil, "Three Views on Revelation and Law," *Judaism* 9 (1960): 296; Mendes-Flohr, *Divided Passions*, 355–56. Arnold Eisen, *Rethinking Modern Judaism Ritual, Commandment, Community*, CSHJ (Chicago, IL: University of Chicago Press, 1998), 208 (and, on Rosenzweig's commitment to autonomy, 350–51, 354).

also challenge us to wonder about the extent to which the specifics of its bindings laws are of divine origin.

This combination of traditionalism in regard to the authoritative status of the Torah's legal system and openness to questioning the provenance of its specific laws is not new. The Torah's narrative of revelation at Sinai in Exodus 19–20 hints that the laws Moses presented to the nation Israel may have originated in part with Moses himself. These hints raise the possibility that the connection between the divine voice and the text of the Torah is not simple.

## Participatory theology in Exod 19–20

Several textual ambiguities in Exod 19–20 raise the question: Did the people Israel hear the Decalogue directly from God or only through Moses' mediation? That is, did the people hear specific words and commandments directly from heaven, or did they hear all of them through an intermediary human voice? To answer this question, I will examine five ambiguities in the text of Exod 19–20.

The *first ambiguity* centers around the word קוֹל (*qol*), which allows several translations.[36] This word often means "voice"—that is, the sound a human being makes when uttering words.[37] But it also can mean "thunder," especially when it is accompanied by other terms that denote thunder, by a term for lightning, or by other meteorological vocabulary. Finally, the term can be part of an idiom in which literal senses of *qol* is less important. In particular, the phrase שָׁמַע בְּקוֹל denotes obedience in biblical Hebrew.[38] Appearing seven times in Exod 19–20, *qol* serves as what Martin Buber and Franz Rosenzweig call a *Leitwort* or "guiding word." The repetition and variation of such a word reveals, clarifies, or emphasizes something crucial to that passage.[39] Which meanings does this guiding word carry in

---

[36] The information in what follows can be found in almost any dictionary of biblical Hebrew. As is so often the case, the most thorough and subtle treatment is Francis Brown, Samuel R. Driver, and Charles A. Briggs, *A Hebrew and English Lexicon of the Old Testament* (Oxford: Oxford University Press, 1907), 876–77.

[37] Especially clear cases of this word's association with human speech occur, e.g., in 1 Sam 1:13; 24:17; 26:17; Judg 7:9; Psalm 86:6, to mention only a few examples. It can also refer to the voice of God speaking what seem to be specific words (Isaiah 6:8).

[38] On *qol* as command even outside this idiom, see Thomas Krüger, "Die Stimme Gottes: Eine ästhetisch-theologische Skizze," in *Gottes Wahrnehmungen: Helmut Utzschneider zum 60. Geburtstag*, eds. Stefan Gehrig and Stefan Seiler (Stuttgart: Kolhammer, 2009): 2, and cf. 17.

[39] I paraphrase the definition of the phenomenon found in Buber's essay, Martin Buber, "Leitwort Style," in *Scripture and Translation*, 114–28, esp. 114. See further his essay "*Leitwort* and Discourse Type," in *Scripture and Translation*, 143–50; Robert Alter, *The Art of Biblical Narrative* (New York:

this narrative? At the beginning of 19:16 and at the beginning of 20:18,[40] *qol* clearly refers to thunder, because it appears next to a term meaning "lightning." In the middle of 19:16, at the beginning of 19:19, and in the middle of 20:18, it refers specifically to the sound of a horn (קוֹל הַשּׁוֹפָר). In its first occurrence, at 19:5, the term is part of the idiom, שָׁמַע בְּקוֹל, "to obey" and thus it refers to the Israelites' compliance with God's covenant. As part of this standard phrase, the term does not literally refer to a voice, though it does imply some command or commands with which the Israelites are to be compliant. Because our term becomes associated with obedience very early in this chapter, the audience may hear an echo of this idea when the word appears later in the text; as is often the case in biblical narrative, the guiding word picks up a meaning in one verse that it drops off later on.

The most important case—because the least clear—occurs in the second half of 19:19: מֹשֶׁה יְדַבֵּר וְהָאֱלֹהִים יַעֲנֶנּוּ בְקוֹל: "Moses would speak, and God answered him with a *qol*."[41] Does this mean that God answered Moses with thunder, or with a voice that spoke specific words? On the one hand, the two cases in which *qol* clearly refers to thunder before and after 19:19 may lead the audience to assume that *qol* means thunder here as well. The presence throughout chapters 19–20, and especially immediately before our verse in 19:18, of lightning, clouds, and an earthquake (which, acquaintances from California tell me, sounds like thunder) may lead us to presume that "thunder" is the default value of *qol* in this narrative. Further, the verb יַעֲנֶנּוּ (*ya'anennu*, "answer him") in this clause sounds similar to the noun עָנָן (*'anan*, "cloud"), and this similarity also prompts an association between meteorological phenomena and the word *qol* in this clause.[42] On the other hand, the context at the end of our verse is one of speaking and answering—activities that are normally associated with a voice and with words. In short, both translations,

---

Basic, 1981), 92–112; Ronald Hendel, "Leitwort Style and Literary Structure in the J Primeval Narrative," in *Sacred History, Sacred Literature: Essays on Ancient Israel, the Bible, and Religion in Honor of R. E. Friedman*, ed. Shawna Dolansky (Winona Lake, IN: Eisenbrauns, 2008): 93–109.

**40** There are three systems for versification of Exod 20 and Deut 5 in different editions of the Masoretic text. As a result, Bibles variously number the first verse after the Decalogue in Exod 20 as v. 14, 15, or 18 and in Deut 5 as 18, 19, or 22. Throughout this article, I number the first verse after the Decalogue in Exodus as 20:18 and in Deuteronomy as 5:22. On these systems and their development, see Mordechai Breuer, "Dividing the Decalogue Into Verses and Commandments," in *The Ten Commandments in History and Tradition*, eds. Ben-Zion Segal and Gershon Levi, Publications of the Perry Foundation for Biblical Research of the Hebrew University of Jerusalem (Jerusalem: Magnes Press, 1990): 291–330.

**41** All translations from the Hebrew (including the translation from ibn Tibbon's Hebrew version of Maimonides Mishnah commentary in n. 47) are my own.

**42** My thanks to Chazzan Henry Rosenblum for this fine observation.

"thunder" and "voice," are legitimate,⁴³ but the difference between them is significant. Did God communicate with Moses using a human voice or a very loud noise? Our understanding of revelation's nature and its very content changes drastically depending on which understanding we adopt. If *qol* is a voice, the Israelites heard God providing specific information in verbal form to Moses. If it means thunder, then what occurred at Sinai was an overwhelming experience, but not necessarily one in which Israelites acquired heard distinct words and commands directly from God. The stenographic theory of revelation grows out of the former translation; participatory theories can align themselves with the latter.

The *second ambiguity* also raises the question of whether and to what extent the nation heard specific laws directly from God. It emerges when we read the passage immediately after the Decalogue, Exod 20:18–22. The content of these verses is straightforward: the people are frightened by what they have already heard, and they ask Moses to approach God so that they do not have to continue experiencing something so terrifying, whereupon Moses calms the people and agrees to serve as intermediary. What is not clear is when this conversation takes place. One might assume that the people spoke to Moses after the giving of the Decalogue, since the verses in question immediately follow the text of the Decalogue. In that case, the people heard the Decalogue in its entirety. When it ended, the nation asked to be spared any more direct revelations, pleading that Moses notify them of subsequent communications from God. Moses approves this plan, and consequently he is alone when he goes into the presence of God. Upon doing so he receives additional laws, presumably those found in Exod 20:23–23:33. The rest of the laws are the product of Mosaic mediation; but the people did hear, directly from the mouth of God, one group of commands.

But the norms of biblical Hebrew narrative syntax and style suggest that we should understand the order of events in Exod 19–20 differently. The past tense in biblical Hebrew narrative is normally indicated by a grammatical form known as the *waw*-consecutive, which indicates that the verb in question describes the next past event narrated in a chain of events; thus, ויקם וילך וישא את־עיניו וירא means, "Next, he got up; next he walked; next he lifted his eyes; next he saw." But the initial verb in 20:18 is not a *waw*-consecutive form (which would have been וַיִּֽרְאוּ), as many translations imply.⁴⁴ Rather, this verse begins with a particular construction, *waw* + noun + participle (וְכָל־הָעָם רֹאִים אֶת־הַקּוֹלֹת), which is often used to indicate that the event reported occurred simultaneously with a previously narrated occur-

---

43 On the unresolved nature of the ambiguity, see Brevard Childs, *Exodus: A Commentary*, OTL (London: SCM Press, 1974), 343. In light of Childs' discussion, any attempt to claim that קול must be translated one way or the other is unfaithful to the text.
44 E.g., NJPS, NEB, NRSV, KJV, Luther, Buber-Rosenzweig, Hirsch, Mendelssohn.

rence.⁴⁵ Thus the phrase in question should be rendered, "The whole people had seen the *qolot*" or "Meanwhile, the whole people were seeing the *qolot*." The question then is which previous occurrence our verse (20:18) coincided with, or how far back the "meanwhile" extends. One possibility is that the event narrated in 20:18 happened along with the previous *waw*-consecutive verb, which appeared in 20:1. In that case, the conversation between Moses and the people took place during the giving of the Decalogue; the narrator avoids interrupting the text of the commandments, however, and thus the narrative does not begin again until Exod 20:18.⁴⁶ According to this understanding of the narrative sequence in Exod 19–20, the nation heard only part (which part?) of the Decalogue and were immediately seized by fear, so that they asked Moses to act as intermediary; Moses, upon approaching "the thick cloud where God was" (20:21), was vouchsafed the text of the remainder of the Decalogue. Further, Moses subsequently obtained the additional legislation found in Exod 20:23–23:33.

But it may be that the verb at the beginning of 20:18 describes an action that took place simultaneously with some event earlier than 20:1, such as those narrated at Exodus 19:19 or 19:25. In that case, so that the people did not hear any of the Decalogue at all. The people's fear may have resulted from the extraordinary seismic and meteorological events that were already occurring prior to the lawgiving, in which case they must have urged Moses to approach God on their behalf before the lawgiving began. Naḥmanides (a thirteenth-century biblical commentator, halakhic authority, and kabbalist) supports this reading in his commentary to 20:18–19, pointing out that the people say to Moses not, "Let not God speak to us anymore, lest we die," nor "Let not God continue speaking to us. . .," but simply, "Let not God speak to us, lest we die." If this is the case, then the nation did not hear the Decalogue at all; the entirety of that text, along with all the other commandments in the Torah, came to the nation exclusively through Moses.

A *third ambiguity* occurs in Exod 20:1: "God spoke all these words, saying." This sort of phrasing (viz., "God/Yhwh spoke/said. . .saying") is exceedingly common; verses with the subject "God" or "Yhwh" and the *waw*-consecutive verb "spoke"

---

45 See, e.g., Paul Joüon and Takamitsu Muraoka, *A Grammar of Biblical Hebrew*, SB (Rome: Pontificium Institutum Biblicum, 1991), §121f, and cf. §118d, §167h, 166j. Alternatively, (as some of Joüon-Muraoka's examples in §121f show) the participle can indicate an action that was ongoing in the past and was followed by a new action. Thus the syntax of 20:18 may tell us that the people were witnessing the thunder for some time, and then they spoke to Moses—perhaps towards the end of the giving of the Ten Commandments, or even when it was complete. But the latter possibility is less likely; to indicate clearly that 20:18 took place after the giving of the Ten Commandments, *waw*-conversive could have been used.

46 See Ḥazzequni's commentary to Exod 20:18.

(וַיְדַבֵּר) or "said" (וַיֹּאמֶר) occur 339 times in the Bible. In every occurrence other than Exod 20:1, the text uses the word אֶל or the particle לְ- to tell us explicitly whom God addressed (thus, "Yhwh spoke to Moses, saying," or "God said to Moses and Aaron, saying").[47] Only in the verse introducing the Decalogue in Exodus is there any doubt about the recipient of divine speech. This fact is jarring to an audience whose ears are familiar with the hundreds of cases of the normal form.[48] It bothered ancient translators: the *Codex Alexandrinus* of the Septuagint adds the words, "to Moses," while the Old Latin translation adds "to the people." It is striking that this ambiguity crops up precisely at the central case of divine revelation in the entire Bible. One might view all previous revelations as leading to the event at Sinai and all subsequent ones as echoing it, repeating it, building upon it, or pointing towards its importance; certainly, this is the way Jewish tradition has come to regard the Sinai revelation.[49] As a result, the absence of a prepositional phrase indicating the recip-

---

**47** Two apparent exceptions are not exceptions at all. 2 Kings 21:10 introduced the recipients of divine speech with בְּיַד, and Gen 17:3 does so with אֵת. As Richard Tupper points out to me, other exceptions occur in Gen 1, in which God speaks the world into existence. In these cases, with the exception of v. 26, God is not addressing anyone at all; and in v. 26, the absence of the dative reflects the text's strategy of reminding us of the heavenly council while also belittling it.
**48** See Aryeh Toeg, *Lawgiving at Sinai* [in Hebrew] (Jerusalem: Magnes, 1977), 62–64, though Toeg explains the reasons for the unusual phrasing here differently, on the basis of the theory (which I find unconvincing) that the Decalogue was added to the redacted text of Exodus much later than the narrative surrounding them.
**49** On Sinaitic revelation as the mother of all subsequent revelations in Judaism, see the notion, discussed in chapter 5 of Sommer, *Revelation and Authority*, that all Jewish teachings through the ages were already revealed in some form to Moses at Sinai. Cf. Maimonides' Seventh Principle (in his commentary to Mishnah Sanhedrin 10:1), which describes Moses as "the father of all prophets who preceded him or who came after him." The importance of Sinai for all subsequent revelations is discussed throughout George J. Brooke, Hindy Najman, and Loren T. Stuckenbruck, eds., *The Significance of Sinai: Traditions about Sinai and Divine Revelation in Judaism and Christianity*, TBN 12 (Leiden; Boston: Brill, 2008). On the conviction in Second Temple Judaism that later revelations receive authority through their connection or resemblance to the Sinai revelation, see Hindy Najman, *Seconding Sinai: The Development of Mosaic Discourse in Second Temple Judaism*, JSJSup 77 (Leiden; Boston, MA: Brill, 2003); on a similar idea in Jewish mysticism, see Gershom Scholem, "Revelation and Tradition as Religious Categories in Judaism," trans. Michael A. Meyer, in *The Messianic Idea in Judaism: and Other Essays on Jewish Spirituality* (New York: Schocken, 1971), 288–90. The importance of Sinai is not only a postbiblical development; Shimon Gesundheit, "Das Land Israels als Mitte: einer jüdischen Theologie der Tora Synchrone und diachrone Perspektiven," *ZAW* 123 (2011): 333, notes that Deut 18:15–19 sees all later prophecy as a continuation of the event at Horeb. This connection was made already by ancient scribes in the Samaritan Pentateuch (in an interpolation located immediately after Exod 20:21) and in 4QGen-Exodus[1], 4QpaleoExodus[m], 4QBibPar *ad loc*. See further William H. Propp, *Exodus 19–40: A New Translation with Introduction and Commentary*, AB 2A (New York: Doubleday, 2006), vol. 2, 115 on v. 21 (18).

ient of the revelation commands our attention. The unprecedented phrasing calls us to wrestle with the question: from whom did Israel receive the text of the Decalogue?

The *fourth ambiguity* focuses our attention on the mode of the nation's perception at Sinai. Exod 20:18 reads: וְכָל־הָעָם רֹאִים אֶת־הַקּוֹלֹת וְאֶת־הַלַּפִּידִם וְאֵת קוֹל הַשֹּׁפָר וְאֶת־הָהָר עָשֵׁן "All the people had seen the voices/thunders and the blazing lightning and the sound of the shofar and the smoke from the mountain." The verb רֹאִים normally means "to see." For this reason, commentators such as Rabbi Akiva (a second-century sage, one of the greatest authorities in the Mishnah) and Rashi (an eleventh-century sage, the most influential and beloved Jewish biblical commentator) point out that the verse presents us with the paradox of visible sound.[50] Thus it suggests that whatever act of cognition took place during the lawgiving was singular; it was not the sort of cognition that takes place when one human being talks to another.[51] To be sure, other commentators, including Rabbi Yishmael (a contemporary of Akiva and also one of the most influential Mishnaic sages) and ibn Ezra (a twelfth-century biblical commentator renowned for his linguistic precision and independent judgement) reject the notion that the phrasing is paradoxical. Yishmael claims that the verse means to say that the Israelites saw the visible but heard the aural.[52] Ibn Ezra points out that the verb רא"ה sometimes means "perceive" in a general sense, not just perceive through the eyes.[53] This proposal is not entirely persuasive. In Gen 2:19, 27:27, Jer 33:24, Hab 2:1 רא"ה does not refer to sight, but there the verb means "think about," "attend to," or "understand," rather than as "perceive non-visually."[54] Further, even if ibn Ezra's explanation is valid, the nar-

---

[50] See Mekhilta deRabbi Yishmael, Baḥodesh, §9 and (with even greater emphasis on the paradoxical nature of the phrasing) the parallel passage in Mekhilta deRabbi Shimon bar Yoḥai. See Rashi to Exod 20:18 and to b. Shabbat 88b. For additional rabbinic and medieval sources, see Menahem M. Kasher, *Torah Sheleimah* [in Hebrew], 48 vols. (Jerusalem: Beit Torah Sheleimah, 1979), 16: 136–37, notes to §§ 131 and 143.

[51] For overviews of the exegetical problem, see Michael Carasik, "To See a Sound: A Deuteronomic Rereading of Exodus 20:15," *Prooftexts* 19 (1999): 262; Assnat Bartor, "Seeing the Thunder: Narrative Images of the Ten Commandments," in *The Decalogue in Jewish and Christian Tradition*, ed. Henning Graf Reventlow and Yair Hoffman, LHBOTS (New York: T&T Clark, 2011): 13–14 and notes there.

[52] See references into his debate with Akiva in n. 50 above.

[53] See both of ibn Ezra's commentaries to our verse. The same interpretation is found in August Dillmann and Victor Ryssel, *Die Bücher Exodus und Leviticus*, Kurzgefasstes exegetisches Handbuch zum Alten Testament 12 (Leipzig: S. Hirzel, 1897), 245.

[54] See Brown, Driver, Briggs, *A Hebrew and English Lexicon of the Old Testament*, 906 §6d,g and §7; Ludwig Koehler and Walter Baumgartner, *Hebrew and Aramaic Lexicon of the Old Testament*, trans. and ed. under the supervision of Mervyn E. J. Richardson (Leiden: Brill, 1994–1999), s.v. רא"ה §§2, 6e, 13; Isac Leo Seeligmann, "Knowledge of Yhwh and Historical Consciousness in Antiquity"

rator's decision to use the verb רא"ה in a rare sense ("perceive through any sense organ, including the ear") rather than its most typical sense ("perceive through the eye") encourages the reader to slow down and to ponder how, precisely, the perceived matter came into the people's mind. A modern Italian-Israeli scholar, Umberto (Moshe David) Cassuto, also attempts to downplay the oddity, but in a different way. He suggests that the phrase involves zeugma— that is, the use of this verb is suited to some of its direct objects (the lightning and the smoke from the mountain) but not to others (the various sounds).[55] Even if Cassuto is correct,[56] the narrator's decision to put the inappropriate accusative first rather than one of the accusatives that matches the verb focuses our attention on something that, at least initially, appears paradoxical.[57] It seems reasonable to agree with Nahum Sarna, who maintains that "the figurative language indicates the profound awareness among the people of the mystery of God's self-manifestation; an experience that cannot be adequately described by the ordinary language of the senses."[58]

The *fifth ambiguity* results from the fact that one can punctuate the crucial verses where chapter 19 leads into chapter 20 in two different ways. One might understand Exod 19:25–20:2 as follows:

> [25]Moses came down to the people and spoke to them. 20 [1]Then God spoke all these words, saying, [2]"I am Yhwh your God who took you out of Egypt, out of the house of bondage..."

---

[in Hebrew], in *Studies in Biblical Literature* [in Hebrew], eds. Avi Hurvitz, Emanuel Tov, and Sara Japhet (Jerusalem: Magnes Press, 1996), 155–58.

55 Umberto (Moshe David) Cassuto, *A Commentary on the Book of Exodus* [in Hebrew] (Jerusalem: Magnes, 1944) *ad loc.*; Martin Noth, *Exodus, a Commentary*, trans. John Bowden (Philadelphia, PA: Westminster Press, 1962), 168; Propp, *Exodus 19–40*, 181. (This explanation essentially restates the position of Yishmael and the commentators discussed by Kasher on the top of 137; see above, n. 50.) For a different suggestion that attempts to explain the phraseological oddity on a rational plane, see Samson Raphael Hirsch, *Der Pentateuch übersetzt und erläutert* (Frankfurt am Main: J. Kaufmann, 1899), 218, who maintains that the phrasing signifies that they were able to perceive that the lightning they saw and the voice they heard were coming from the same place.

56 Carasik, "To See a Sound", 262, notes that Cassuto himself does not seem fully convinced by his explanation, since he goes on to provide another one, to wit, that (following ibn Ezra) the verb רא"ה can mean "perceive" more generally.

57 The Samaritan Pentateuch eliminates the problem with an expansive reading that adds the verb שָׁמַע to govern the aural phenomena: וכל העם שמע את הקולות ואת קול השופר וראים את הלפידים ואת ההר עשן. MT's רא"ה is the lectio difficilior and calls out for exegetical attention.

58 Nahum Sarna, *Exodus*, The JPS Torah commentary (Philadelphia, PA: Jewish Publication Society, 1991), 115. Cf. Robert Alter, *The Five Books of Moses: A Translation with Commentary* (New York: W.W. Norton & Co., 2004), *ad loc.*: "The writer presents the Sinai epiphany as one tremendous synesthetic experience that overwhelms the people [...]" Similarly, Abraham Joshua Heschel, *God in Search of Man*, 249, 250: "The voice of God is incongruous with the ear of man [...] We do not *hear* the voice; we only *see* the words in the Bible."

But it would be just as defensible to render these verses as follows:

> [25]Moses came down to the people and said to them, 20 [1]"God spoke all these words, saying, [2]'I am Yhwh your God who took you out of Egypt, out of the house of bondage...'"

In the former rendering, we first hear the narrator's voice, and then we hear the narrator quoting God's voice. Thus understood, the text reports that the people hear God's voice pronouncing the Decalogue. In the latter rendering, however, the text informs us that the Israelites hear Moses reciting the Decalogue, which he had heard earlier from God.[59] In that case the nation received the Decalogue only through human mediation. Both translations are legitimate—and both have strikes against them. Against the former, we can note that the verb that appears in 19:25, וַיֹּאמֶר, typically introduces direct speech. It is properly translated, "he said" (rather than what I suggested in the first rendering, "he spoke"), and it is normally followed by the words that the verb's subject utters.[60] But we can also find faults in the second rendering. The phrase "God spoke" in 20:1 is formulated using a *waw*-consecutive. This formulation suggests that God's act of speaking came immediately after Moses' act of speaking. If that is so, then the phrase "God spoke" are the words of the narrator, not of the character Moses.[61] Further, it would have been odd for the character Moses to begin a new statement with a *waw*-consecutive, which correctly is the *continuation* of a narration that was already taking place in a previous sentence.[62] In short: this phrasing forces us to debate whether God or Moses uttered the Decalogue to the nation, and it precludes us from bringing the debate to any definite conclusion.

---

[59] See Propp, *Exodus 19–40*, 167.

[60] In other words, אָמַר always takes an object, whether quoted material (in which case we translate אָמַר as "say") or a noun or a relative pronoun (in which case "mention, specify, designate"). See Brown, Driver, Briggs, *A Hebrew and English Lexicon of the Old Testament*, 55, § 1, under the rubric "*mention, name, designate*". When the verb means "command," the object is sometimes implied (section 4 in the same lexicon); even in these cases, one cannot translate the verb as "speak." Other than Exod 19:25, there are only three cases in which the verb does not have an object stated or implied, and which thus suggests that the verb might be translated as "speak" (as argued by Propp, *Exodus 19–40*, 145). Two of these, Gen 4:8 and 2 Chron 32:24 are textually suspect (see the critical commentaries *ad loc.*). The third is Judg 17:2, but the object "imprecation" is clearly implied by the immediately preceding verb. Thus Exod 19:25 presents at the very least an unusual use of the verb that avoids the clarity that could easily have been achieved by דִּבֶּר. On this anomaly, see Samuel R. Driver, *The Book of Exodus*, The Cambridge Bible for Schools and Colleges (Cambridge: Cambridge University Press, 1911), 168 and 175.

[61] Hence my literal translation of the וַיְ of the *waw*-consecutive in the first rendering as "Then."

[62] Propp, *Exodus 19–40*, 145 rightly notes: "If Moses were reciting the Decalog in Exod 20:1, he would surely begin, 'thus said Yhwh,' not, 'And Deity spoke.' That sounds like a narrator."

These five ambiguities raise a single issue: the extent to which the Israelites were in contact with the divine at Sinai, and, more specifically, the nature of their apprehension of the lawgiving. These ambiguities force the audience to contemplate two related questions: (1) What was the basic nature of the revelation the nation experienced? Did it consist of an overwhelming event without communicating specific words (*qol*=thunder), or did it involve specific words that enunciated the laws found in Exod 20:1–17 (*qol*=voice)? (2) Did the nation Israel hear the text of the Decalogue (or parts thereof) directly from God, or did they hear them exclusively as the product of prophetic mediation? This second question might be recast: to what extent was the lawgiving a private event involving Moses, and to what extent was it a public one involving the whole nation?[63] Three answers emerge: they heard all ten statements of the Decalogue (if we understand the textual location of Exod 20:18–22 as reflecting temporal sequence); they heard some of them (if we understand the conversation in 20:18–22 as occurring during the lawgiving); or they heard none of them (if we understand the conversation as preceding the lawgiving). Given the norms of biblical Hebrew syntax, the first of these is the least likely possibility; the second and third are both strong possibilities. Our five ambiguities are manifestations of a single concern, which the text poses insistently. This narrative does not want the audience to know whether the lawgiving was direct, mediated, or a mix of the two. The narrative does, however, encourage the audience to wonder about this issue, to think through various possibilities, to see their strengths and weaknesses, and perhaps to think about their implications. It endorses a question, but not an answer, a debate, not a resolution.

From a theological and also a halakhic point of view, a great deal is at stake in the equivocation that centers around the people's perception and Moses' mediation. For the many Jewish thinkers who subscribe to the stenographic theory of revelation, Jewish law is based on the actual words of God found in the Torah, which were revealed to all Israel at Sinai. To be sure, the law as observed in rabbinic communities follows specifics found in Talmudic literature; while those specifics are built upon human interpretations of Pentateuchal texts, the texts being interpreted (according to the stenographic theory) contain God's actual words precisely as God dictated them to Moses. According to the participatory theory, the biblical texts themselves are largely or even entirely products of human beings who respond to the revelation at Sinai.[64] Now, the extent to which human beings might feel free

---

63 See Toeg, *Lawgiving at Sinai*, 351–60.
64 This theme appears throughout Heschel's *oeuvre*, but of particular importance for understanding the practical and halakhic implications of Heschel's theology of revelation are Heschel, *Torah min Hashamayim* (1st ed.) esp. vol. 3, 49–138 (and, in somewhat different form, Heschel, *Torah min Hashamayim*, esp. 2nd. ed. vol. 2, 1047–120, and Heschel, *Heavenly Torah as Refracted Through the*

to alter or correct laws based on revelation at Sinai will be limited if one believes those laws are rooted in a legislation whose wording came down from heaven. But the extent to which humans are willing to participate in the unfolding of revelation by altering those laws will be less limited if one believes that the biblical texts themselves were already the product of human interpretation, so that their wording is the work of Moses and those who followed him.[65] If human intermediaries wrote the laws found in the Torah, even those in the Decalogue, as an attempt to translate God's nonverbal *qol* into human language, then the authority behind the law in general remains fully divine, but the specifics of any given law are human.

The insistent focus of Exod 19–20 on the question of Mosaic mediation represents an attempt by biblical authors themselves to raise the sorts of questions central to the work of Rosenzweig, Heschel, Jacobs, and kindred thinkers. If the nation Israel heard the Decalogue in its entirety directly from God, then we know that God does indeed speak with a voice, using words found in a human language—specifically, in the dialect of ancient Canaanite we call Hebrew. In that case, it is possible that other laws found in the Torah were also literally the word of God; when the text reports that God "spoke" to Moses and gave him this or that commandment (as the Torah does throughout the Exodus, Leviticus, and Numbers), "speaking" can reasonably be interpreted as speaking in the sense that one human speaks to another. The people, having heard one sample of divine speech in human language, can presume that the laws they subsequently received through Mosaic mediation were conveyed in words, as the Decalogue was. It follows that Moses, when acting as God's intermediary, is functioning as a stenographer, not as an interpreter, or to use Heschel's terminology: as a vessel rather than a partner. On the other hand, if the nation never heard the Decalogue from God but experienced an overwhelming sense of God's presence, then the laws they received from Moses may have been couched in Moses' own formulation of God's nonverbal communication. In that case, whatever the Israelites know of the laws, they know from a fellow-human and not from God. It remains possible that when Moses or the narrator says that God "spoke" to Moses, they mean that God literally uttered words to him (in which case we can return to

---

*Generations*, esp. 680–769); Abraham Joshua Heschel, "Toward an Understanding of Halacha," in *Abraham Joshua Heschel, Moral Grandeur and Spiritual Audacity: Essays*, ed. Susannah Heschel (New York: Farrar, 1996): 127–45; Heschel, *God in Search of Man*, 213–17. See also the discussion in Even-Chen, *A Voice from the Darkness*, 154–79, and in Arnold Eisen, "Re-Reading Heschel on the Commandments," *Modern Judaism* 9 (1989): 1–33. From among Jacob's works, see esp. Jacobs, *A Tree of Life*, and Jacobs, *Beyond Reasonable Doubt*, 106–31. For other presentations of this sort of approach, see Gillman, *Sacred Fragments*, esp. 39–62; Dorff and Rosett, *A Living Tree*; Elliot Dorff, *The Unfolding Tradition*.

65 See further Eisen, "Re-Reading Heschel on the Commandments," 16–17.

the stenographic theory of revelation), but it is also possible that "spoke" in such a sentence (perhaps: in any sentence where God is the subject) refers to a communication that had to be translated into human language. If the people never heard any of the Decalogue's wording from God own voice, then they could not know which theory of revelation is correct; and neither can we. We can go a step further: because Exod 19–20 repeatedly calls attention to the question of mediation without allowing us to be certain about its answer, these chapters force us to hover between two models for understanding revelation. The audience of Exodus must contemplate each possibility seriously but skeptically, without rejecting either one.

One might argue against my whole line of reasoning by pointing out that, regardless of the complexities of chapters 19–20, the Torah tells us hundreds of times that God "spoke" (וַיְדַבֵּר) to Moses and "said" (וַיֹּאמֶר) certain words to him. The crucial question we confront throughout the Torah, however, is what these verbs mean when their subject is God (as we learn from the most influential Jewish philosopher, Maimonides, who lived in Spain and Egypt in the twelfth century).[66] The purpose of the ambiguities in chapters 19–20, which are at once insistent and consistent, is to render sentences that link this subject to those two verbs problematic: the pattern of ambiguity suggests we should think carefully about such sentences, because they may contain more than one might initially assume, or something different than one might think. These chapters, then, shed light on all cases of divine speech, or, to speak more precisely, they set a dark cloud over them. One cannot use the frequent occurrence of verses like, "God spoke to Moses, saying," to show that God really does talk in human language. The Pentateuch encourages us to conclude from the web of ambiguities in Exod 19–20 that we are unsure whether God talks, even to Moses, in human language.[67] In so doing, the Pentateuch problematizes its own authority without in any way renouncing that authority. The Pentateuch's project, then, is inherently correlational, in Tillich's sense of "designat[ing] the real interdependence of things or events in structural wholes," and more particularly in the sense of "qualif[ying] the divine-human relationship within religious experience."[68] In fact the Pentateuch is doubly correlational. First, it presents its own claim to authority but simultaneously and in the very same narrative forces its audience to wonder about that authority. Thus, it renders its own authority and questions about that authority inseparable and

---

**66** Moses Maimonides, *The Guide of the Perplexed*, trans. Shlomo Pines (Chicago, IL: University of Chicago Press, 1963), Book 1, chapters 65–67. On a proper, which is to say, non-idolatrous, understand of the biblical phrase, "God spoke," see also Heschel, *God in Search of Man*, 177–83; regarding the implied issue of idolatry in those pages, see Held, *Abraham Joshua Heschel*, 268 n. 45.
**67** My thanks to Dan Baras for encouraging me to express myself more fully on this point.
**68** Tillich, *Systematic Theology*, vol.1, 60, 61.

interdependent. Second, it puts God and Israel, commander and commanded, into a relationship in which both participate in laying out what the law requires of Israel.

I have focused here on the way one central narrative in the Book of Exodus forces its audience to engage in a correlational project. I should add now that the verses we have been examining stem specifically from one strand in that book. Four of the five ambiguities we examined occur specifically in the E or Elohist strand found in these chapters.[69] (The fifth one I mentioned, regarding the punctuation of the verses at the end of Exod 19 and the beginning of 20, occurs at the juncture of J and E verses.) Thus, the participatory theology that emerges from my analysis belongs to the E source; we should regard it as *a* Pentateuchal theology, but not as *the* Pentateuchal theology. Elsewhere, the P source also puts forward its own version of the participatory theology, especially in Num 7:89 and in several narratives regarding human-initiated revisions to divine law.[70] P presents its partici-

---

[69] Some contemporary scholars of the Pentateuch reject the notion that we should distinguish between J and E strands in the non-P, non-D sections of the Pentateuch. These scholars propose newer approaches to understanding the origin of the Pentateuch, especially in non-P, non-D passage. These scholars include Rolf Rendtorff, Erhard Blum, Konrad Schmid, David Carr, Jan Gertz and Thomas Dozeman, to name but a few. I myself, however, am convinced by scholars like Menahem Haran, Baruch Schwartz, Joel Baden, and Jeffrey Stackert that we can identify two more or less continuous narrative strands in the non-P, non-D sections of the Pentateuch, which we may term "J" and "E." Nevertheless, the reading of Exodus 19–20 I proposed above is independent of any particular compositional analysis of the book of Exodus. Consequently, supporters of the newer theories can evaluate my exegetical claims about this narrative independently of our disagreement about the continuity or existence of an E strand throughout the Pentateuch. For the delineation of E in Exod 19–24 I follow, see especially Baruch Schwartz, "What Really Happened at Mount Sinai?" *BRev* (1997, Oct.): 21–46. Similar source critical analyses are found Dillmann and Ryssel, *Die Bücher Exodus und Leviticus*, 206–26, 245–58, 284–92 and J. Estlin Carpenter and G. Harford-Battersby, *The Hexateuch According to the Revised Version* (London): Longmans, Green and Co., 1900), vol. 1, 109–19. Note in particular that I believe that E contained some early and unrecoverable version of the Decalogue; the text of Exod 20:1–17 in our Pentateuch has many supplements that are later than E (and in fact later than the compilation of the four sources). For this view, see Baruch Schwartz, "The Horeb Theophany in E: Why the Decalogue Was Proclaimed," paper presented at the SBL Annual Meeting (San Antonio, TX: 2004), and Joel Baden, *J, E, and the Redaction of the Pentateuch*, FAT 68 (Tübingen: Mohr Siebeck, 2009), 153–58, both of whom follow an approach found in Dillmann and Ryssel, *Die Bücher Exodus und Leviticus*, 217, and Driver, *The Book of Exodus*, 168, 174, 201. Similarly, for Julius Wellhausen, *Die Composition des Hexateuchs und der historischen Bücher des Alten Testaments* (Berlin: Georg Reimer, 1899), 86–89, Exod 19:10–19 and 20:1–17 are a compositional unit, and the Decalogue was proclaimed to the people specifically in E (see Wellhausen's helpful summary on 95, and 329–30, where he adds that 20:18–21 are also from E).

[70] For a summary of P's participatory theory of revelation, see Sommer, *Revelation and Authority*, 53–60, and, with greater attention to the relation between P's theory of revelation and P's theory

patory theology so much more briefly than E, but rather more straightforwardly; whereas E presents us with a series of ambiguities that force us to ponder both a stenographic and a participatory understanding of revelation, P simply endorses the latter.

## 2 The rejection, and reappearance, of correlational theology in the book of Deuteronomy

Deuteronomy, on the other hand, rejects the participatory theology. It is clear that the authors of Deuteronomy (whom biblical scholars refer to as "D") have read the E narrative; they noticed precisely the four ambiguities I have identified in E, and they respond to them decisively. Thus, in Deut 4, a D writer has Moses, addressing the people Israel shortly before his death, recall:

> [10]the day you stood before Yhwh your God at Horeb, when Yhwh said to me, "Assemble the people to Me so that I may cause them to hear My words, which they should learn so that they will hold Me in awe all the days that they live on the earth, and so that they will teach their children." [11]Then you drew near and stood at the base of the mountain; the mountain burned with fire to the very heart of the heavens. There was darkness, cloud, and fog. [12]Yhwh spoke to all of you from within the fire; you were hearing a voice of words (קוֹל דְּבָרִים), but you saw no form—just a voice. [13]He declared His covenant to you, which He commanded you to carry out, the ten utterances. Then He wrote them down on two stone tablets. [14]As for me, Yhwh commanded me at that time to teach you laws and statutes so that you carry them out in the land that you are entering so as to own it. [15]So be very careful, for this is a life-and-death point: you saw no form on the day Yhwh spoke to you at Horeb from the midst of the fire (Deut 4:10–15).

These verses were written with two specific questions in mind, which are precisely the questions that emerged in our study of Exod 19–20—and, it seems, from the Deuteronomists' study of this material as well: (1) What does the word *qol* in those chapters mean? (2) How much of the Decalogue did the Israelites hear? Deuteronomy 4:12 informs us that the nation heard a קוֹל דְּבָרִים, a sound of words. D's addition of the clarifying word דְּבָרִים ("of words") to E's *qol* responds to an ambiguity we noticed in Exodus: the *qol* was a voice articulating sounds to communicate meaning. Further, this speech makes clear that the whole people, not just Moses,

---

of legal change, Benjamin Sommer, "Tradition and Change in Priestly Law: On the Internal Coherence of the Priestly Worldview," in *The Pentateuch and Its Readers: Essays in Honor of Baruch Schwartz*, eds. Jeffrey Stackert and Joel Baden, FAT (Tübingen: Mohr Siebeck, 2023): 269–84.

heard the Decalogue. Second-person plural forms fill in the gap we noticed in Exod 20:1, which left out the recipient of the Decalogue text: "Yhwh spoke to all of you (אֲלֵיכֶם) [...] You (אַתֶּם) were hearing a voice of words [...] He declared His covenant to you (לָכֶם), which he commanded you (אֶתְכֶם) to carry out, the ten utterances [...] on the day Yhwh spoke to you (אֲלֵיכֶם) at Horeb [...]" (The rhetorical effect of the second person plural forms is lost in English; I attempt to regain it once by translating "all of you" at its first appearance.) To be sure, in v. 14 Moses was commissioned to act as intermediary, but only for subsequent legislative disclosures.[71]

In addition to clarifying the ambiguities in E, the Deuteronomists in this passage also take issue with a view found in sections of the Exodus narrative that stem from the Pentateuch's P source and from what some scholars call the J strand of the Pentateuch. In 4:12 and 4:15, D insists that the people "saw no form" of the divine body, thus repudiating the view found in J verses such as Exod 19:11 and 24:10–11, as well as P verses such as Exod 24:17 and Lev 9:4–24, which explicitly claim that the Israelites or some of their leaders saw God at Sinai. It is characteristic that D puts a voice in place of a visual form, for Deuteronomy's is a "religion of the ear and not of the eye" (to borrow a phrase Tillich used to characterize Protestant Christianity in distinction from Catholicism and Orthodoxy).[72] Deuteronomy insists that the Temple contains not God's bodily presence (which is located exclusively in heaven and never on earth) but a symbol of God's presence that D terms God's "Name."[73] D emphasizes verbal symbolism rather than cultic sight as an avenue to God when, in texts like Deut 6:4–5 and 31:10–13,[74] it requires Israelites to listen to God's teaching

---

[71] Further, this verse is likely to be a secondary addition, for reasons I adduce below; see the reference to Loewenstamm in note 86.

[72] See Paul Tillich, *On Art and Architecture*, eds. John and Jane Dillenberger, trans. Robert Sharlemann (New York: Crossroad, 1989), 215, as well as the useful discussion in Richard Kieckhefer, *Theology in Stone: Church Architecture from Byzantium to Berkeley* (Oxford: Oxford University Press, 2004), 120. On this aural/Protestant tendency in D and the historical prophetic traditions under D's influence (such as Kings and Jeremiah), see Benjamin D. Sommer, *The Bodies of God and the World of Ancient Israel* (New York: Cambridge University Press, 2009), 135.

[73] On this theology in D, see Moshe Weinfeld, *Deuteronomy and the Deuteronomic School* (Oxford: Clarendon, 1972), 191–209; Tryggve N. D. Mettinger, *The Dethronement of Sabaoth: Studies in the Shem and Kabod Theologies*, ConBOT 18 (Lund: Almqvist and Wiksell, 1982), 48–80; Stephen Geller, *Sacred Enigmas: Literary Religion in the Hebrew Bible* (London: Routledge, 1996), 30–61; Sommer, *The Bodies of God and the World of Ancient Israel*, 62–68. All these studies are indebted to Gerhard von Rad, *Studies in Deuteronomy*, trans. David M.G. Stalker (London: SCM Press, 1953), 37–44.

[74] Non-D material appears in Deuteronomy from 31:14 on; the verses from chapter 31 with which we are concerned, however, belong to D. See, e.g., Samuel R. Driver, *Deuteronomy*, 3rd ed., ICC (Edinburgh: T&T Clark, 1902), 336–38; Wellhausen, *Die Composition des Hexateuchs und der historischen Bücher des Alten Testaments*, 118; Joel Baden, *The Composition of the Pentateuch: Renewing the Documentary Hypothesis* (New Haven, CT: Yale University Press, 2012), 146–7.

on a regular basis.[75] This substitution of voice for picture speaks volumes not only about D's understanding of revelation but about D's theological project altogether. Hermann Cohen describes what he calls Deuteronomy's "reflective repetition" on the preceding books, insightfully connecting the replacement of form with voice to D's abhorrence of anthropomorphism:

> the criticism of this reflection penetrates even deeper in that it considers above anything else those doubts in regard to revelation that must be raised from the point of view of God's spirituality [...] The danger of a material conception of God was concealed in the theophany itself. It is very instructive to learn how Deuteronomy strives to avert this danger [...][76]

—and here Cohen quotes our passage from Deut 4 (specifically, vv. 15–16). As part of this move away from sight toward sound, the D authors redeploy the verbal root רא"ה throughout chapter 4 (and also in chapter 5). The texts we examined in Exodus use verbs and nouns from this root to denote the vision of God that the people or the elders see; so in both J (Exod 3:3; 19:21; 24:10) and P (24:17); a similar idea occurs with the term לְעֵינֵי ("in the sight of," or, more literally, "in the eyes of") in J (19:11) and P (24:17; 40:38). P also uses the root רא"ה when speaking of the plan for the tabernacle that God showed Moses in Exod 25:9; 25:40; 26:30; 27:8; Num 8:4. This verb appears throughout the Deuteronomic authors' Horeb narratives, but D repeatedly finds new uses for the verb, which now refers to what the people learn in an abstract sense (Deut 4:5; 4:25), to what the nation did *not* see (to wit, the deity, 4:12; 4:15), and to enticements that might lead them astray if they pay too much attention to what they might one day see (4:9; 4:19). Only twice in Deuteronomy's Horeb narratives does this verb refer to what Israelites really saw with their eyes (4:36; 5:24). These verses insist that what they saw were accompaniments of theophany but not God's bodily manifestation. Moreover, both of these verses go on to use שמע ("hear"), as if the verb רא"ה ("see"), by itself and unchaperoned by a

---

[75] On cultic sight of the Temple as an avenue to God in (non-deuteronomic) Israelite religion, see, e.g., Mark Smith, "'Seeing God' in the Psalms: The Background to the Beatific Vision in the Hebrew Bible," *CBQ* 50 (1988): 171–83. On D's movement away from this form of religiosity, see Ronald Hendel, "Aniconism and Anthropomorphism in Ancient Israel," in *The Image and the Book: Iconic Cults, Aniconism, and the Rise of Book Religion in Israel and the Ancient Near East*, ed. Karel van der Toorn (Leuven: Peeters, 1997): 205–28, and Karel van der Toorn, "The Iconic Book: Analogies Between the Babylonian Cult of Images and the Veneration of the Torah," in *The Image and the Book: Iconic Cults, Aniconism, and the Rise of Book Religion in Israel and the Ancient Near East*, ed. Karel van der Toorn (Leuven: Peeters, 1997): 228–48.

[76] Cohen, *Religion of Reason Out of the Sources of Judaism*, 73. On this theme in Cohen's work and its anti-mythological tendency, see Erlewine, "Reclaiming the Prophets," 188. On the philosophical context of Cohen's demythologizing reading of Deuteronomy, see Seeskin, *Autonomy in Jewish Philosophy*, 163–64.

more responsible verb, might get the Israelites into troubling situations. In fact in 4:36 "hear" appears once before "see" and again after it, so that the audience contextualizes seeing within a context controlled by hearing. Similarly 5:24 specifies that what the people *saw* is that God *speaks*. Thus, רא"ה here—and also, D wants us to realize, in any case where it is used with something divine as the object—really means "understand," not "perceive with one's eyes." The Deuteronomist moves the verb's meaning away from sight towards something of a verbal and intellectual nature, thus making רא"ה subservient to שמ"ע, and emptying the former of its central meaning to make more room for the latter.[77] This tendency to put hearing where other Israelite thinkers put seeing also appears in 4:33, where, in contrast to the biblical norm, it is the sound of God's voice rather than the sight of God's body that poses a mortal danger to human beings.

Moses' speech in Deut 5 responds to the ambiguities of Exod 19–20 in similar ways:

> [2]Yhwh our God formed a covenant with us at Horeb. [3]It was not with our parents that Yhwh formed this covenant, but with us, all of us, we who are here today, we who are alive! [4]It was directly[78] that Yhwh spoke with you at the mountain from within the fire [. . .] [5bβii] saying:
> "[6]I am Yhwh your God, who led you out of the land of Egypt [. . .]
>
> [. . .]

---

[77] On the use of רא"ה and שמ"ע as guiding words in Deut 4, see the brilliant treatment in Geller, *Sacred Enigmas*, 36–44, 52–53, esp. 39. Geller establishes this chapter reverses the normal hierarchy of ancient Near Eastern wisdom: "hearing is promoted and seeing demoted in significance as regards revelation, and, by extension, all religious experience." On the hierarchical relationship of visual and aural knowledge in the Bible generally, see Seeligmann, "Knowledge of Yhwh and Historical Consciousness in Antiquity," 141–68, esp. 155–58. On the complex interplay of visual and aural elements in both Exod 19–20 and Deut 4–5 and their relationship to the interplay of *fascinans* and *tremendum*, see further George W. Savran, *Encountering the Divine: Theophany in Biblical Narrative*, JSOTSup 420 (London: T&T Clark International, 2005), 109–16.

[78] Heb. פָּנִים בְּפָנִים. In light of Deuteronomy's theology of transcendence, which insisted that God dwells only in heaven and never comes to dwell on earth, it is clear that D intends this phrase idiomatically ("directly, without intermediary") and not literally ("face to face"). On the possibility that this phrase disturbed later Deuteronomistic tradents due to its implications if taken literally, and on their reaction to this problem, see Carasik, "To See a Sound," 263. For a compelling defense of my understanding of the phrase that does not rely on reference to D's theology, see ibn Ezra's commentary to this verse. The difference between this phrase here and the same phrase as used by E in Exod 33:11 is instructive. There E adds several words: "God would speak to Moses face-to-face, as a man speaks to his fellow." The added clause at the end may be intended to specify that the phrase is not merely an idiom intending "directly" but refers to genuine physical proximity, as indicated also by 33:9, which tells us that God (or at least a significant avatar of God) descended from heaven to the Tent of Meeting to speak with Moses. (On the notion of avatar in J and E, see Sommer, *The Bodies of God and the World of Ancient Israel*, 78, 232, 254.)

²¹ᵇ You shall not desire your neighbor's house, his field, his worker, his maid, his ox, his ass, or anything that belongs to him."

²²It was these words that Yhwh spoke to your whole congregation on the mountain from within the fire, the cloud, and the fog—a great voice (קוֹל), which did not continue. Then He wrote them down on two tablets of stone and gave them to me. ²³And it came about that when you all heard the voice (קוֹל) from within the darkness—and the mountain was on fire—that the leaders of your tribes and the elders drew near to me, ²⁴and you said, "Look, Yhwh has shown us His glory⁷⁹ and His greatness; it was His voice (קוֹל) that we heard from the midst of the fire; today we saw that God can speak with a human, and the human lives. ²⁵So now, why should we die? For this huge fire will devour us! If we continue to hear the voice (קוֹל) of Yhwh our God anymore, we will die! ²⁶For who among all flesh has heard the voice of the living God speaking from the midst of the fire like us, and then lived? ²⁷You go and hear whatever Yhwh our God may say; *you* can tell us all that Yhwh our God tells you, and we will listen, and we will carry it out." ²⁸Yhwh heard the voice (קוֹל) consisting of your words as you spoke to me, and Yhwh said to me, "I have heard the voice (קוֹל) consisting of the words of this people as they spoke to you. Everything they said is fine."

Here again D responds specifically to the elements of E we noted earlier in order to reject a participatory theology. As in the E verses of Exod 19–20, the guiding world *qol* appears precisely seven times in Moses' speech in Deut 5. But D stipulates at 5:26 that the people heard a *qol* that speaks, not just a *qol* that accompanies lightning and clouds. Underscoring this idea, *qol* appears in close proximity to the word "speak" in two of its additional occurrences (vv. 24 and 28). The passage also resolves the oddity in Exod 20:18, which told us that the people "saw the voices/thunders (קוֹלֹת) and the blazing lightning and the sound of the shofar and the smoke from the mountain." Like Rabbi Yishmael in the midrash cited earlier, Deut 5:24 clarifies that the people saw the visible but heard the aural by adding verbs from the root רא"ה ("see") in its paraphrase of the verse from Exodus: "Yhwh has let us see (הֶרְאָנוּ) His glory and His greatness; it was His voice (קֹלוֹ) that we heard from the midst of the fire; today we saw (רָאִינוּ) that God can speak with a human, and the human lives." This verse closely tracks the vocabulary and imagery of Exod 20:18 while removing any element of paradox.⁸⁰

Furthermore, our passage addresses the question insistently raised in E concerning how much of the Decalogue the nation heard. Deut 5:23–31 echo Exod 20:18–22 (where the people request that Moses act as intermediary), but the verses

---

**79** I do not capitalize "glory" here, because D, unlike P, does not use the word כָּבוֹד as a technical term for God's body. See Sommer, *The Bodies of God and the World of Ancient Israel*, 64.
**80** I am indebted to Hillel Ben-Sasson for pointing out this exegetical aspect of Deut 5:24.

in Deuteronomy are not phrased ambiguously.[81] Exodus 20:19 did not specify whether the people heard the revelation: "Let not God speak to us, lest we die." But Deut 5:24 makes clear they did: "If we *continue* to hear the voice of Yhwh our God *any more*, we shall die."[82] (D has Moses repeat the same point in Deut 18:16, where we again find the crucial terms "continue" [אֹסֵף] and "any more" [עוֹד].) Moses' task on his own is to receive the remainder of the legislation, which 5:31 calls "the *whole* command."[83] The events recounted in 5:23–31 follow the giving of the Decalogue not only textually but temporally; by using *waw*-consecutive verbs in v. 23 the Deuteronomist eliminates the possibility that the people heard only part of the Decalogue or none of it. D insists that this revelation involved not just Moses or elders but "the *whole* congregation" (5:22). To the same end, Deuteronomy revises the line introducing the Ten Commandments: while Exod 20:1 stated merely, "God spoke all these words, saying," the parallel sentence in Deut 5:4–5 reads, "Yhwh spoke to you [עִמָּכֶם; the Hebrew is plural, addressing the nation] [...] saying." Like the Old Latin translation of Exod 20:1, the Deuteronomist attempts to remedy the earlier verse's failure to specify the addressee of the divine speech by making it clear that God spoke to the whole people. Finally, D stresses

---

[81] Childs, *Exodus*, 351, 343, points out the ambiguity of *qol* in Exod 19:19 and also notes that Deut 4:10; 4:33; 5:4; 5:24 decisively resolve the ambiguity.

[82] Naḥmanides notes this contrast in the opening section of commentary on Exod 20:18–19. He concludes that Exod 20:18–19 and Deut 5:24 narrate two completely different events, the former before the revelation of the Decalogue and the latter after it. His solution differs from that of a modern scholar, but his literary sensitivity is an important tool for the modern scholar all the same. Similarly, he notes that in Exod 20:18 the people are frightened by sounds and sights, while in Deut 5:23–26 they are frightened by the divinity's speech (דבור השבינה). Even if we do not agree that this shows the texts narrate different events altogether, Naḥmanides helps us to see that Deuteronomy unambiguously identifies the voice the people hear as God's, while in Exodus E forces us to wonder what the noise the people hear is and how (or whether) it relates to God's person.

[83] Here we see another subtle difference between D and its source. Schwartz, "The Horeb Theophany in E," explains that in D, "God's original intention was to impart to them the whole of his teaching, and he [...] thought better of it only in light of their resistance [...] In the Elohistic account, the assumption the entire body of laws is going to be communicated to the people by means of a messenger is present from the beginning. In E, the purpose of the proclamation of the Decalogue from the outset is to establish the credibility of the prophet, whose task it will then be to convey the laws and statutes." In light of this contrast, it becomes clear that Rashbam imports the attitude of Deuteronomy into his reading of Exod 20:19 (see his commentary *ad loc.*). In this regard Rashbam is a predecessor of many modern scholars, e.g. Ernest W. Nicholson, "The Decalogue as the Direct Address of God," *VT* 27 (1977): 424–27, Frank Crüsemann, *The Torah: Theology and Social History of Old Testament Law*, trans. Allan W. Mahnke (Minneapolis, MN: Fortress Press, 1996), 253, and Patrick D. Miller, *The Way of the Lord: Essays in Old Testament Theology* (Grand Rapids, MI: William B. Eerdmans, 2007), 4, 19–23.

that the people had direct contact with God in 5:4.⁸⁴ The revelation was public, not mediated; on this point Deuteronomy is both insistent and clear.

Clear, yet equivocal. Deuteronomy 5:5 contradicts the verse that comes before it (as well 4:12–13 and 5:19–20). Immediately after the vivid description of the unmediated meeting of God and Israel in Deut 5:4, there follows a comment announcing that Moses acted as intercessor:

> ⁴It was directly that Yhwh spoke with you at the mountain from within the fire—⁵I was standing between Yhwh and all of you at that time, so as to tell you God's word, for you were afraid of the fire, and you did not go up the mountain—saying: "⁶I am Yhwh your God [. . .]"

The medieval commentators Rashi, Rashbam, and ibn Ezra point out that the word לֵאמֹר ("saying") in v. 5 belongs to the sentence found in v. 4, since it completes the phrase in v. 4 which begins with the words "Yhwh spoke."⁸⁵ This renders the remainder of v. 5 parenthetical. We can go a step further than these commentators: v. 5 (other than the word "saying") is a later addition to the text. It includes the formula, "at that time," which (as the scholar Samuel Loewenstamm has demonstrated) consistently serves in Deuteronomy to indicate redactional interpolations.⁸⁶ This interpolation reintroduces E's idea of a mediated revelation into Deuteronomy. Exodus 19–20 forced the audience to contemplate the possibilities of direct, public revelation of the Decalogue and a mediated one. Deuteronomy 5, acting as a commentary on (more precisely, a revision of) these passages in Exodus, decides in favor of the view that revelation at Sinai was direct. However, a glossator who agrees with the older notion (which was one of the options E allows, and the only

---

84 Here again D neatens up E's enigmatic or messy categories. For D lawgiving at Horeb was entirely unmediated: the whole people heard the whole of the Ten Commandments; and all lawgiving thereafter was entirely private and mediated through Moses. E, on the other hand, portrays lawgiving at Sinai itself as combining public and private aspects, as partially mediated and partially direct, without letting us know how and when the public/national revelation gave way to the private/Mosaic lawgiving. On this contrast, see also Alan Lenzi, *Secrecy and the Gods: Secret Knowledge in Ancient Mesopotamia and Biblical Israel*, SAA 19 (Helsinki: Neo-Assyrian Text Corpus Project, 2008), 302, who points out that for D the people are never "distant" as they are in Exodus; they are either present and fully involved or entirely absent.
85 See their commentaries to Deut 5:5, especially ibn Ezra's discussion of the biblical narrative style as it relates to the displacement of לֵאמֹר.
86 See Samuel E. Loewenstamm, "The Formula 'At That Time' in the Introductory Speeches in the Book of Deuteronomy" [in Hebrew], *Tarbiz* 38 (1969): 99–104. Loewenstamm collects 14 other examples in chapters 1–10 in which context shows that the sections starting with this formula, "at that time," are secondary. On pp. 103–104 he points out the contradiction between 5:5 and 5:4 in particular. For the view that 5:5 is a later interpolation that modifies the claim in 5:4, see also Krüger, "Die Stimme Gottes," 15–16; Alexander Rofé, *Deuteronomy: Issues and Interpretation* (London: T&T Clark, 2002), 29–30.

possibility in P) acts as a supercommentator, adding a line that eliminates both D's notion of public revelation and E's equivocation so that the text agrees with the position that we know from P—but only in the gloss itself, since the surrounding context remains intact. In the end, both Exodus and the final form of Deuteronomy present two possibilities, but it is important to notice the difference between them: In Exodus, we find ambiguity, while in Deuteronomy, we find debate or, to use the rabbinic term, מחלוקת. The former contains a pattern of verses that could be understood in more than one way. This pattern focuses our attention on the question, "Did they hear all or part or none?" but makes it impossible to give a definitive answer. The original text of Deut 5, on the other hand, provides one answer to the question: they heard all, without mediation. But the gloss in 5:5 gives the other answer: they heard none directly and received Torah only through mediation. The final form of Deuteronomy converts E's deliberate indeterminacy into multivocalic disputation.

By utilizing the formula "at that time," the supercommentator in 5:5 has clearly marked his interpolation as such. Like a page in a midrashic collection or a Rabbinic Bible, Deut 5 presents more than one reading of Exod 19–20. As a result of the interpolation, the final version of the text contradicts itself: Deut 5 in its present form does not achieve the univocal clarity D originally sought.[87] In this way the final form presages a tendency that will become prominent in later Jewish literature: texts that attempt to reduce complex traditions to definitive compendia are typically subject to commentaries that reinscribe the earlier complexity.[88] This was the fate of the Mishnah, whose clarity and brevity are followed by the Gemaras' intricate and extended discourses. It was also the fate of Maimonides' law code, which became canonical only alongside the whole literature of commentary and

---

[87] Driver, *Deuteronomy*, 84, argues that 5:5 is not really contradictory: "the people heard the 'voice' of God, but not distinct words; the latter Moses declared (הִגִּיד) to them afterwards." Thus, Driver argues, Deut 5 as a whole, and not just Deut 5:5, agrees with Exod 19:9 and 19:19. Moshe Weinfeld, *Deuteronomy 1–11: A New Translation with Commentary*, AB 5 (New York: Doubleday, 1991) ad loc., and Thomas Krüger, "Die Stimme Gottes," 16, both adopt a similar reading, acknowledging that Deut 5:5 is an interpolation but arguing that it does not necessarily contradicts 5:4. Similar attempts at reconciling verse 5 to its context appear in ibn Ezra *ad loc.* (who argues that 5:5 refers to a later exposition of the law by Moses) and Cohen, *Religion of Reason Out of the Sources of Judaism*, 75–76. These interpretations are not compelling. They contradict Deut 4:12 (according to which the people heard not an indistinct noise but the "sound of words"). Further, they do not even agree with Exod 19, since Deut 5:4 still emphasizes the direct revelation that does not occur in the former.

[88] On this tendency in Jewish learning, see David Weiss Halivni, *Midrash, Mishna, and Gemara: The Jewish Predilection for Justified Law* (Cambridge: Harvard, 1986), 108–15. On the parallel between the multivocality of postbiblical Jewish commentary and that of biblical texts generally, see Moshe Greenberg, *'Al Hammiqra Ve'al Hayyahadut* [in Hebrew] (Tel Aviv: 'Am 'Oveid, 1984), 345–49.

super-commentary it attracted. Maimonides' decision to borrow a traditional Jewish appellation for Deuteronomy, "*Mishneh Torah*" ("repetition of the Torah")[89] for his code was unintentionally apt, for Maimonides' code came to share a particular type of multivocality with Deut 5. I refer here to comments found throughout almost all editions of Maimonides' *Mishneh Torah*. Known as the השגות or *Reservations*, these passages were written by Rabbi Abraham ben David of Posquières (known as the Rabad) and are now printed within the text of the *Mishneh Torah*, usually in a different typeface, or indented into Maimonides' own text. In the *Reservations* the Rabad often disagrees with Maimonides' rulings; he presents alternatives to them and transmits rulings from earlier rabbinic texts that Maimonides had rejected. In a strikingly similar fashion, the interpolator in Deut 5:5 puts forward precisely the view that D rejected. Indeed, the literary genre of 5:5 might be termed a השגה or "reservation," and we may dub the unknown scribe who wrote the verse "Proto-Rabad." The parallel between D and Maimonides' code goes further. The *Mishneh Torah* that became canonical and authoritative in Judaism was less Maimonides' *Mishneh Torah* than the *Mishneh Torah* of tradition: what Jews study as a central part of the curriculum of rabbinic Judaism are editions of the *Mishneh Torah* that include Rabad's *Reservations* interpolated into the Maimonides' text along with a host of commentators positioned around Maimonides' text. These commentators reinstated the disputes, discourses, and legal derivations that Maimonides intended his *Mishneh Torah* to render avoidable.[90] Precisely the same dynamic is at work in Deuteronomy's depiction of Sinai: what serves as Jewish scripture is not D's Deuteronomy but tradition's; the canonical version of Deuteronomy includes both D and the tradition-restoring interpolations of Proto-Rabad.[91] Thus Deuteronomy is a classical Jewish text—one might be so bold as to call it a rabbinic text—for two reasons: first, because it functions as commentary and revision;[92] and, second, because already in the biblical period it is subject to commentary and revision.

---

[89] The term is borrowed from Deut 17:18, which directs future kings of Israel to write out אֶת־מִשְׁנֵה הַתּוֹרָה הַזֹּאת. Though often taken to be Deuteronomy's title for itself, in its own literary context the phrase in fact means "a copy of this Teaching." The text refers to itself here simply as "this Teaching"; the מִשְׁנֵה (copy) of which the text speaks to the physical copy the king writes out.

[90] The השגות of the Rabad have been a standard element of printed editions of Maimonides' Code since the Constantinople edition of 1509—that is, since very shortly after the invention of printing.

[91] Proto-Rabad also inserts a Reservation at 1:18 that moves away from D's notion of revelation as a one-time event (at Horeb) that Moses conveyed to the nation at another one-time event (in Moab). In this verse, Proto-Rabad inserts an element more typical of P, according to which Moses provided legal instruction to Israel at other times as well. Proto-Rabad further emphasizes Moses' intermediary role in 4:14.

[92] Cf. the notion of Deuteronomy as a "proto-Mishnah" suggested by Jacob Weingreen, *From Bible to Mishna: The Continuity of Tradition* (Manchester: Manchester University Press, 1976), 143–54.

## 3 Multiple perspectives within the Pentateuch

One more voice from within scripture requires attention: that of the final, canonical form of the text of the Pentateuch. What is most remarkable when we compare the Pentateuch's sources (J, E, P, and D) to the Pentateuch itself is the difference between the relative self-consistency of the former and the disarray of the latter. Each source presents its story about the giving of the law without any sense that other laws were given at some other point in time. In E and D, God gives the law to Moses on the mountain immediately after they arrive at Horeb, whereas in P God gives Moses the law roughly eight months after they arrive at Sinai, starting at Lev 1:2.[93] In the former, God gives the law to Moses on top of the mountain, whereas in P God does so at the entrance to the tabernacle, which was located at the bottom of the mountain. Moreover, in Exod 25:22 P makes clear that *all* the laws were given at the tabernacle. (The only exception is the law of Passover in Exod 12, which had to be given prior to the exodus event.[94]) Some laws were given at the tabernacle after the Israelites left Mount Sinai, in Numbers, and thus for P the location of lawgiving is the tabernacle, not the mountain. Because in Exod 25:22 P states that God gives *all* the laws to Moses from the holy of holies of the tabernacle, it is impossible to read the legislation in Leviticus and Numbers as the product of a second lawgiving that supplements an earlier one, which took place on the mountain roughly two months after the Exodus—yet the compiled Torah forces us to do just that. Though E and D agree on the timing and location of the divine lawgiving, they differ regarding the time when Moses passed the law on to the people. In E, Moses read the laws to them shortly after he received them (Exod 24:3–7), while in D Moses does not convey the

---

The exegetical nature of Deuteronomy's repetition of the story of lawgiving is also evident in Deuteronomy's treatment of the tablets produced after the Golden Calf incident. We saw earlier that in Exod 34:1 God announced that He would write the second set of tablets, yet in 34:28 the narrator allows the possibility—in fact, the likelihood—that Moses wrote them. The tension between those verses was typical of E, who, by introducing ambiguity as to the origin of the tablets, again encourages the readers to wonder about the provenance of the laws' wording and hints at a greater role for Moses. In Deut 10:1–4 D entirely eliminates the contradiction by stating clearly that God wrote the second set of tablets. Thus D achieves the perspicuity that E studiously avoids when reporting this event. On the exegetical nature of D's treatment of the tablets, see Jean-Pierre Sonnet, *The Book Within the Book: Writing in Deuteronomy* (Leiden: Brill, 1997), 42–45.

**93** Baruch Schwartz, "The Priestly Account of the Theophany and Lawgiving at Sinai," in *Texts, Temples, and Traditions: A Tribute to Menahem Haran*, ed. Michael Fox et al. (Winona Lake, IN: Eisenbrauns, 1996), 116.

**94** God gave Moses directions for constructing the tabernacle in Exod 25–31 on top of Mount Sinai. Of course these directions (which are not laws to be obeyed in the future but architectural and sartorial plans to be executed as soon as Moses comes down from the mountain) had to be given before the tabernacle existed.

law to them until forty years later (and the people do not observe them until they enter the promised land).⁹⁵

If anything, this contrast between the sources' unity and the final version's disarray is even stronger on a thematic level. For E and D, lawgiving was punctual, while for P it was a process that lasted decades. D insists that lawgiving took place stenographically, not correlationally. (To be sure, Proto-Rabad's Reservation or השגה in Deut 5:5 undermines D's point, but the original attempt still comes through clearly.) Even E is consistent, though in a deliberately perplexing way. In light of the frequency with which E forces us to wonder whether divine revelation to the people was verbal and unmediated or non-verbal and mediated, it is clear that the ambiguity in E is intentional and self-consistent. But when the redactors combined the sources, the thematic unity of each source is obscured. The redacted text depicts multiple moments of lawgiving, some of which are clearly stenographic and others of which are not. All the sources want to locate these important events in a single place, whether at Sinai, at Horeb, or at a tent that moves around the wilderness. But the unity of place each source championed is gone from the redacted text. The final form of the Torah relativizes the sources, replacing their clarity with cacophony.

The canonical version of the Pentateuch presents a jumbled set of memories of lawgiving, how it happened, why and when and where it happened. By forcing its audience to wonder about revelation and to contemplate its nature, the final form of the Pentateuch continues E's correlational thrust. A reader of any one source has a specific picture of the revelation in her head, but a reader committed to accepting the whole witness of scripture cannot produce any such picture without doing damage to parts of the text or ignoring large swaths of it. A person who attends only to D or perhaps P can achieve that most dangerous of things in religion, certainty. A premodern reader of the final form of the text, constitutionally unable to become aware of the self-contradictions the text contains, might also achieve certainty, though only after a fair amount of exegetical struggle, which might undermine the sense of certainty. But the modern reader has no reason to privilege any one source over others. If that reader accepts the Pentateuch as authoritative scripture, she is forced to accept that lawgiving occurred, that it is vitally important, but that we can never be sure precisely what it entails. In this respect, the final form, in its broad thematic sweep, most closely resembles E, though it goes even further than E in the direction of equivocation. What the Pentateuch presents to us is not univocality

---

**95** The fact that each source intends to tell the one and only story of the lawgiving has been demonstrated especially convincingly by Schwartz; see, e.g., Baruch Schwartz, "The Torah—Its Five Books and Four Documents" [in Hebrew], in *The Literature of the Hebrew Bible: Introductions and Studies*, ed. Zipora Talshir (Jerusalem: Yad Ben-Zvi Press, 2011), 181–2.

but argument. It leads its audience not to clarity but to perplexity.[96] It highlights revelation as the central theme of the Pentateuch; after all, much more of the Pentateuch is devoted to revelation and lawgiving than, say, the exodus from Egypt, the wandering through the wilderness, the creation of the world, or the lives of the Patriarchs.[97] Yet the final form undermines our ability to truly know about the revelation with any certainty. Its combination of traditions both emphasizes and problematizes the lawgiving, whether by design or by its refusal to decide among those traditions. This tendency is a hallmark of the Torah as a theological document: the Pentateuch accentuates a theme's importance even as it bewilders us with self-contradictory positions.[98]

The Pentateuch, in short, presents us with blatantly repetitious and contradictory narratives concerning revelation. It does not suggest how we might harmonize these narratives or decide among them. Indeed, it does not even hint that doing so would be desirable. What sort of view of revelation is implicit in such a presentation? I would like to suggest that the three narratives of revelation preserved in Exodus, along with a fourth, from Deuteronomy, were written centuries after the event (or events?) that took place at a mountain or mountains variously

---

[96] Here I borrow phrasing from Ward, *Religion and Revelation*, 22–23, from the section with the subtitle, "The Ambiguity of Revelation."

[97] Lawgiving at Sinai/Horeb and the tabernacle takes up Exod 19–40, Lev 1–27, and Num 1–10, along with significant sections of the remainder of Numbers and Deuteronomy. The exodus narrative is found in Exod 1–15; the wandering, in Num 13–36; creation, in Gen 1–3; and patriarchs, in Gen 12–50.

[98] Something similar happens with the Pentateuch's three divergent pictures of divine presence, I have argued in Sommer, *The Bodies of God and the World of Ancient Israel*. A very similar debate occurs among D, P, and H in regard to holiness in the Pentateuch: Is it a characteristic of space or of people? Is it automatically granted by the divine presence, or is it something towards which Israelites must always strive? On this rich topic, see especially Walter Kornfeld and Helmer Ringgren, "קד״ש," in *Theological Dictionary of the Old Testament*, eds. Helmer Ringgren G. Johannes Botterweck, and Heinz-Josef Fabry, trans. John T. Willis et al. (Grand Rapids: Eerdmans, 2003), vol. 12, 521–45; Israel Knohl, *The Sanctuary of Silence: The Priestly Torah and the Holiness School* (Minneapolis: Fortress, 1995); Jan Joosten, *People and Land in the Holiness Code: An Exegetical Study of the Ideational Framework of the Law in Leviticus 17–26*, VTSup 67 (Leiden: Brill, 1996); Sara Japhet, "Some Biblical Concepts of Sacred Space," in *Sacred Space: Shrine, City, Land: Proceedings of the International Conference in Memory of Joshua Prawer*, eds. Benjamin Kedar and Raphael Judah, R. J. Zwi Werblowsky (New York: Macmillan, 1998): 54–72; Baruch Schwartz, *The Holiness Legislation: Studies in the Priestly Code* [in Hebrew] (Jerusalem: Magnes Press, 1999), and, more briefly, Baruch Schwartz, "Israel's Holiness: The Torah Tradition," in *Purity and Holiness: The Heritage of Leviticus*, eds. Marcel Poorthuis and Joshua J. Schwartz, Jewish and Christian Perspectives Series 2 (Leiden: Brill 1999): 39–52; Eyal Regev, "Priestly Dynamic Holiness and Deuteronomic Static Holiness," *VT* 51 (2001): 243–61; Gary Anderson, "To See Where God Dwells: The Tabernacle, the Temple, and the Origins of the Christian Mystical Tradition," *Letter and Spirit* 4 (2008): 13–45.

known as Sinai and Horeb. Each narratives preserves memories going back to the event.[99] Because the revelation was so overwhelming, the way people perceived it as it was happening must have varied; different Israelites noticed, and missed, different aspects of what took place. As these perceptions were transmitted over generations, the differences among them grew further, and they evolved into the varied historical memories preserved in the Pentateuchal sources.

We should not regard this variety of perception, or the even greater variety of historical accounts that followed, as an error or a problem. Rather, it may be God's intentional strategy of overcoming the limits of human perception, which could not assimilate the extraordinary event. Revelation, then, is (to borrow the words of the contemporary Anglican theologian Keith Ward) something that "God has not, in the working-out of Divine providence, seen fit to do [. . .] in [. . .] [a] clear and unequivocal way" but rather in a way that produces argument and perplexity.[100] This strategy affords the human participants in the event and its aftermath the gift of interpretive freedom. By isolating each of the sources, scholars have recovered a valuable variety of older voices from the history of Israelite theology, voices that are able to speak more distinctly when we hear each one by itself. The diverse memories found in the Pentateuchal sources serve as religiously useful testimonies that provide guidance to people for whom the Bible functions as scripture.[101] Attending to these testimonies allows us, first, to sense the extent to which teachings about revelation were already subject to rich debate in the biblical period itself, and, second, to see how the modern debates about revelation recall and re-enact this older debate.

---

[99] Cf. Edward L. Greenstein, "Understanding the Sinai Revelation," in *Exodus: A Teacher's Guide*, eds. Ruth Zielenziger, Marcia Lapidus Kaunfer, Barry Holtz, and Miles Cohen (New York: Melton Research Center of the Jewish Theological Seminary, 1994): 277–8, who points out that the differences among the memories preserved in Exod 19–24 reflect not only different perceptions of the event itself but different ways of preserving, interpreting, and passing on those perceptions.

[100] Ward, *Religion and Revelation*, 22–23. On the religious value of a plurality of understandings of the divine, especially for monotheists, see further the references to Moses Mendelssohn in the first two footnotes above.

[101] For the argument that source criticism is religiously valuable because it allows us to recover theologically meaningful views of the revelation that existed in ancient Israel that are harder to see if we focus on the final form of a biblical text, see, Baruch Schwartz, "The Origin of the Law's Authority: 'Grundnorm' and Its Meaning in the Pentateuchal Traditions" [in Hebrew], *Shnaton Ha-Mishpat Ha-Ivri* 21 (2000): 254, and cf. Schwartz, "The Torah," 213–18. The same point has been made in relation to other issues, such as conceptions of God in the Torah and the theme of the promises to the patriarchs; see Sommer, *The Bodies of God and the World of Ancient Israel*, 124–26, and Joel Baden, *The Promise to the Patriarchs* (New York: Oxford University Press, 2013), chapter 5.

## 4 Conclusions

I have suggested that the debate between participatory and stenographic theories of revelation is not the invention of the modern era or even of the Middle Ages but can be found in the varied positions of the Pentateuchal sources. The Torah's accounts of revelation at Sinai consistently raise the issue of how the nation Israel came to know the law. Did they hear God's commands directly, or exclusively through Moses' mediation, which inevitably involves some degree of interpretation? This question points to several larger ones: Is God's voice similar to a human voice, or does God communicate in nonverbal ways even with the intermediator himself? If God does not speak in any human sense, where do the specifics of the Torah's law originate? These questions received attention not only from texts in Exodus but from the tradition of interpretation that began within the Bible itself, in Deuteronomy's deliberate revision of the E narrative preserved in Exod 19–20. The E source suggests—but does not confirm—the possibility that the revelation, while real and commanding, was non-verbal. The P source also raises this possibility, but without simultaneously hinting at the opposite point of view. These traditions, one maximalist and one minimalist, developed further among the rabbinic interpreters in antiquity and among commentators and philosophers in the Middle Ages.[102] The theologians I discussed at the outset of this chapter, Rosenzweig and Heschel, build on an implication of nonverbal revelation by proposing that the specific words found in scripture are a human response to God's commanding but nonverbal self-disclosure.

A critic of my argument might argue that I place too much weight on a few elements of the texts in Exod 19–20 and their interpreters.[103] In attempting to trace a trajectory that leads from E to the theologies of Rosenzweig and Heschel, I am, such a critic would maintain, pushing too hard, because the modern theologians develop the participatory theology in ways that are far more ramified and systematic than E does. It is hardly the case that E (or P) would agree with many details of the theologies of revelation that those two modern thinkers espouse, much less with halakhic changes that might receive license from such theologies. One may wonder, therefore, if it is really legitimate to look to E as a precursor to modern correlational theologians, since the latter take the ideas in question so much further than the biblical authors did. The connection I draw is based, at best, on implica-

---

[102] For a review of the growth of these two traditions in biblical, rabbinic, and medieval Jewish literature, see Sommer, *Revelation and Authority*, 75–98.
[103] My thanks to Yair Lorberbaum and Yehudah Mirsky, who helped me think through this issue more carefully.

tions of the biblical authors' positions, implications those authors do not draw out and might not even recognize. Is drawing such a connection legitimate?

I submit that it is. It is always the case that a thinker may not articulate crucial implications of his own ideas. This phenomenon is well-known to any teacher who attempts to convey material of a certain complexity. On occasion, I have known a student to make a comment that shows she understood what I said better than I did; at other times, students have asked questions I was able to answer immediately—but my answer entailed ideas I myself only came to realize at the moment that the student asked the question. The existence of unrealized implications is an inevitable feature in the history of ideas, for changing circumstances create new vantage points from which to observe and extend earlier observations.[104] One thinker may have an insight that cannot be easily expressed or even fully understood in the conceptual language of his own day, but a later author, equipped with habits of thought unavailable earlier, can take up that insight, grasp it more thoroughly than the thinker who first propounded it, and articulate it in ways the original thinker could not imagine.[105] To use Aristotelian terminology: the new formulation actualizes a potential that was present in the original insight. The inability of the earlier thinker, using the tools of his own day, to imagine all the consequences of the insight hardly vitiates the link between that insight and the later author's proposals. (Here it is useful to recall the distinction that the historian of religion Wilfred Cantwell Smith draws between continuity and unchangingness.[106] The former, I think, is essential to authenticity in a religious tradition; the latter is inimical to its endurance.) As the Catholic theologian Yves Congar teaches: within a tradition, a doctrine may contain the solution to a problem not yet encountered when the doctrine emerged.[107] We may add that the sages who first propounded the doctrine might find the problem itself surprising; that is, they might not understand why it is a problem at all. Further, the way their doctrine funds a particular solution might startle them even more. Their surprise does not mean, however, that the solution is any less organic to the tradition those sages embodied and passed on.

---

**104** Cf. Brown, *Tradition and Imagination*, 374; Alon Goshen-Gottstein, "The Promise to the Patriarchs in Rabbinic Literature," in *Divine Promises to the Fathers in the Three Monotheistic Religions*, ed. Alviero Niccacci (Jerusalem: Franciscan Printing Press, 1995): 97.
**105** Similarly, it is possible that later readers understand an earlier text better than that text's first readers understood it. See Eric Donald Hirsch, Jr., *Validity in Interpretation* (New Haven, CT: Yale University Press, 1967), 43. This is especially the case in poetry and in scripture, as noted by Wilfred Cantwell Smith, *What Is Scripture? A Comparative Approach* (Minneapolis: Fortress Press, 1993), 230.
**106** Smith, *What Is Scripture?*, 148.
**107** Yves Congar, *The Meaning of Tradition*, trans. A. N. Woodrow (San Francisco, CA: Ignatius Press, 2004), 14.

This phenomenon of unstated or unrealized implications that emerge only as a tradition evolves is especially important in religious discourse. One does not have to be associated with progressive movements to recognize this. One theologian already alluded to has explained this phenomenon especially well, though this theologian is not reputed to harbor an overenthusiastic attachment to radical change. I refer to Joseph Ratzinger (Pope Benedict XVI), who writes that "it is necessary to keep in mind that any human utterance of a certain weight contains more than the author may have been immediately aware of at the time." This is especially the case when we speak of a scripture, Ratzinger explains, because in scripture:

> older texts are reappropriated, reinterpreted, and read with new eyes in new contexts. They become Scripture by being read anew, evolving in continuity with their original sense, tacitly corrected and given added depth and breadth of meaning. This is a process in which the word gradually unfolds its inner potentialities, already somehow present like seeds, but needing the challenge of new situations, new experiences and new sufferings, in order to open up [...] The author is not simply speaking for himself on his own authority. He is speaking from the perspective of a common history that sustains him and that already implicitly contains the possibilities of its future, of the further stages of its journey [...] The author does not speak as a private, self-contained subject. He speaks in a living community, that is to say, in a living historical movement not created by him, nor even by the collective, but which is led forward by a greater power that is at work.[108]

Thus, a religious thinker may begin to perceive, and to express, some aspect of a divine reality whose significance cannot be fully understood in her own day, and this tentative perception may bear fruit many generations later. It is just such a latent possibility that the E source experiments with; and as Solomon Schechter rightly notes, "no creed or theological system which has come down to us from antiquity can afford to be judged by any other standard than by its spiritual and poetic possibilities."[109] The fact that the biblical authors I cite in this chapter would not have agreed with all the participatory implications I associate with their words is of no relevance for evaluating the validity of my claim that those implications grow out of their work. It is the very nature of scripture that it illuminates crucial matters for later audiences in ways the first authors and audiences did not foresee. The correlations with which my own theological reading are concerned, then, are not only those between heaven and earth but also those within the tradi-

---

**108** Ratzinger, *Jesus of Nazareth*, xviii–xx. On the communal nature of biblical authorship in Catholic thought, see further Harrington's remarks in Marc Zvi Brettler, Peter Enns, and Daniel J. Harrington, *The Bible and the Believer: How to Read the Bible Critically and Religiously* (New York: Oxford University Press, 2012), 87.
**109** Solomon Schechter, *Studies in Judaism, First Series* (Philadelphia, PA: Jewish Publication Society, 1896), xxiv–xxv.

tion that begins within scripture and continues to grow and flourish down to the present day and, no doubt, long into the future.

# Bibliography

Albrektson, Bertil. *History and the Gods*. Lund: CWK Gleerup, 1967.
Alter, Robert. *The Art of Biblical Narrative*. New York: Basic, 1981.
Alter, Robert. *The Five Books of Moses: A Translation with Commentary*. New York: W. W. Norton, 2004.
Amir, Yehoyada. *Reason Out of Faith: The Philosophy of Franz Rosenzweig* [in Hebrew]. ʾAron Sefarim Yehudi. Tel Aviv: Am Oveid, 2004.
Amir, Yehoyada. *A Small Still Voice: Theological Critical Reflections* [in Hebrew]. Tel-Aviv: Yediʿot Aḥaronot: Sifre Ḥemed, 2009.
Anderson, Gary. "To See Where God Dwells: the Tabernacle, the Temple, and the Origins of the Christian Mystical Tradition." *Letter and Spirit* 4 (2008): 13–45.
Baden, Joel. *J, E, and the redaction of the Pentateuch*. FAT 68. Tübingen: Mohr Siebeck, 2009.
Baden, Joel. *The Composition of the Pentateuch: Renewing the Documentary Hypothesis*. New Haven, CT: Yale University Press, 2012.
Baden, Joel. *The Promise to the Patriarchs*. New York: Oxford University Press, 2013.
Bartor, Assnat. "Seeing the thunder: Narrative Images of the Ten Commandments." In *The Decalogue in Jewish and Christian Tradition*, edited by Henning Graf Reventlow and Yair Hofman, 13–31. LHBOTS. New York: T&T Clark, 2011.
Batnitzky, Leora. *Idolatry and Representation: The Philosophy of Franz Rosenzweig Reconsidered*. Princeton, NJ: Princeton University Press, 2000.
Bigman, David. "A Ladder Upon the Earth, Whose Top Reaches the Heavens." *Conversations: The Journal of the Institute for Jewish Ideas and Ideals* 11 (2011): 1–18.
Bland, Kalman. "Moses and the Law According to Maimonides." In *Mystics, Philosophers and Politicians: Essays in Jewish Intellectual History in Honor of Alexander Altman*, edited by Jehuda Reinharz, Daniel Swetschinski and Kalman Bland, 49-66. Durham, NC: Duke University Press, 1982.
Brettler, Marc Zvi, Enns Peters, and Daniel J. Harrington. *The Bible and the Believer: How to Read the Bible Critically and Religiously*. New York: Oxford University Press, 2012.
Breuer, Mordechai. "Dividing the Decalogue into Verses and Commandments." In *The Ten Commandments in History and Tradition*, edited by Ben-Zion Segal and Gershon Levi, 291–330. Jerusalem: Magnes Press, 1990.
Brooke, George J., Hindy Najman, and Loren T. Stuckenbruck, eds. *The Significance of Sinai: Traditions about Sinai and Divine Revelation in Judaism and Christianity*. TBN 12. Leiden: Brill, 2008.
Brown, David. *Tradition and Imagination: Revelation and Change*, Oxford: Oxford University Press, 1999.
Brown, Francis, Samuel R. Driver, and Charles Briggs, eds. *A Hebrew and English Lexicon of the Old Testament*. Oxford: Oxford University Press, 1907.
Buber, Martin, and Franz Rosenzweig. *Scripture and Translation*, trans. Lawrence Rosenwald. Bloomington, IN: Indiana University Press, 1994. Orig. edition: *Die Schrift und ihre Verdeutschung*. Schocken: Germany, 1936.
Carasik, Michael. "To See a Sound: A Deuteronomic Rereading of Exodus 20:15." *Prooftexts* 19 (1999): 257–65.

Carpenter, J. Estlin and G. Harford-Battersby. *The Hexateuch According to the Revised Version*. 2 vols. London: Longmans, Green and Co., 1900.
Cassuto, Umberto (Moshe David). *A Commentary on the Book of Exodus*. Jerusalem: Magnes Press, 1952.
Childs, Brevard. *Exodus: A Commentary*. OTL. London: SCM Press, 1974.
Cohen, Hermann. *Religion of Reason Out of the Sources of Judaism*. AARTTS 7. Atlanta, GA: Scholars Press, 1995.
Congar, Yves. *The Meaning of Tradition*, trans. A. N. Woodrow. San Francisco, CA: Ignatius Press, 2004.
Crüsemann, Frank. *The Torah: Theology and Social History of Old Testament Law*, trans. Allan W. Mahnke. Minneapolis, MN: Fortress Press, 1996.
Dillmann, August, and Victor Ryssel. *Die Bücher Exodus und Leviticus*. Kurzgefasstes exegetisches Handbuch zum Alten Testament 12. Leipzig: S. Hirzel, 1897.
Dorff, Elliot, and Arthur Rosett. *A Living Tree: The Roots and Growth of Jewish Law*. Albany: State University of New York Press, 1988.
Dorff, Elliot. *The Unfolding Tradition: Jewish Law After Sinai*. New York: Aviv Press, 2011.
Driver, Samuel R. *Deuteronomy*, 3rd edition. ICC. Edinburgh: T&T Clark, 1902.
Driver, Samuel R. *The Book of Exodus*. The Cambridge Bible for Schools and Colleges. Cambridge: Cambridge University Press, 1911.
Driver, Samuel R. *Introduction to the Literature of the Old Testament*. New York: Meridian, 1956.
Dulles, Avery. *Models of Revelation*. New York: Doubleday, 1983.
Eisen, Arnold. "Re-Reading Heschel on the Commandments." *Modern Judaism* 9 (1989): 1–33.
Eisen, Arnold. *Rethinking Modern Judaism Ritual, Commandment, Community*. CSHJ. Chicago, IL: University of Chicago Press, 1998.
Enns, Peter. *Inspiration and Incarnation: Evangelicals and the Problem of the Old Testament*. Grand Rapids, MI: Baker Academic, 2005.
Erlewine, Robert. "Reclaiming the Prophets: Cohen, Heschel, and Crossing the Theocentric/ Neo-Humanist Divide." *Journal of Jewish Thought and Philosophy* 17 (2009): 177–206.
Even-Chen, Alexander. *A Voice from the Darkness: Abraham Joshua Heschel Between Phenomenology and Mysticism* [in Hebrew]. Tel Aviv: Am Oveid, 1999.
Even-Chen, Alexander and Ephraim Meir. *Between Heschel and Buber: A Comparative Study*. Emunot: Jewish Philosophy and Kabbalah. Boston, MA: Academic Studies Press, 2012.
Fackenheim, Emil Ludwig. *God's Presence in History: Jewish Affirmations and Philosophical Reflections*. New York: Harper Collins, 1972.
Geller, Stephen. "Were the Prophets Poets?" *Prooftexts* 3 (1983): 211–221.
Geller, Stephen. *Sacred Enigmas: Literary Religion in the Hebrew Bible*. London: Routledge, 1996.
Gesundheit, Shimon. "Das Land Israels als Mitte: Einer jüdischen Theologie der Tora Synchrone und diachrone Perspektiven." *ZAW* 123 (2011): 325–35.
Gillman, Neil. *Sacred Fragments: Recovering Theology for the Modern Jew*. Philadelphia, PA: Jewish Publication Society, 1990.
Glatzer, Nahum Norbert, ed. *Franz Rosenzweig: His Life and Thought*. New York: Schocken, 1961.
Glatzer, Nahum Norbert. "Introduction to OJL." In *On Jewish Learning*, by Franz Rosenzweig, edited by Nahum N. Glatzer, 9–24. New York: Schocken Books, 1965.
Goodman, Micah. *The Secrets of he Guide to the Perplexed* [in Hebrew]. Or Yehudah: Dvir, 2010.
Goshen-Gottstein, Alon. "The Promise to the Patriarchs in Rabbinic Literature." In *Divine Promises to the Fathers in the Three Monotheistic Religions*, edited by Alviero Niccacci, 60–97. Jerusalem: Franciscan Printing Press, 1995.
Gottlieb, Michah. "Mendelssohn's Metaphysical Defense of Religious Pluralism." *JR* 86 (2006): 205–25.
Greenberg, Moshe. *Al Hammiqra Ve'al Hayyahadut* [in Hebrew]. Tel Aviv: 'Am 'Oveid, 1984.

Greenstein, Edward. "Understanding the Sinai Revelation." In *Exodus: A Teacher's Guide*, edited by Ruth Zielenziger, Marcia Lapidus Kaunfer, Barry Holtz, and Miles Cohen, 273–317. 2nd edition. New York: Melton Research Center of the Jewish Theological Seminary, 1994.

Halivni, David Weiss. *Midrash, Mishna, and Gemara: The Jewish Predilection for Justified Law*. Cambridge: Harvard University Press, 1986.

Heinemann, Isaac. *Ta'amei Hamitzvot Besifrut Yisrael* [in Hebrew]. 2 vols. Jerusalem: Jewish Agency and Horeb, 1993 and 1996.

Held, Shai. *Abraham Joshua Heschel: The Call of Transcendence*. Bloomington, IN: Indiana University Press, 2013.

Hendel, Ronald. "Aniconism and Anthropomorphism in Ancient Israel." In *The Image and the Book: Iconic Cults, Aniconism, and the Rise of Book Religion in Israel and the Ancient Near East*, edited by Karel van der Toorn, 205–28. Leuven: Peeters, 1997.

Hendel, Ronald. "Leitwort Style and Literary Structure in the J Primeval Narrative." In *Sacred History, Sacred Literature: Essays on Ancient Israel, the Bible, and Religion in Honor of R. E. Friedman*, edited by Shawna Dolansky, 93–109. Winona Lake, IN: Eisenbrauns, 2008.

Heschel, Abraham Joshua *God in Search of Man: A Philosophy of Judaism*. New York: Farrar Straus and Giroux, 1955.

Heschel, Abraham Joshua. *Torah min Hashamayim B'aspaqlarya shel Hadorot* [in Hebrw]. 3 vols. London – New York: Soncino and the Jewish Theological Seminary, 1965 and 1990.

Heschel, Abraham Joshua. *Moral Grandeur and Spiritual Audacity: Essays*, edited by Susannah Heschel. New York: Farrar, Straus & Giroux, 1996.

Heschel, Abraham Joshua. *The Prophets*. New York: Harper Collins, 2001.

Heschel, Abraham Joshua. *Heavenly Torah as Refracted Through the Generations*. Edited and translated by Gordon Tucker with Leonard Levin. New York: Continuum, 2005.

Hirsch, E. D., Jr. *Validity in Interpretation*. New Haven, CT: Yale University Press, 1967.

Hirsch, Samson Raphael. *Der Pentateuch übersetzt und erläutert*. Frankfurt am Main: J. Kaufmann, 1899.

Idel, Moshe. "On the Theologization of Kabbalah in Modern Scholarship." In *Religious Apologetics— Philosophical Argumentation*, edited by Yossef Schwartz and Volkhard Krech, 123–74. Tübingen: Mohr Siebeck, 2004.

Idel, Moshe. "Abraham J. Heschel on Mysticism and Hasidism" [in Hebrew], *Modern Judaism* 29 (2009): 80–105.

Jacobs, Louis. *A Tree of Life: Diversity, Flexibility, and Creativity in Jewish Law*. Littman Library of Jewish Civilization. Oxford: Oxford University Press, 1984.

Jacobs, Louis. *Beyond Reasonable Doubt*. Littman Library of Jewish Civilization Oxford. London: Oxford University Press, 1999.

Japhet, Sara. "Some Biblical Concepts of Sacred Space." In *Sacred Space: Shrine, City, Land: Proceedings of the International Conference in Memory of Joshua Prawer*, edited by Benjamin Kedar and R. J. Zwi Werblowsky, 54–72. New York: Macmillan, 1998.

Joosten, Jan. *People and Land in the Holiness Code: An Exegetical Study of the Ideational Framework of the Law in Leviticus 17–26*. VTSup 67. Leiden: Brill, 1996.

Joüon, Paul, and Takamitzu Muraoka *A Grammar of Biblical Hebrew*. SB. Rome: Pontificium Institutum Biblicum, 1991.

Kaplan, Lawrence. "'I Sleep, but My Heart Waketh': Maimonides' Conception of Human Perfection." In *The Thought of Moses Maimonides: Philosophical and Legal Studies*, edited by Ira Robinson, Lawrence Kaplan, and Julien Bauer, 130–66. Lewiston: Mellen Press, 1990.

Kasher, Menahem M. *Torah Sheleimah* [in Hebrew]. 48 vols. Jerusalem: Beit Torah Sheleimah, 1979.

Kellner, Menachem M. *Dogma in Medieval Jewish Thought: From Maimonides to Abravanel*. The Littman Library of Jewish Civilization. Oxford: Oxford University Press, 1986.

Kepnes, Steven. "Revelation as Torah: From an Existential to a Postliberal Judaism." *Journal of Jewish Thought and Philosophy* 10 (2000): 205–37.

Kieckhefer, Richard. *Theology in Stone: Church Architecture from Byzantium to Berkeley*. Oxford: Oxford University Press, 2004.

Kimelman, Reuven. "Abraham Joshua Heschel's Theology of Judaism and the Rewriting of Jewish Intellectual History." *Journal of Jewish Thought and Philosophy* 17 (2009): 207–38.

Knohl, Israel. *The Sanctuary of Silence: The Priestly Torah and the Holiness School*. Minneapolis, MI: Fortress Press, 1995.

Koehler, Ludwig, Walter Baumgartner, Johann Jakob Stamm. *The Hebrew and Aramaic Lexicon of the Old Testament*. Translated and edited under the supervision of Mervyn E. J. Richardson. Leiden: Brill, 1994–1999.

Kornfeld, Walter and Helmer Ringgren. "קד״ש." In *Theological Dictionary of the Old Testament*, edited by G. Johannes Botterweck, Helmer Ringgren, and Heinz-Josef Fabry, vol. 12, 521–45. Translated by John T. Willis et al. Grand Rapids, MI – Cambridge: Eerdmans, 2003.

Krüger, Thomas. "Die Stimme Gottes: Eine ästhetisch-theologische Skizze." In *Gottes Wahrnehmungen: Helmut Utzschneider zum 60. Geburtstag*, edited by Stefan Gehrig and Stefan Seiler, 41–65. Stuttgart: Kolhammer, 2009.

Kurzweil, Zvi. "Three Views on Revelation and Law." *Judaism* 9 (1960): 292–98.

Lenzi, Alan. *Secrecy and the Gods: Secret Knowledge in Ancient Mesopotamia and Biblical Israel*. SAA 19. Helsinki: Neo-Assyrian Text Corpus Project, 2008.

Loewenstamm, Samuel E. "The Formula 'At That Time' in the Introductory Speeches in the Book of Deuteronomy" [in Hebrew]. *Tarbiz* 38 (1969): 99–104.

Maimonides, Moses. *The Guide of the Perplexed*. Translated by Shlomo Pines. Chicago, IL: University of Chicago Press, 1963.

McDonald, Hugh Dermot. *Theories of Revelation: An Historical Study 1860–1960*. London: George Allen and Unwin, 1963.

Mendelssohn, Moses. *Jerusalem, or, On Religious Power and Judaism*. Translated by Allan Arkush. Hanover: Published for Brandeis University Press by University Press of New England, 1983.

Mendes-Flohr, Paul. *Divided Passions: Jewish Intellectuals and the Experience of Modernity*. The Culture of Jewish Modernity. Detroit, CT: Wayne State University Press, 1990.

Mettinger, Tryggve N. D. *The Dethronement of Sabaoth: Studies in the Shem and Kabod Theologies*. ConBOT 18. Lund: Almqvist and Wiksell, 1982.

Miller, Patrick D. *The Way of the Lord: Essays in Old Testament Theology*. Grand Rapids, IN: Eerdmans, 2007.

Najman, Hindy. *Seconding Sinai: The Development of Mosaic Discourse in Second Temple Judaism*. JSJSup 77. Leiden: Brill, 2003.

Nicholson, Ernest W. "The Decalogue as the Direct Address of God." *VT* 27 (1977): 422–33.

Noth, Martin. *Exodus: A Commentary*, trans. John Bowden. Philadelphia, PA: Westminster Press, 1962.

Pannenberg, Wolfhart ed. *Revelation as History*, trans. David Granskou. New York: Macmillan, 1969.

Perlman, Lawrence. *Abraham Heschel's Idea of Revelation*. BJS 171. Atlanta, GA: Scholars Press, 1989.

Propp, William. *Exodus 19–40: A New Translation with Introduction and Commentary*. AB 2A. New York: Doubleday, 2006.

Ratzinger, Joseph. *Jesus of Nazareth: From the Baptism in the Jordan to the Transfiguration*. Translated by Adrian J. Walker. New York: Doubleday, 2007.

Regev, Eyal. "Priestly Dynamic Holiness and Deuteronomic Static Holiness." *VT* 51 (2001): 243–61.

Reines, Alvin. "Maimonides' Concept of Mosaic Prophecy." *HUCA* 40–41 (1969–1970): 325–61.

Rofé, Alexander. *Deuteronomy: Issues and Interpretation*. London: T&T Clark, 2002.
Rosenzweig, Franz. *On Jewish Learning*. Edited by Nahum Norbert Glatzer. New York: Schocken, 1965.
Rosenzweig, Franz. *The Star of Redemption*. Translated by William W. Hallo. Boston: Beacon Press, 1972. (= *The Star of Redemption*. Translated by Barbara E. Galli. Modern Jewish Philosophy and Religion. Madison, WI: University of Wisconsin Press, 2005.)
Rosenzweig, Franz. *Der Mensch und sein Werk: Gesammelte Schriften*, vol. 3: *Zweistromland: Kleinere Schriften zu Glauben und Denken*. Edited by. Reinhold Mayer and Annemarie Mayer. Dordrecht – Boston – Lancaster: Martinus Nijhoff, 1984.
Rosenzweig, Franz. *Scripture and Translation*. Translated by Lawrence Rosenwald. ISBL. Bloomington, IN: Indiana University Press, 1994.
Ross, Tamar. "The Cognitive Value of Religious Truth Claims: Rabbi A. I. Kook and Postmodernism." In *Hazon Nahum: Jubilee Volume in Honor of Norman Lamm*, edited by Yaakov Elman and Jeffrey Gurock, 479–528. New York: Yeshiva University Press, 1997.
Ross, Tamar. *Expanding the Palace of Torah: Orthodoxy and Feminism*. Waltham, MA: Brandeis University Press, 2005.
Ross, Tamar. "Orthodoxy and the Challenge of Biblical Criticism: Some Reflections on the Importance of Asking the Right Question." In *The Believer and the Modern Study of the Bible*, ed. Tovah Ganzel, Yehudah Brandes, and Chayuta Deutsch, 263–87. Boston, MA: Academic Studies Press, 2019.
Ross, Tamar. "R. Kook: A This-Worldly Mystic." In *The Cambridge Companion to Jewish Theology*, edited by Steven Kepnes, 185–212. New York: Cambridge University Press, 2021.
Rowley, Harold H. *The Relevance of the Bible*. London: James Clark, 1942.
Samuelson, Norbert M. *Revelation and the God of Israel*. New York: Cambridge University Press, 2002.
Sarna, Nahum. *Exodus*. The JPS Torah commentary. Philadelphia, PA: Jewish Publication Society, 1991.
Savran, George W. *Encountering the Divine: Theophany in Biblical Narrative*. JSOTSup 420. London: T&T Clark, 2005.
Schechter, Solomon. *Studies in Judaism, First Series*. Philadelphia, PA: Jewish Publication Society, 1896.
Scholem, Gershom. "Revelation and Tradition as Religious Categories in Judaism." In *The Messianic Idea in Judaism*, 282–303. Translated by Michael A. Meyer. New York: Schocken, 1971.
Schwartz, Baruch. "The Priestly Account of the Theophany and Lawgiving at Sinai." In *Texts, Temples, and Traditions: A Tribute to Menahem Haran*, edited by Michael Fox et al., 103-34. Winona Lake, IN: Eisenbrauns, 1996.
Schwartz, Baruch. "What Really Happened at Mount Sinai?" *BRev* (1997 Oct.): 21–46.
Schwartz, Baruch. *The Holiness Legislation: Studies in the Priestly Code* [in Hebrew]. Jerusalem: Magnes Press, 1999.
Schwartz, Baruch. "Israel's Holiness: The Torah Tradition." In *Purity and Holiness: The Heritage of Leviticus*, edited by Marcel Poorthuis and Joshua J. Schwartz, 39–52. Leiden: Brill, 1999.
Schwartz, Baruch. "The Origin of the Law's Authority: 'Grundnorm' and Its Meaning in the Pentateuchal Traditions" [in Hebrew]. *Shnaton Ha-Mishpat Ha-Ivri* 21 (2000): 241–65.
Schwartz, Baruch. "The Horeb Theophany in E: Why the Decalogue Was Proclaimed," paper presented at the SBL Annual Meeting (San Antonio, TX: 2004).
Schwartz, Baruch. "The Torah—Its Five Books and Four Documents" [in Hebrew]. In *The Literature of the Hebrew Bible: Introductions and Studies*, edited by Zipora Talshir, 161– 226. Jerusalem: Yad Ben-Zvi Press, 2011.
Seeligmann, Isac Leo. "Knowledge of Yhwh and Historical Consciousness in Antiquity" [in Hebrew]. In *Studies in Biblical Literature*, edited by Avi Hurvitz, Emanuel Tov, and Sara Japhet, 141–68. Jerusalem: Magnes Press, 1996.

Seeskin, Kenneth. *Autonomy in Jewish Philosophy*. Cambridge – New York: Cambridge University Press, 2001.
Silman, Yochanan. *The Voice Heard at Sinai: Once or Ongoing?* [in Hebrew]. Jerusalem: Magnes, 1999.
Simon, Uriel. *Seek Peace and Pursue It. Pressing Questions in Light of the Bible, and the Bible in Light of Pressing Questions* [in Hebrew]. Tel Aviv: Yedi'ot Aḥaronot: Sifrei Ḥemed, 2002.
Smith, Mark. "'Seeing God' in the Psalms: the Background to the Beatific Vision in the Hebrew Bible." *CBQ* 50 (1988): 171–83.
Smith, Wilfred Cantwell. *What Is Scripture? A Comparative Approach*. Minneapolis, MI: Fortress Press, 1993.
Sommer, Benjamin David. *The Bodies of God and the World of Ancient Israel*. New York: Cambridge University Press, 2009.
Sommer, Benjamin David. *Revelation and Authority: Sinai in Jewish Scripture and Tradition*. AYBRL. New Haven, CT: Yale University Press, 2015.
Sommer, Benjamin David. "Tradition and Change in Priestly Law: On the Internal Coherence of the Priestly Worldview." In *The Pentateuch and Its Readers: Essays in Honor of Baruch Schwartz*, edited by Jeffrey Stackert and Joel Baden, 269–84. FAT. Tübingen: Mohr Siebeck, 2023.
Sonnet, Jean-Pierre. *The Book within the Book: Writing in Deuteronomy*. Leiden: Brill, 1997.
Tillich, Paul. *Systematic Theology*. Chicago, IL: University of Chicago Press, 1967.
Tillich, Paul. *On Art and Architecture* Edited by John and Jane Dillenberger, translated by Robert Sharlemann. New York: Crossroad, 1989.
Toeg, Aryeh. *Lawgiving at Sinai* [in Hebrew]. Jerusalem: Magnes Press, 1977.
Van der Toorn, Karel. "The Iconic Book: Analogies Between the Babylonian Cult of Images and the Veneration of the Torah." In *The Image and the Book: Iconic Cults, Aniconism, and the Rise of Book Religion in Israel and the Ancient Near East*, edited by Karel van der Toorn, 228–48. Leuven: Peeters, 1997.
Viezel, Eran. "The Divine Content and the Words of Moses: R. Abraham Ibn Ezra on Moses' Role in Writing the Torah" [in Hebrew]. *Tarbiz* 80 (2012): 387–407.
Viezel, Eran. "Moses' Literary License in Writing the Torah: Joseph Hayyun's Response to Isaac Abrabanel" [in Hebrew]. In *Zer Rimonim: Studies in Biblical Literature and Jewish Exegesis Presented to Prof. Rimon Kasher*, edited by Michael Avioz, Elie Assis, and Yael Shemesh, 603–19. SBL/IVS. Atlanta, GA: Society of Biblical Literature, 2013.
Viezel, Eran. "Rashbam on Moses' Role in Writing the Torah" [in Hebrew]. *Shnaton: An Annual for Biblical and Ancient Near Eastern Studies* 22 (2013): 167–88.
Von Rad, Gerhard. *Studies in Deuteronomy*. Translated by David M.G. Stalker. London: SCM Press, 1953.
Von Rad, Gerhard. *Old Testament Theology*. Translated by David M.G. Stalker. Edinburgh: Oliver and Boyd, 1962–1965.
Ward, Keith. *Religion and Revelation: A Theology of Revelation in the World's Religions*. Oxford: Clarendon, 1994.
Weinfeld, Moshe. *Deuteronomy and the Deuteronomic School*. Oxford: Clarendon, 1972.
Weinfeld, Moshe. *Deuteronomy 1–11: A New Translation with Commentary*. AB 5. New York: Doubleday, 1991.
Weingreen, Jacob. *From Bible to Mishna: The Continuity of Tradition*. Manchester: Manchester University Press, 1976.
Wellhausen, Julius. *Die Composition des Hexateuchs und der historischen Bücher des Alten Testaments*. Berlin: Georg Reimer, 1899.
Wolfson, Elliot R. "Light Does Not Talk but Shines: Apophasis and Vision in Rosenzweig's Theopoetic Temporality." In *New Directions in Jewish Philosophy*, edited by Aaron Hughes and Elliot Wolfson, 87–148. Bloomington, IN: Indiana University Press, 2010.

## Reception as Revelation?

Régis Burnet

# 7 New Testament Inspiration and Apocryphal Subtext: The Case of the Epistle of Jude

In Christianity, there is another Sinai, and it stands in Emmaus. In Judaism, the account of what occurred at Sinai constructs a stenographic ideal of revelation according to which God would dictate his will to humankind; in Christianity, the Emmaus narrative shows that Jewish and Christian Scriptures stand in perfect continuity, as if God had performed the same revelation in two stages. In this well-known pericope, the evangelist Luke recounts the meeting of the risen Jesus and two disciples who are grieving over his death. They rail about what had happened to him and lament the end of their hopes. Jesus replies:

> "Oh, how foolish you are, and how slow of heart to believe all that the prophets have declared! [26] Was it not necessary that the Messiah should suffer these things and then enter into his glory?" [27] Then beginning with Moses and all the prophets, he interpreted to them the things about himself in all the scriptures. (Luke 24:25–27)[1]

Most interpreters understand this passage as the hermeneutic key to the relationship between the two Testaments. Such a sophisticated exegete as Luke Timothy Johnson exemplifies the widespread idea, expressed since the Church Fathers.[2]

> The Emmaus story showed that Moses and the prophets foretold the suffering and resurrection of the Messiah. Now the suffering and resurrection of the Messiah are shown to be the interpretive key both to the words of Jesus and to Law, Prophets, and Writings. It is the risen Lord who teaches the Church to read Torah properly. He "opens their mind to understand the Scriptures." And this is necessary if those who have been "eyewitnesses" are also to be "ministers of the word" (1:2) in preaching these events and interpreting them from Torah.[3]

In other words, the text of the New Testament presents itself as a continuation of the Scriptures of Israel, seen from a messianic viewpoint. Inspired Scripture begets inspired Scripture, as if the Jewish canon of Scripture had been fixed from all eternity and had produced another rigid canon, the one of the Christian Scriptures.

---

[1] All bible translations in this article come from the NRSV.
[2] Arthur A. Just, ed., *Luke*, ACCS 3 (Downers Grove, IL: InterVarsity Press, 2003), 380–1; Joel B. Green, *The Gospel of Luke*, NICNT (Grand Rapids, MI: Eerdmans, 1997), 848–9; Hans Klein, *Das Lukasevangelium*, KEK 1/3/10 (Göttingen: Vandenhoeck & Ruprecht, 2006), 732; John T. Carroll, *Luke: A Commentary*, NTL (Louisville, KY: Westminster John Knox Press, 2012), 485–6.
[3] Luke Timothy Johnson, *The Gospel of Luke*, SP 3 (Collegeville, MN: Liturgical Press, 1991), 405.

Did it really happen that way? As he showed in the preceding lecture and in his book *Revelation and Authority*, Benjamin Sommer advocates a participatory theology of revelation. Relying on the work of Franz Rosenzweig and Abraham Heschel, Sommer defines revelation as "a joint effort involving heavenly and earthly contributions; or the wording may be an entirely human response to God's real but nonverbal revelation."[4] This means a dialogue between God and Israel, in which human words are provisional rather than definitive.[5] Taking this idea to its logical final stage, Sommer then concludes that this never-ending dialogue inevitably muddles the boundaries between inspired Scripture and tradition. More accurately, the written Torah is a subset[6] of the Oral Torah, and thus the fringes of the canon are shifting and blurring. I would like to show that the same applies to Christianity. If the Emmaus episode serves to build a kind of *regulatory ideal* of transmission according to which only inspired Scripture generates inspired Scripture, a precise investigation of the New Testament proves that things did not turn out this way.

The Epistle of Jude is a case in point. In this letter, the one who presents himself as "the brother of James" and therefore, indirectly, the brother of Jesus,[7] quotes, both implicitly and explicitly, texts that do not belong to the Torah-Prophets set. A historical analysis of what the Christian communities have done with it does not only enable us to generalize Benjamin Sommer's thesis; it also helps to understand why and how the Christian churches have maintained in the canon writing that deviated so much from the Emmaus regulatory ideal.

# 1 A Scripture born of tradition

In recounting how Jesus interprets the events of his life ἀπὸ Μωϋσέως καὶ ἀπὸ πάντων τῶν προφητῶν, the evangelist constructs a kind of fuzzy canon that would be composed of the Pentateuch of Moses and an ill-defined set, the prophets. Irrespective of this rule, Jude quotes a text which is authoritative for him, but does not belong to this group, since it relates to a patriarch, Enoch. Jude demonstrates, in the words of Sommer, that Scripture can be born of other traditions.

---

[4] Benjamin D. Sommer, *Revelation and Authority: Sinai in Jewish Scripture and Tradition*, AYBR (New Haven, CT: Yale University Press, 2015), 2.
[5] Sommer, *Revelation and Authority*, 147.
[6] Sommer, *Revelation and Authority*, 170.
[7] Richard Bauckham, *Jude and the Relatives of Jesus in the Early Church*, T&T Clark Academic Paperbacks (London/New York: T&T Clark International, 2004).

## 1.1 Jude and his quote from Enoch

The Epistle of Jude is a short letter of 24 verses which aims to resist the ascendancy in a Christian community of individuals whom the author violently opposes. It is very difficult to know who they were. The fact that "Jude" refers to them as "dreamers" (ἐνυπνιαζόμενοι, Jude 8) has often led commentators to view them as charismatics, fond of mystical experience.[8] Whatever they were, "Jude" reviles them and accuses them of all the biblical evils (Jude 5–13): they have the sexual perversity of the people of Sodom and Gomorrah, they are without faith like the rebellious angels, they are ungodly like the devil, Cain, Balaam and the sons of Korah, they are similar to clouds without rain, or the foam of the wave, or wandering stars. Eventually, he condemns them in a radical way with the help of the patriarch Enoch:

> [14] It was also about these that Enoch, in the seventh generation from Adam, prophesied, saying, "See, the Lord is coming with ten thousand of his holy ones, [15] to execute judgment on all, and to convict everyone of all the deeds of ungodliness that they have committed in such an ungodly way, and of all the harsh things that ungodly sinners have spoken against him." (Jude 14–15)

Three verbs pertaining to divine action (come/ἔρχομαι, judge/ ποιεῖν κρίσιν, convince/ ἐλέγχω) are set alongside a threefold emphasis on the ungodliness (ἀσεβεία) of behaviours, both of deeds (ἔργον) and of speech (λαλέω).[9] Such vigor should not be surprising. These imprecations are extremely oratorical,[10] since mobilizing eschatology does not necessarily mean preaching the doomsday; there exists a rhetorical use of the end of time whose purpose is simply to reinforce the identity of a community by confronting it with a radical choice for the future that is relevant in the present.[11]

"Jude" not only alludes to the son of Jared (Gen 5:18), of whom Genesis says that he lived 365 years, walked with God; then he was no more, because God took him (Gen 5:22–24); more crucially, he quotes a phrase from a work often referred to as the "Book of Watchers" (1 En 1:9), attributed to this same Enoch and preserved in a book usually called 1 Enoch (a collection of different treatises, actually). The

---

[8] Richard Bauckham, *Jude, 2 Peter*, WBC 50 (Waco, TX: Word Books, 1983), 11; Jerome H. Neyrey, *2 Peter, Jude: A New Translation with Commentary*, AB 37C (New York: Doubleday, 1993), 31; Steven J. Kraftchick, *Jude, 2 Peter*, ANTC (Nashville, TN: Abingdon Press, 2002), 33.
[9] William F. Brosend, *James and Jude*, NCBC (Cambridge/New York: Cambridge University Press, 2004), 179.
[10] Lauri Thurén, "Hey Jude! Asking for the Original Situation and Message of a Catholic Epistle," *NTS* 43 (1997): 451–65.
[11] Robert L. Webb, "The Eschatology of the Epistle of Jude and Its Rhetorical and Social Functions," *BBR* 6 (1996): 139–51.

Hebrew or Aramaic original of this writing is lost. The text cited by the author of Jude cannot be found exactly in the versions now available and looks like a sort of combination of Ethiopic and Greek, which suggests that Jude has his own version or that he quotes from memory.[12]

## 1.2 The recourse to particular traditions within Second Temple Judaism

By referring in this way to the book of Enoch, and also, by veiled allusion, to several other texts identified by Jeremy Hultin and David A. deSilva,[13] the epistle of Jude makes use of a corpus of traditions that flourished in the last centuries before the common era. These traditions support a particular vision of the universe, as George Nickelsburg and Michael Stone have shown.[14] It portrays a world haunted by evil, originating from angelic sin, which precipitated the Flood. On our post-diluvian earth, this evil persists, and is perpetuated and nurtured by the demonic order, stemming from antediluvian wickedness. Hopefully, this sin, depicted as a sign of rebellion against the divine sovereignty, will be annihilated by God himself who will come as a judge to restore justice and as a savior to reinstate his elect in his mercy.

The quote describes this energetic move by God, accompanied by his "saints," who refer to the heavenly creatures. This verse itself seems to be inspired by two prophetic passages, Jer 25:30–31 and Isa 66:16–16, although it introduces a major difference: sin, ostensibly pervasive, is manifested in deeds and words.[15] By mentioning the term κύριος, which the scholars still do not know if it was part of the

---

12 Henning Paulsen, *Der Zweite Petrusbrief Und Der Judasbrief*, KEK 12,2 (Göttingen, Vandenhoeck & Ruprecht, 1992), 74–6. See also Lewis R. Donelson, *I & II Peter and Jude: A Commentary*, NTL (Louisville, KY: Westminster John Knox Press, 2010), 191.
13 Jeremy Hultin, *Judes's Citation of 1 Enoch*, in *Jewish and Christian Scriptures: The Function of "Canonical" and "Non-Canonical" Religious Texts*, eds. James Hamilton Charlesworth and Lee Martin McDonald, Jewish and Christian Texts in Contexts and Related Studies 7 (London/New York: T&T Clark, 2010): 113–28; David A. deSilva, *The Jewish Teachers of Jesus, James, and Jude: What Earliest Christianity Learned from the Apocrypha and Pseudepigrapha* (New York: Oxford University Press, 2012), 101–40, 175–236. See also Peter H. Davids, "The Use of Second Temple Traditions in 1 and 2 Peter and Jude," in *The Catholic Epistles and the Tradition*, ed. Jacques Schlosser, BETL 176 (Leuven: Peeters, 2004): 409–32.
14 George W.E. Nickelsburg, *1 Enoch: A Commentary on the Book of 1 Enoch*, Hermeneia (Minneapolis, MN: Fortress, 2001), 37–57; Michael E. Stone, *Ancient Judaism: New Visions and Views* (Grand Rapids, MI: Eerdmans, 2011), 31–58.
15 Nickelsburg, *1 Enoch*, 149.

original text, "Jude" operates a Christological reading of the book of the Watchers. Jesus is this very Messiah who is going to swiftly take action with the support of angelic forces.[16] One might ask whether the author opts for this assimilation because he is familiar with a pre-existing Christology based on the figure of the Son of Man drawn from the Enochic traditions (and which is also at work in Matthew, for example), or whether he makes a personal innovation, but this would be the subject of another work.[17] What is certain, however, is that "Jude" considers that this tradition has authority,[18] perhaps because of the antiquity and dignity of Enoch.[19]

## 1.3 The reception of Enoch and Jude in the first centuries

The appeal to this Enochian tradition is not eccentric in Second Temple Judaism.[20] Many fragments of the text have been discovered in caves 1 and 4 of Qumran and a number of parallels can be drawn between these texts and the writings of the sect, which constructs itself as an eschatological Israel established by divine revelation.[21] In the early days of Christianity, many authors likewise refer to it.[22] One can cite in particular the epistle of Barnabas (c. 96) which makes several allusions to it (Barn 16). Many authors tell the account of the fall of the angels, present in the book of the Watchers: Athenagoras in his *Embassy for the Christians*, around 176–180, Irenaeus of Lyon in the *Against the Heresies* (Adv. Hær. 4,16,2 & 4,36,4), but also Justin Martyr, Tatian, Clement of Alexandria, Bardaisan, Tertullian, Commo-

---

[16] Simon J. Joseph, "'Seventh from Adam' (Jude 1:14–15): Re-Examining Enochic Traditions and The Christology of Jude," *JTS* 64 (2013): 463–81.
[17] See Nickelsburg, *1 Enoch*, 123–4. See also George W.E. Nickelsburg and David N. Freedman, "Son of Man," *ABD* 6: 137–50.
[18] Paulsen, *Judasbrief*, 74.
[19] Neyrey, *2 Peter, Jude*, 81.
[20] John C. Reeves and Annette Yoshiko-Reed, *Enoch from Antiquity to the Middle Ages* (Oxford: Oxford University Press, 2018).
[21] Nickelsburg, *1 Enoch*, 77. References are 1Q19; 4Q201; 4Q204; 4Q213; 4Q227; 4Q228; 4Q369; 4Q534; 5Q13; 11Q12.
[22] James C. VanderKam, "1Enoch, Enochic Motives and Early Christian Literature," in *The Jewish Apocalyptic Heritage in Early Christianity*, eds. James C. VanderKam and William Adler, CRINT (Assen/Minneapolis, MN: Van Gorcum/Fortress Press, 1996): 33–101. See also Wolfgang Grünstäudl and Tobias Nicklas, "Searching for Evidence: The History of Reception of the Epistles of Jude and 2 Peter," in *Reading 1–2 Peter and Jude: A Resource for Students*, eds. Eric F. Mason and Troy W. Martin, RBS 77 (Atlanta, GA: Society of Biblical Literature, 2014): 215–28.

dian, Cyprian, and Lactantius.[23] Origen's case is especially relevant, since he uses the book in his theological works such as the *Treatise on Principles*, but also in his exegetical works.[24] As Anette Yoshiko Reed, who thoroughly studied the myth, comments, it is not impossible that early Christians believed that some elements of the Enochian text were simply part of the biblical story.[25]

In this respect, the same Anette Yoshiko Reed shows they did not differ fundamentally from other authors from Judaism of the period. Philo of Alexandria in his writing *On the Giants* and Flavius Josephus in *Jewish Antiquities* 1:73 seem to read a text from the LXX where angels would have replaced the sons of men in Gen 6:2.[26]

Therefore, Jude illustrates well what Benjamin Sommer asserts and confirms our point of departure. The composition of Jude takes place thanks to written traditions, which are doubtless the result of an oral tradition. Consequently, the Emmaus episode is but a very general allegory explaining a much more complex process that could be extrapolated to the entire New Testament. In which book of the Jewish scriptural canon is there an expression of messianism similar to that of Jesus? Where is communicated the belief in the resurrection of the dead? Where is the description of the Last Judgment found? All these beliefs come from traditions that do not belong to the Moses and Prophets collection and are usually referred to as Second Temple literature. The epistle of Jude presents an interesting example because it explicitly claims to have drawn from this literature, but it is certainly not an isolated case.

## 2 Which are the criteria of inspiration or how to keep a text referring to an Apocrypha in the Canon

The epistle of Jude presents another interest. It provides a glimpse into the process of canonization, i.e., the criteria by which Churches could recognize that a given writing was inspired by God. In that respect, the end of the second century struck

---

**23** VanderKam, "Enochic Motives," 62–84; Reeves and Yoshiko-Reed, *Enoch*. See Barnabas 4:3; 16:5–6; 1 Clement 9–11; Clement of Alexandria, *Adumbrationes*, Jude 13–14; Irenaeus, *Adv. Hær.* 1.10.1; 4.16.2: 5.30.2; Origen, *Comm. Jo.* 6.42; *Contra Cels.* 5.52–55; *Princ.* 1.3.3; Tertullian, *Apologeticum* 22.3; *De Fem. Cult.* 1.2–3; *De idololatria* 4.2–3.
**24** VanderKam, "Enochic Motives," 54–9.
**25** Annette Yoshiko-Reed, *Fallen Angels and the History of Judaism and Christianity: The Reception of Enochic Literature* (Cambridge/New York: Cambridge University Press, 2005), 151.
**26** Yoshiko-Reed, *Fallen Angels*, 106.

a severe blow to the 24-verse letter. Many voices rose in the Jewish and Christian communities to distance themselves from the book of Enoch. This partial disapproval inevitably had a knock-on effect on Jude's letter: how could James' brother dare quote a text that was beginning to be rejected? Those wishing to retain it in the list of the Christian books were compelled to make explicit their reasons for doing so: their arguments show the criteria of inspiration at work.

## 2.1 The third and fourth centuries and the fading of Enoch's authority

The first evidence of a certain fading of Enoch's authority is found in Tertullian's *De Feminarum Cultu*. Tertullian wrote:

> I am aware that the Book of Henoch which assigns this role to the angels is not accepted because it is not admitted into the Jewish Library (*armarium Iudaicum*). I suppose it is not accepted because they did not think that a book written before the flood could have survived that catastrophe which destroyed the whole world (...) But, since Henoch in this same book preached us our Lord, we must not reject anything at all which really pertains to us. Do we not read that every word of Scripture useful for edification is divinely inspired? As you very well know, it was afterwards rejected by the Jews for the same reason that prompted them to reject almost all the other portions which prophesied about Christ. Now, it is not at all surprising that they refused to accept certain Scriptures which spoke of Him when they were destined not to receive Him when He spoke to them Himself. Moreover, Enoch has in his favor the testimony of the apostle Jude.[27]

Several details useful to our investigation emerge from this text. First of all, by evoking the *armarium Iudaicum*, Tertullian suggests that there is a kind of canon of the Jews in the making, which excluded the book of Enoch. The reason for rejecting the epistle is unexpected for a modern reader: a book attributed to Enoch could not survive the Flood. The argument seems naive, but it is based on a criterion that will play a significant role in later debates on inspiration: the authority of a book rests on its *auctoritas*, in both senses of the Latin term, that is, the fact that the book was indeed written by a given person (authorship) and that this person enjoyed an undeniable prestige (authority). Tertullian proposes a second explanation for the Jews' abandonment of the book: it would have prophesied about Christ. Of course,

---

27 Tertullian, *De Feminarum Cultu* 1.3. Translation: Tertullian, *Disciplinary, Moral, and Ascetical Works*, trans. Rudolph Arbesmann, Fathers of the church 40 (New York: Fathers of the Church, 1959), 122. We correct the translation thanks to the critical edition: Tertullian, *La Toilette Des Femmes (De Cultu Feminarum)*, trans. Marie Turcan, Sources chrétiennes 173 (Paris: Cerf, 1970), 56–60.

Tertullian is talking about himself, not about these so-called Jews: he read in the "Son of Man" appearing as a vindicator in 1 En 46 the figure of Christ, something that the non-messianic communities of Judaism of his time certainly did not do. And finally, he uses the authority of Jude to preserve the authority of Enoch, which seems like a definitive way of settling all quarrels.[28] After this demonstration, he can freely invoke *1 Enoch*, and scholars can detect many allusions to the book in his work.[29]

Let us stop for a moment on the second point of Tertullian's reasoning, for it raises the question of the Parting of the Ways, i.e., the separation between Judaism and Christianity. Would not the use of 1 Enoch be one of those points on which Jews and Christians conflicted?[30] Indeed, in contrast to the Christian sources, the rabbinic documents make no reference to the Book of Enoch. Moreover, a passage in the Targum *Genesis Rabbah* seems to imply a strong rejection against the interpretation of *bene Elohim* as angels (as the Book of Enoch did):[31]

> *And the sons of God saw the daughters of men.* R. Simeon b. Yohai called them 'sons of judges' R. Simeon b. Yohai cursed all who called them 'sons of God'.[32]

While Christians were the promoters of the book of Enoch, the rabbis were not. Rather than a process of self-definition between those who believe in the fall of the angels and those who do not, Annette Yoshiko Reed prefers to see here the result of two completely independent processes at work.[33] Indeed, the dismissal of Enoch in Judaism can be explained by the well-known rejection of apocalyptic aspirations after the Bar-Kokhba revolt and by the fact that the Talmud is almost exclusively interested in oral tradition and does not make use of this famous Second Temple literature. Taken together, these two reasons largely justify the removal of Enochian sources in the Talmudic literature. This has nothing to do with a polemic between communities.

In the Christian sources, the Enochian material disappeared as well. From the fourth century onwards, not only the cult of the patriarch, but also the popular theme of the fall of the angels, suffered a certain decline, even if this motif was still

---

**28** David R. Nienhuis, *Not by Paul Alone: The Formation of the Catholic Epistle Collection and the Christian Canon* (Waco, TX: Baylor University Press, 2011), 40.
**29** See *De virginibus velandis* 7, *De idololatria* 4.15. Nickelsburg, *1 Enoch*, 89.
**30** Lawrence VanBeek, "1 Enoch among Jews and Christians: A Fringe Connection?," in *Christian-Jewish Relations Through the Centuries*, eds. Stanley E. Porter and Brook W.R. Pearson, JSNTsup 192 (Sheffield: Sheffield Academic Press, 2000): 93–115.
**31** Philip S. Alexander, "The Targumim and Early Exegesis of 'Sons of God' in Genesis 6," *JJS* 23 (1972): 60–71, esp. 62. Cited by Yoshiko-Reed, *Fallen Angels*, 137.
**32** *Genesis Rabbah* 26.5. Translation from Yoshiko-Reed, *Fallen Angels*, 137.
**33** Yoshiko-Reed, *Fallen Angels*, 140–7.

important until the fourth century.³⁴ A very characteristic case of this marginalization is Lucifer of Cagliari (died in 370 B.C.). In his *De non conveniendo cum hæreticis* (On Not Coming Together with Heretics), written around 355, he rants about Arians and sermonizes on the necessity to separate from them. He equates them with Jude's opponents, whose epistle he quotes extensively. However, the cited verses (vv. 1–4, 5–8, 11–13, 17–19)³⁵ carefully avoid any reference to the book of Enoch. If Lucifer considered Jude as a canonical writing, he was careful *not* to endorse its use of an apocryphal book.

## 2.2 How to keep in the canon a writing that quotes a text without authority? The criteria of Inspiration in the fourth-seventh centuries and the primacy of the apostolic origin of the writing

How then to keep in the canon a scripture that cites a rejected book? Much more than for books that are not "problematic" such as the four gospels, Jude is a testcase or the criteria of legitimization during the centuries. The first to discuss Jude's entry into a canon in the making is Eusebius of Caesarea, who, in his *Ecclesiastical History* (3:25), classifies the epistle among the disputed texts (ἀντιλεγομένα).

> It is to be observed that its authenticity [of the Letter of James] is denied, since few of the ancients quote it, as is also the case with the Epistle called Jude's, which is itself one of the seven called Catholic; nevertheless we know that these letters have been used publicly with the rest in most churches.³⁶

Eusebius provides a first touchstone for canonicity: the universality of the reading of the text. In other words, a writing is inspired if it is received by all communities, this is the criterion of catholicity. This is based on two parameters: the prevalence of its usage among the ancients (οὐ πολλοὶ τῶν παλαιῶν) and the pervasiveness of its use in the churches. Why is Eusebius so concerned? The ancients in question are apparently the Christian writers who preceded Eusebius: very few of the Fathers quote the epistle of Jude. As for the consensus of the communities, Eusebius is content with "most of the churches" (ἐν πλείσταις ἐκκλησίαις). A geographical investigation shows that Jude is mostly attested in the Greek realm, and especially

---

**34** VanderKam, "Enochic Motives," 100–1; Yoshiko-Reed, *Fallen Angels*, 190–232.
**35** Grünstäudl and Nicklas, "Searching for Evidence," 219.
**36** Eusebius, *Eccl. Hist.* 2.23,25; translation: Kirsopp Lake, *The Ecclesiastical History*, vol. 1, LCL 153 (Cambridge, MA: Harvard Univ. Press, 1926), 179.

in Alexandria, but that its use is rarer in the Latin and Syriac world: this may justify Eusebius' hesitancy.[37]

Jerome of Stridon provides another explanation:

> Jude, the brother of James, left behind a brief epistle which is among the seven Catholic ones, because he alleges the testimony of the book of Enoch, which is apocryphal, the epistle is rejected by many. However, because of its antiquity and use, it has gained authority and is counted among the holy writings.[38]

Another criterion is here at work: the content of the text. Citing a book now classified as *apocryphus* threatens to make Jude lose its place in the canon in certain Churches (and again, one thinks of the Eastern Churches) and calls into question the validity of its message. However, the Stridonian intends to keep the letter within the canon and counterattack with two additional criteria: its "antiquity," which no doubt alludes to the criterion of apostolicity, and the criterion of usage.

Jerome's quotation is very important, because it shows that a hierarchy of criteria is at work here, since apostolicity and usage take precedence over content. This hierarchy of criteria is confirmed by Priscillian. In his *Liber de fide et de apocryphis* (Book on the Faith and the Apocrypha), he defends his interest in visionary literature, which corresponds to his own ecstatic conceptions,[39] by the fact that even apostles like Jude, the Lord's brother, quote from 1 Enoch. If Jude and other canonical writings used apocryphal texts and traditions, the reading of these apocryphal texts cannot be censured. His argument is crystal clear: "either the witness of the condemned is accepted or the authority of the writer of the scriptures is not maintained."[40] This glorification of the apostolic origin should not come as a surprise. It is consistent with the construction, since the fourth century, of the apostolic age as a time of perfect orthodoxy, of perfect orthopraxy, an epoch when miracles

---

[37] Nicholas J. Moore, "Is Enoch Also among the Prophets? The Impact of Jude's Citation of 1 Enoch on the Reception of Both Texts in the Early Church," *JTS* 64 (2013): 498–515.

[38] *Judas, frater Iacobi, parvam quae de septem catholicis est epistolam reliquit. Et quia de libro Enoch, qui apocryphus est, assumit testimonium, a plerisque reicitur. Tamen auctoritatem vetustate iam et usu meruit et inter sanctas scripturas computatur*. Text in Ernest C. Richardson, *Hieronymus liber De viris inlustribus. Gennadius liber De viris inlustribus*, TUGAL 14.1 (Leipzig: J.C. Hinrichs, 1896), 9.

[39] Andrew S. Jacobs, "The Disorder of Books: Priscillian's Canonical Defense of Apocrypha," *HTR* 93 (2000): 135–59.

[40] Tract. 3.50: "...si extra canonem tota damnanda sunt aut qualiter vel damnatorum testimonium recipitur, vel in his quae scribta sunt scribentis auctoritas non tenetur." Quoted by Virginia Burrus, "Canonical References to Extra-Canonical "Texts": Priscillian's Defense of the Apocrypha," in *Society of Biblical Literature Seminar Papers*, vol. 126, ed. David J. Lull (Atlanta, GA: Scholars Press, 1990): 60–7; citations on p. 61.

were commonplace, proof of God's exceptional favor toward the first generation of witnesses.[41]

The importance of this criterion is also observed in Augustine, who manages to find a solution that clears the character of James' brother of any complicity with apocrypha. It is worth quoting the text extensively:

> We cannot deny that Enoch, the seventh from Adam, left some divine writings, for this is asserted by the Apostle Jude in his canonical epistle. But it is not without reason that these writings have no place in that canon of Scripture which was preserved in the temple of the Hebrew people by the diligence of successive priests; for their antiquity brought them under suspicion, and it was impossible to ascertain whether these were his genuine writings, and they were not brought forward as genuine by the persons who were found to have carefully preserved the canonical books by a successive transmission. So that the writings which are produced under his name, and which contain these fables about the giants, saying that their fathers were not men, are properly judged by prudent men to be not genuine; just as many writings are produced by heretics under the names both of other prophets, and, more recently, under the names of the apostles, all of which, after careful examination, have been set apart from canonical authority under the title of Apocrypha.[42]

Augustine, who elsewhere needs the testimony of Enoch to establish the antiquity of revelation (Civ. Dei 18:37–38) cannot tackle the son of Yared head-on. He therefore relies on the testimony of Jude. This once again proves the hierarchy of criteria: apostolic origin takes precedence over content. However, he cannot overlook the issues of 1 Enoch. So, he makes a distinction between the patriarch and his writing. If the character is praiseworthy, the book is not. Indeed, echoing Tertullian's argument, Augustine assumes that the original volume is too old to have survived, and that the text being read in his time is forged. He identifies 1 Enoch as a pseudepigrapha to better dismiss it, while affirming that Jude never quoted the book, but the patriarch himself.

Eventually, it was Bede the Venerable who produced the synthesis that closed the case in the West for a thousand years.

> But nevertheless we must know that the book of Enoch from which he took this is classed by the Church among the apocryphal scriptures,[22] not because the sayings of so great a patriarch in any way can or ought to be thought worthy of rejection but because that book which is presented in his name appears not to have been really written by him but published by someone else under his name. For if it were really his, it would not be contrary to sound truth. But now because it contains many incredible things, such as the statement that the giants did not have human beings for fathers but angels,[23] it is deservedly evident to the learned that writ-

---

**41** Régis Burnet, "La notion d'apostolicité dans les premiers siècles," *RSR* 103 (2015): 185–202.
**42** Augustine, *City of God* 15.23. Augustine, *The City of God*, trans. Marcus Dods (New York: Modern Library, 1950), 514.

ings tainted by a lie are not those of a truthful man. Hence this very Letter of Jude, because it contains a witness from an apocryphal book, was rejected by a number of people from the earliest times. Nonetheless because of its authority and age and usefulness it has for long been counted among the holy scriptures, particularly because Jude took from an apocryphal book a witness which was not apocryphal and doubtful but out standing because of its true light and light-giving truth.[43]

Bede makes a kind of synthesis of all the preceding arguments, some of which he quotes verbatim without giving their origin. He first makes the same distinction as Augustine between the patriarch and his writing, which is declared apocryphal by the crime of pseudonymy. Then he takes up Jerome's argument for the preservation of the epistle. His original contribution consists of a gloss on Jerome's term *usus*. If the epistle is in use in the churches, it is because it is useful, and if it is useful, it is because it is not contrary to the truth. Bede therefore ratifies the content of the quotation, not because of the criterion of patriarchal authenticity, but on behalf of a criterion of analogy of faith.

## 2.3  The evolution of the criteria of canonicity since Bede the Venerable

What has happened to the criteria of inspiration since the modern era? Did the Reformation reshuffle the deck? Surprisingly for the clichés, it was mainly on the Catholic side that criticism arose. Erasmus, in the successive editions of his *Novum Instrumentum omne*, appears more and more harsh for the epistle. In 1516, he limits himself to recall the doubts of Jerome[44]: "Moreover, the quotation he makes comes from an apocryphal text of the Hebrews, and because of this the epistle itself has not failed to be suspected." But in the separate publication of his annotations to the *Novum Instrumentum omne* in 1527, he adds more clearly: "It seemed to many not to be very apostolic to quote from apocrypha."[45] The Dominican Thomas de Vio, Cardinal Cajetan, is much more incisive in his commentary of 1532. In his presentation of the epistle, after quoting Jerome's words, he proceeds with a somewhat impertinent "This is it" (*hæc ille*) and develops: "It appears from this that the

---

**43** Bede the Venerable, *The Commentary on the Seven Catholic Epistles*, trans. David Hurst, Cistercian Studies 82 (Kalamazoo, MI: Cistercian Publications, 1985), 249–50.
**44** *Porro locus quem hic citat Iudas sumptus est ex apocryphis Hebraeorum, unde & ipsa epistola non caruit suspicione.* Desiderius Erasmus, *Novum Instrumentum Omne* (Germaniæ Basileam [Basel]: Apud Inclytam [Froben], 1516), 670.
**45** *Quod quibusdam uideatur parum apostolicum quicquam ex apocryphis.* Desiderius Erasmus, *In Novum Testamentum Annotationes* (Rauracorum Basileam [Basel]: Apud Inclytam [Froben], 1527), 702.

authority of this letter seems weaker than those which are certainly part of the Holy Scriptures."⁴⁶ In his commentary on the verses, he gives the substance of his thought: "Since it is much more permissible to quote an apocryphal text than poets, he derogates from the authority of Holy Scripture, since he describes the apocrypha as prophecy and pure prophecy. This is clearly shown by the words [Enoch] prophesied."⁴⁷

Despite these prejudices, the epistle of Jude soon returned to the canonical sphere.⁴⁸ On the Protestant side, Luther comments on it. He explains in his *Ennarationes* of 1524 that the passage is nowhere to be found in the Scriptures, but that this is no reason to reject the epistle, just as one does not dismiss 2 Timothy for identifying the two magicians of Ex 7:10–12 as Jannes and Mambres, although neither of these names is found anywhere.⁴⁹ Calvin, for his part, glosses Bede by pointing out that the letter contains nothing that is not "accordant à la pureté de la doctrine apostolique" (consistent with the purity of apostolic doctrine).⁵⁰ And he even makes a fairly audacious hypothesis: "I rather think that this prophecy was kept and carried on from hand to hand without being written, than to say that it was taken from some apocryphal book."⁵¹ If the book is apocryphal, the sentence is not. Eventually, Bullinger minted the most decisive defense. After returning to Bede's reasoning that nothing can be found that runs counter to the Scriptures, and after giving the example of Paul who quotes Menander, Epimenides and Aratos in his letters, he concludes: "True piety despises nothing, however obscure and humble, but with discernment gathers gold from dung."⁵² In other words, and to speak very

---

**46** *Ex quibus apparet minoris esse autoritatis hanc epistolam iis quae sunt certe scripturae sacrae.* Thomas de Vio [Cajetan], *In Omnes D. Pauli et Aliorum Apostolorum Epistolas Commentarii*, vol. 5 (Lugduni [Lyon]: Prost, 1639), 399.
**47** *Quoniam etsi citare apocrypha multo magis licet quam poëtas, authoritati tamen sacræ scripturæ derogat, vt apocrypha prophetia vt simpliciter & absolutem prophetia inducatur. Quod hic fieri clare apparet: dum absolutem dicitur, prophetiam autem.* De Vio [Cajetan], *Epistolas Commentarii*, 401.
**48** Beth Langstaff, "The Book of Enoch and the Ascension of Moses in Reformation Europe: Early Sixteenth-Century Interpretations of Jude 9 and Jude 14–15," *JSP* 23 (2013): 134–74.
**49** *Hic locus nusquam in scriptura legitur, quae altera ratio est, quare Patrum aliqui hanc epistolam non recepereunt, quanquam hoc satis non sit, ad rejiciendum librum aliquem ; cum et Paulus 2 Timo 3 duos adversarios, Iannem et Mambrem nominent, quorum tamen nomina in scripturis haud leguntur.* Martin Luther, *Enarrationes Martini Lutheri in Epistolas D. Petri Duas, et Iudae Unam* (Rauracorum Basileam [Basel]: Hervagius, 1524), 160.
**50** Jean Calvin, *Commentaires de M. Iehan Calvin sur toutes les épistres de l'apostre S. Paul, & aussi sur l'épistre aux Hebrieux: Item sur les épistres canoniques de S. Pierre, S. Iehan, S. Iaques & S. Iude, lesquelles sont aussi appelées catholiques* (Genève: Conrad Badius, 1556), 160.
**51** Calvin, *Commentaires*, 166.
**52** *Quod si vitio non vertitur Paulo citavit Menandri, Epimenidis et Arati testimonia, cur unus Iudas ab omnibus male audit quod quaedam citavit ex apocryphis. Solet vera pietas nihil asper-*

vulgarly, 1 Enoch is crap, but Jude's quotation is a nugget. On the Catholic side, another Dominican provided a scathing rebuttal to Cajetan: Lancelotto Politi, in religion Brother Ambrosius Catharinus (1484–1553). In his *Commentary on the General Epistle of Jude*, he violently attacks Cajetan and recalls all the grounds in favor of the canonicity of the epistle.[53] His rationale is threefold: Paul's use of non-canonical texts (as in Bullinger), the analogy of faith and the fact that the epistle in no way contradicts the rest of Scripture, and finally the fact that Jude claims Enoch prophesied does not imply that he is quoting the apocrypha, but the oral testimony of Enoch (Calvin's assertion). Ultimately, he puts forward a decisive reason: it is not the task of Scripture to prove Scripture, the Church proves it[54]. Catharinus published his commentary in 1551, having been preparing it for about ten years. In this way, he adopted the dogmatic formulation of the Council of Trent (1546): the Church guarantees the text and is responsible for preserving the Vulgate, which is now the typical version of the Bible.

What can be drawn from this overview? Even if the arguments given between Catholics and Protestants may be slightly divergent, they are very consistent and converge on one point: the abandonment of the criterion of apostolicity. Instead, the criterion of analogy of faith and ecclesiastical usage (or the authority of the Church) was emphasized. In the middle of the eighteenth century, two centuries after the Reformation, and after so many struggles, two exegetes as different as the pietist Bengel and the abbot of Senones, Dom Calmet, arrived at the same point. Bengel writes about the combat of Michael on the body of Moses, which he identifies as apocrypha: "It matters not whether the apostle received the knowledge of this contention from revelation only, or from the tradition of the elders: it is sufficient that he writes true things, and even admitted to be true by the brethren."[55] Dom Calmet notes: "This book is regarded as apocryphal. But the apostle, instructed elsewhere either by tradition or by a particular revelation, was able to draw this passage from it, which is of an incontestable and divine truth."[56] This dismissal of

---

*nari quantumvis sit obscurum et humile, sed cum iudicio ex stercoribus colligit aurum*. Heinrich Bullinger, *In omnes Apostolicas epistolas, divi videlicet Pauli XIIII. et VII. Canonicas, commentarii* (Zürich: apud Christophorum Froschouerum, 1537), 149–50.

53 Patrick Preston, "Ambrosius Catharinus' Commentary on the General Epistle of St Jude," *Reformation & Renaissance Review* 4 (2002): 217–29.

54 *Non opportet scriptura a scriptura probari, sed ab ecclesia.* Aurelius Ambrosius Catharinus, *Commentaria R. P. F. Ambrosii Catharini Politi in Omnes Divi Pauli, et Alias Septem Canonicas Epistolas* (Venetiis [Venezia]: in officina Erasmiana Vincentii Valgrisii, 1551), 545.

55 Johann Albrecht Bengel, *Gnomon of the New Testament*, trans. William Fletcher (Edinburgh: T&T Clark, 1865), 165.

56 "Ce livre passe pour apocryphe. Mais l'apôtre, instruit d'ailleurs ou par tradition, ou par une révélation particulière, en a pu tirer ce passage, qui est d'une vérité incontestable et divine."

the criterion of apostolic origin allowed doubts about the authorship of Judas to be expressed, notably by Eichhorn at the beginning of the nineteenth century,[57] without questioning its presence in the canon. Most present-day exegetes can therefore assume that the letter is pseudepigraphal, without this preventing them from commenting on it.[58]

## 3 Conclusion: What justifies the reading of the Epistle of Jude even today?

The specific case of the epistle of Jude, which quotes a text that was authoritative in its time but ceased to be so afterwards, demonstrates two different aspects of the Scripture. First, as Benjamin Sommer said, Scripture is not generated by Scripture alone, but by what might be called a canonization of traditions. By explicitly quoting the book of Enoch, "Jude" reveals the open secret that not all the texts of the New Testament derived from the Law and the Prophets, as the Emmaus pericope claims, but also from the traditions of Second Temple Judaism. Secondly, the hierarchy of criteria used to justify the inspiration of a writing can change drastically in the course of time. While the Fathers of the Church favored apostolicity over catholicity and analogy of faith, these two latter criteria took precedence over apostolicity from Reformation onwards. This progressive weakening of apostolicity's importance led to the questioning of Jude's authorship by critical studies at the beginning of the nineteenth century. This gives rise to a final thought. What is the situation today? What justifies the reading of the epistle of Jude now? I think that, paradoxically, the criterion of apostolicity is making a big comeback. It should not be understood in its restricted sense of identification with an apostle, but rather as participation in a specific community from the Early Christianity. Ultimately, we still read the epistle of Jude, not because of its content, not because we still believe that the one who wrote it is the brother of James and therefore possibly the brother of the Lord; we read Jude because it provides a testimony to the life of a Christian community of Jewish origin in the first century of the common era. In other words,

---

Augustin Calmet, *Commentaire littéral sur tous les livres de l'Ancien et du Nouveau Testament: Les épîtres canoniques et l'Apocalypse* (Paris: Emery, 1726), 361.

57 Johann Gottfried Eichhorn, *Einleitung in Das Neue Testament*, vol. 3.1, 2nd ed. (Leipzig: Weidmann, 1820), 646–8. For a summary of the discussion in the early nineteenth century: Adam Jessien, *De Αὐθεντίᾳ Epistolae Judae. Commentatio Critica* (Lipsiæ [Leipzig]: J.A. Barthius, 1821).

58 Neyrey, *2 Peter, Jude*, 31; Donald P. Senior and Daniel J. Harrington, *1 Peter, Jude and 2 Peter*, SP 15 (Collegeville, MI: Liturgical Press, 2008), 176; Thurén, "Hey Jude!," 464.

the epistle is canonical because it offers a historical documentation. And to substantiate this point, I would like to study four commentaries. I took them purposely from the Catholic world, because it is well known that it was given to conservatism at the beginning of the twentieth century and has the tendency to be more centralized. The evolution that emerges in this context could perfectly be transposed to all the branches of Protestantism, probably with slightly different chronologies.

The first one has a very explicit title, *Catholic Commentary of Scripture*, it received the *nihil obstat* and was covered by *imprimatur*. It dates from 1953 and was therefore written after the encyclical of Pius XII *Divino Afflante Spiritu*, which loosened the stranglehold of the anti-modernist condemnations; it presents the age-old position:

> There is great probability, as St Jerome asserts above that Jude made use of the apocryphal Book of Henoch. This does not prove that Jude considered the contents of Henoch as inspired; nor does it indicate that he approved of every statement contained therein. Henoch was held in high esteem in the early Church, and it may have contained some genuine Jewish traditions.[59]

This work was revised after the Council, in 1969, under the direction of one of the co-editors of the 1953 volume, Reginald Fuller, and it reads:

> The prophecy of Enoch is not contained in the OT but is found almost verbatim in the apocryphal Book of Enoch, 1:9. This book was held in great esteem in the early Church. Jude simply cites the book as an authority which his readers would accept.[60]

The difference is obvious: the reference to inspiration has disappeared. And what justifies Jude's quoting an apocryphal book is the acceptance of the audience.

The same assertion is made by another Catholic publication, the *Jerome Commentary* edited by the illustrious Raymond Brown, which was published in 1968. The explanation is the same: "Jude, however, quotes from the apocryphal Enoch (1:9), referring to it as a prophecy; he reflects the esteem in which this work was held in the early Church."[61] The *Jerome* was also revised, in the 1990s.

> The importance of Enoch lies in the content of his citation and its function in the argument (...) Jude even claims that Enoch was "prophesying" against these very heretics, and so the citation

---

[59] Bernard Orchard and Reginald Fuller, eds., *A Catholic Commentary on Holy Scripture* (London/New York: Nelson, 1953), 1191.

[60] Reginald Fuller, Luke Johnson, and Conleth Kearns, eds., *A New Catholic Commentary on Holy Scripture* (London/New York: Nelson, 1969), 1260.

[61] Raymond Brown, Joseph Fitzmyer, and Roland Murphy, eds., *The Jerome Biblical Commentary*, vol. 2 (Englewood Cliffs, NJ: Prentice-Hall, 1968), 380.

functions as one more traditional judgment against Jude's opponents, alongside the biblical examples of judgment in vv5–7,11.[62]

The evolution is done: no need to justify the use of the apocryphal book anymore, but simply a description of the argumentation and of Jude's usage of the text.

## Bibliography

Alexander, Philip S. "The Targumim and Early Exegesis of 'Sons of God' in Genesis 6." *JJS* 23 (1972): 60–71.
Ambrosius Catharinus, Aurelius. *Commentaria R. P. F. Ambrosii Catharini Politi in Omnes Divi Pauli, et Alias Septem Canonicas Epistolas.* Venetiis [Venezia]: in officina Erasmiana Vincentii Valgrisii, 1551.
Augustine. *The City of God*, trans. Marcus Dods. New York: Modern Library, 1950.
Bauckham, Richard. *Jude, 2 Peter.* WBC 50. Waco, TX: Word Books, 1983.
Bauckham, Richard. *Jude and the Relatives of Jesus in the Early Church*. T&T Clark Academic Paperbacks. London – New York: T&T Clark International, 2004.
Bede the Venerable. *The Commentary on the Seven Catholic Epistles*, trans. David Hurst. Cistercian Studies 82. Kalamazoo, MI: Cistercian Publications, 1985.
Bengel, Johann Albrecht, *Gnomon of the New Testament*, trans. William Fletcher. Edinburgh: T&T Clark, 1865.
Brosend, William F. *James and Jude*. NCBC. Cambridge – New York: Cambridge University Press, 2004.
Brown, Raymond, Joseph Fitzmyer, and Roland Murphy, eds. *The Jerome Bible Commentary*, vol. 2. Englewood Cliffs, NJ: Prentice-Hall, 1968.
Brown, Raymond, Joseph Fitzmyer, and Roland Murphy, eds. *The New Jerome Bible Commentary*. Englewood Cliffs, NJ: Prentice-Hall, 1990.
Bullinger, Heinrich. *In omnes Apostolicas epistolas, divi videlicet Pauli XIIII. et VII. Canonicas, commentarii.* Zürich: apud Christophorum Froschouerum, 1537.
Burnet, Régis. "La notion d'apostolicité dans les premiers siècles." *RSR* 103 (2015): 185–202.
Burrus, Virginia. "Canonical References to Extra-Canonical "Texts": Priscillian's Defense of the Apocrypha," in *Society of Biblical Literature Seminar Papers*, vol. 126, edited by David J. Lull, 60–7. Atlanta, GA: Scholars Press, 1990.
Calmet, Augustin. *Commentaire littéral sur tous les livres de l'Ancien et du Nouveau Testament. Les épîtres canoniques et l'Apocalypse*. Paris: Emery, 1726.
Calvin, Jean. *Commentaires de M. Iehan Calvin sur toutes les épistres de l'apostre S. Paul, & aussi sur l'épistre aux Hebrieux: Item sur les épistres canoniques de S. Pierre, S. Iehan, S. Iaques & S. Iude, lesquelles sont aussi appelées catholiques.* Genève: Conrad Badius, 1556.
Carroll, John T. *Luke: A Commentary*. NTL. Louisville, KY: Westminster John Knox Press, 2012.
Davids, Peter H. "The Use of Second Temple Traditions in 1 and 2 Peter and Jude". In *The Catholic Epistles and the Tradition*, edited by Jacques Schlosser, 409–32. BETL 176. Leuven: Peeters, 2004.

---

**62** Raymond Brown, Joseph Fitzmyer, and Roland Murphy, eds., *The New Jerome Bible Commentary* (Englewood Cliffs, NJ: Prentice-Hall, 1990), 919.

De Vio, Thomas [Cajetan]. *In Omnes D. Pauli et Aliorum Apostolorum Epistolas Commentarii, vol. 5*. Lugduni [Lyon]: Prost, 1639.

DeSilva, David A. *The Jewish Teachers of Jesus, James, and Jude: What Earliest Christianity Learned from the Apocrypha and Pseudepigrapha*. New York: Oxford University Press, 2012.

Donelson, Lewis R. *I & II Peter and Jude: A Commentary*. NTL. Louisville, KY: Westminster John Knox Press, 2010.

Eichhorn, Johann Gottfried. *Einleitung in Das Neue Testament*, vol. 3.1. 2nd edition. Leipzig: Weidmann, 1820.

Erasmus, Desiderius. *Novum Instrumentum Omne*. Germaniæ Basileam [Basel]: Apud Inclytam [Froben], 1516.

Erasmus, Desiderius. *In Novum Testamentum Annotationes*. Rauracorum Basileam [Basel]: Apud Inclytam [Froben], 1527.

Fuller, Reginald, Luke Johnson, and Conleth Kearns, eds. *A New Catholic Commentary on Holy Scripture*. London/New York: Nelson, 1969.

Green, Joel B. *The Gospel of Luke*. NICNT. Grand Rapids, MI: Eerdmans, 1997.

Grünstäudl, Wolfgang and Tobias Nicklas. "Searching for Evidence: The History of Reception of the Epistles of Jude and 2 Peter." In *Reading 1–2 Peter and Jude: A Resource for Students*, edited by Eric Farrel Mason and Troy W. Martin, 215–28. RBS 77. Atlanta, GA: Society of Biblical Literature, 2014.

Hultin, Jeremy. *Jude's's Citation of 1 Enoch, in Jewish and Christian Scriptures: The Function of "Canonical" and "Non-Canonical" Religious Texts*, edited by James Hamilton Charlesworth and Lee Martin McDonald, 113–28. Jewish and Christian Texts in Contexts and Related Studies 7. London/New York: T&T Clark, 2010.

Jacobs, Andrew S. "The Disorder of Books: Priscillian's Canonical Defense of Apocrypha." *HTR* 93 (2000): 135–59.

Jessien, Adam. *De Αὐθεντίᾳ Epistolae Judae. Commentatio Critica*. Lipsiæ [Leipzig]: J.A. Barthius, 1821.

Johnson, Luke Timothy. *The Gospel of Luke*. SP 3. Collegeville, MN: Liturgical Press, 1991.

Joseph, Simon J. "'Seventh from Adam' (Jude 1:14–15): Re-Examining Enochic Traditions and The Christology of Jude." *JTS 64* (2013): 463–81.

Just, Arthur A. *Luke*. ACCS 3. Downers Grove, IL: InterVarsity Press, 2003.

Klein, Hans. *Das Lukasevangelium*. KEK 1/3/10. Göttingen: Vandenhoeck & Ruprecht, 2006.

Kraftchick, Steven J. *Jude, 2 Peter*. ANTC. Nashville, TN: Abingdon Press, 2002.

Lake, Kirsopp. *The Ecclesiastical History*, vol. 1. LCL 153. Cambridge, MA: Harvard Univ. Press, 1926.

Langstaff, Beth. "The Book of Enoch and the Ascension of Moses in Reformation Europe: Early Sixteenth-Century Interpretations of Jude 9 and Jude 14–15." *JSP 23* (2013): 134–74.

Luther, Martin. *Enarrationes Martini Lutheri in Epistolas D. Petri Duas, et Iudae Unam*. Rauracorum Basileam [Basel]: Hervagius, 1524.

Moore, Nicholas J. "Is Enoch Also among the Prophets? The Impact of Jude's Citation of 1 Enoch on the Reception of Both Texts in the Early Church." *JTS 64* (2013): 498–515.

Neyrey, Jerome H., *2 Peter, Jude: A New Translation with Commentary*. AB 37C. New York: Doubleday, 1993.

Nickelsburg, George W.E. *1 Enoch: A Commentary on the Book of 1 Enoch*. Hermeneia. Minneapolis, MN: Fortress, 2001.

Nickelsburg, George W.E. and David N. Freedman. "Son of Man." *ABD* 6: 137–50.

Nienhuis, David R. *Not by Paul Alone: The Formation of the Catholic Epistle Collection and the Christian Canon*. Waco, TX: Baylor University Press, 2011.

Orchard, Bernard and Reginald Fuller, eds. *A Catholic Commentary on Holy Scripture*. London/New York: Nelson, 1953.

Paulsen, Henning. *Der Zweite Petrusbrief Und Der Judasbrief*. KEK 12,2. Göttingen, Vandenhoeck & Ruprecht, 1992.

Preston, Patrick "Ambrosius Catharinus' Commentary on the General Epistle of St Jude." *Reformation & Renaissance Review 4* (2002): 217–29.

Reeves, John C. and Annette Yoshiko-Reed. *Enoch from Antiquity to the Middle Ages*. Oxford: Oxford University Press, 2018.

Richardson, Ernest Cushing. *Hieronymus liber De viris inlustribus. Gennadius liber De viris inlustribus.* TUGAL14.1. Leipzig: J.C. Hinrichs, 1896.

Senior, Donald P. and Daniel J. Harrington. *1 Peter, Jude and 2 Peter*. SP 15. Collegeville, MI: Liturgical Press, 2008.

Sommer, Benjamin D. *Revelation and Authority: Sinai in Jewish Scripture and Tradition*. AYBRL. New Haven, CT: Yale University Press, 2015.

Stone, Michael E. *Ancient Judaism: New Visions and Views*. Grand Rapids, MI: Eerdmans, 2011.

Tertullian, *Disciplinary, Moral, and Ascetical Works*, trans. Rudolph Arbesmann. Fathers of the Church 40. New York: Fathers of the Church, 1959.

Tertullian, *La Toilette Des Femmes (De Cultu Feminarum)*. Translated by Marie Turcan. Sources chrétiennes 173. Paris: Cerf, 1970.

*The Holy Bible: New Revised Standard Version*. Grand Rapids, MI: Zondervan, 1989.

Thurén, Lauri. "Hey Jude! Asking for the Original Situation and Message of a Catholic Epistle." *NTS 43* (1997): 451–65.

VanBeek, Lawrence. "1 Enoch among Jews and Christians: A Fringe Connection?" In *Christian-Jewish Relations Through the Centuries*, edited by Stanley E. Porter and Brook W.R. Pearson, 93–115. JSNTSup 192. Sheffield: Sheffield Academic Press, 2000.

VanderKam, James C. '1 Enoch, Enochic Motives and Early Christian Literature." In *The Jewish Apocalyptic Heritage in Early Christianity*, edited by James C. VanderKam and William Adler, 33–101. CRINT 4. Assen: Van Gorcum, Minneapolis, MN: Fortress Press, 1996.

Webb, Robert L. "The Eschatology of the Epistle of Jude and Its Rhetorical and Social Functions." *BBR 6* (1996): 139–51.

Yoshiko-Reed, Annette. *Fallen Angels and the History of Judaism and Christianity: The Reception of Enochic Literature*. Cambridge – New York: Cambridge University Press, 2005.

Mehdi Azaiez
# 8 Qur'ānic Inspiration: A Triple Rupture? Remarks on the Qur'ānic Process of Revelation

When discussing inspiration in the Qur'ān, three prior distinctions should be made.[1] The first differentiates between the meanings of the roots *w-ḥ-y* and *n-z-l*, commonly translated as "inspiration" and "revelation." While both signify a "self-communication" from God to man, they differ in the nature of the recipients. If *w-ḥ-y*'s root can be used towards non-human creatures,[2] *n-z-l*-root occurrences are mostly attached to the divine revelation to the prophets, and especially the first of them, that of Allah to his "qur'ānic first addressee."[3] A second distinction separates the roots *n-b-'* and *r-s-l*,[4] and derived forms *nabiyy* and *rasūl*, which do not have exactly the same meaning.[5] The former seems to imply the delivery of a law without the gift of a divine book; the term *rasūl*, on the other hand, would rather imply a double

---

**1** See Denis Gril, "Révélation et inspiration," in *Dictionnaire du Coran*, ed. Mohammad Ali Amir-Moezzi (Paris: Robert Laffont, 2007): 749–51. See also the recent dissertation by Khalil Andani, *Revelation in Islam: Qur'ānic, Sunni, and Shi'i Ismaili Perspectives* (Harvard: Harvard University, Graduate School of Arts & Sciences, 2020). See especially Chapter 1, "Revelation in the Qur'ān," 27–107. My deepest thanks to Benjamin Sommer who introduced me to this work.
**2** *Cf.* Q al-Naḥl 16:68 *wa-'awḥā rabbuka 'ilā n-naḥli 'ani ttaḫiḏī mina l-ǧibāli buyūtan wa-mina š-šaǧari wa-mimmā ya'rišūna* (And your Lord *inspired* the bee [saying]: 'Make your home in the mountains, and on the trees and the trellises that they erect) and Q Fuṣṣilat 41:12 *fa-qaḍāhunna sab'a samāwātin fī yawmayni wa-'awḥā fī kulli samā'in 'amrahā wa-zayyannā s-samā'a d-dunyā bi-maṣābīḥa wa-ḥifẓan ḏālika taqdīru l-'azīzi l-'alīmi* (Then He set them up as seven heavens in two days, and *revealed* [to the angels] in each heaven its ordinance. We have adorned the lowest heaven with lamps, and guarded them. That is the ordaining of the All-mighty, the All-knowing.) The translation of the two Quranic verses comes from Ali Quli Qarai, *The Qur'ān: With a Phrase-by-Phrase English Translation* (Clarksville, MD: Khatoons, 2006).
**3** Cf. Simon P. Loynes, *Revelation in the Qur'ān: A Semantic Study of the Roots n-z-l and w-ḥ-y* (Leiden: Brill, 2019), especially "Divine Sending Down (*tanzīl*): Actors, Spatiality, and Interaction," 20–35.
**4** Q al Ḥajj 22:52. *Cf.* 'Abd Allah b.'Umar al-Bayḍāwī (d. 685/1286), *Anwār al-tanzīl wa-asrār al-ta'wīl*, vol. 2 (Beyrouth: Dār al-kutub al-'ilmiyya, 2003): 92–93.
**5** Commenting on Q al Hajj 22:52, I observed that: "The distinction between the notions of 'Prophet' (*nabiyy*) and 'Envoy' (*rasūl*) is not clearly established in the Qur'ān, although a classical interpretation suggests that the former do not deliver a divine law (*sharī'a*) while the latter deliver both a Law and a divine Book." See Mehdi Azaiez, "al-ḥajj. (Le pèlerinage)" in *Le Coran des historiens*, vol. 2a, eds. Mohammad Amir-Ali Moezzi and Guillaume Dye (Paris: Cerf, 2019): 836.

transmission: that of a law and a book.⁶ Based on a single qur'ānic verse,⁷ a third distinction identifies three ways in which qur'ānic inspiration manifests itself, as specified: "it is not (fitting) for any human being that God should speak to him, except (by) inspiration (*'illā waḥy^an*), or behind a veil (*min warā'^i ḥiǧāb^in*), or (that) He should send a messenger and He inspire by His permission (*yursil^a rasūl^an fa-yūḥiy^a bi-'iḏnihī*) whatever He pleases…"⁸

The three distinctions (1. *w-ḥ-y/n-z-l* ; 2. *nabiyy/rasūl* ; 3. *waḥy/ warā'^i ḥiǧāb^in/ yursil^a rasūl^an*) highlight how the Qur'ān speaks about revelation: its nature, its modalities and its addressees. It is a divine communication whose author can only be God. Its modes of manifestation are threefold. They take the form of inspiration, vision or the sending of a messenger. Finally, it is addressed to men, and to prophets in particular, but not exclusively.⁹

While the similarities with the Jewish and Christian monotheistic traditions are obvious,¹⁰ the notions of "revelation" and "inspiration" have certain singularities in the Qur'ān. As this essay suggests, the founding book of Islam could be seen as discontinuous from a triple perspective: Arabic, biblical and Islamic. By proposing a new topography of the sacred, the Qur'ān seems to break with a conception and a vocabulary anchored in pre-Islamic representations (Part 1). This break is also possibly made thanks to the oral and post-biblical traditions of late antiquity, which acquire an authority in the Qur'ān in contrast to the earlier biblical religions (Part 2). Finally, the Qur'ān, through the ambiguities of its discourse and grammar,

---

6 These distinctions are relative and we can specify, with Denis Gril, that "only certain prophets or envoys are said to have received a Book." Gril, "Révélation et inspiration," 749.
7 Q aš-šūrā 42:51. Translation by Arthur J. Droge, *The Qur'ān: A new Annotated Translation* (Sheffield: Equinox, 2014), 327.
8 For a better appreciation of these three modalities, particularly as they are considered in Islamic exegesis, see Michaël Fitzgerald's article: Michaël Fitzgerald, "Islam and Revelation," *Islamochristiana* 4 (1978): 113-25.
9 We agree with Daniel Madigan's caution about *waḥy*'s meanings in the Qur'ān: "Nor does *waḥy* have any necessary connection with written communication as many others have suggested. It indicates a kind of communication that appears impenetrable and perhaps exotic to a third person observing it, yet remains full of meaning for the one receiving it. Given the range of its use, it seems possible, perhaps even preferable, to translate wahy simply as "communication," understanding that it normally refers to divine communication." Daniel Madigan, "Revelation and Inspiration," in *Encyclopedia of the Qur'ān*, vol. 4, ed. Jane Dammen MacAuliffe (Leiden: Brill, 2003): 441.
10 On the subject of the three monotheisms and "Revelation," Denise Masson writes: "Revelation is considered by the three monotheistic religions, which go back to Abraham, as a supernatural manifestation attributed to the eternal Word, the divine Word, the Voice of God, which uses the organ of the Prophets. These act under the impulse of the Holy Spirit." Denise Masson, *Monothéisme coranique et monothéisme biblique*, 2nd edition (Paris: Desclée de Brouwer, 1976), 230.

could stand in contrast to later exegetical claims about the possible participatory nature of Muḥammad in qur'ānic inspiration (Part 3).

## 1 A renewal of sacred topography?

The qur'ānic use of the root *w-ḥ-y* is part of a radical reimagining of what can be called the topography of sacredness as it was conceived in pre-Islamic society.[11] In order to show the full extent of this upheaval, we outline the conception of Arabic cosmology before Islam. Secondly, we will explain how the Qur'ān disrupts these representations.

The people of seventh-century Arabia conceived of the existence of a supernatural, invisible and mysterious world: the *ghayb*. This space was occupied by supernatural beings: the *ǧinn*. The latter had the capacity to make this invisible world known thanks to men endowed with particular gifts and very precise social functions: these are the *kāhin*, the *sāḥir* or the *shā'ir*. By *ghayb*, we mean a fearsome and supernatural space occupied by "metamorphic powers of the invisible such as the Jinns."[12] But it is also (and curiously) a place where the destiny of men and their tribe is inscribed in a "supernatural script," the *kitāb*, "hidden and invisible in the present."[13] To access the *ghayb* and the knowledge of their destiny, tribesmen could rely on intermediary figures called *ǧinn*. They were metamorphic beings inhabiting desert spaces with the ability to move quickly on the ground as well as in the air.[14] Their importance was explained by their role as mediators and vectors of the sacred through their ability to access the *ghayb*. These *ǧinn* were feared. Contact with them was always indirect and synonymous with entry into the sacred sphere. It was only possible through human mediators.

The first of these mediators, the diviner or *kāhin*, had at his service a *ǧinn* called *tābi'*, whose function was to make known the destiny inscribed in the *ghayb*. As Esma Hind Tengour explains:

> These soothsayers had at their command a jinn named *tābi'*, the one who follows, or *tālī*, the one who attaches himself to the footsteps, whose function was to whisper to them the news of the *Ghayb*. The active participle, *tābi'*, is built on the root *t-b-'* which connotes the idea of

---

11 For similar considerations about pre-Islamic conceptions of *waḥy*, see Toshihiko Izutsu, *God and Man in the Qur'ān: Semantics of the Qur'anic Weltanschauung*, 2nd reprint (Kuala Lumpur: Islamic Book Trust, 2008), 181–99.
12 Jacqueline Chabbi, Le *Seigneur des tribus: L'islam de Mahomet* (Paris: Noêsis, 1997), 124.
13 Chabbi, *Le Seigneur des tribus*, 527.
14 Chabbi, *Le Seigneur des tribus*, 187.

immediate proximity, and derives from the verb *tabi'a, yatba'u* which means to follow. The *tābi'* is part of the jinn and seems to lend a hand and provide answers only at the request of the diviner to whom it is attached.[15]

A second character, the sorcerer or *sāḥir*, had as a companion a *shayṭān* who was none other than a local *ǧinn* who mediated between the supernatural world and the world of men. His power, which aroused fear, was recognized by his ability to do or undo evil deeds, which the Qur'ān itself seems to echo.[16] A third figure, that of the poet, *shā'ir*, also had a *ǧinn* or *shayāṭīn* at his service, who was the source of his inspiration. But the latter had the particularity of being ambivalent. He could be a good genie and inspire positively. He could also be the source of a bad inspiration, making the person who received him a *majnūn* or a person possessed by an evil genie (*shayṭān*).

Therefore, in the peculiar pre-Islamic cosmology and demonology, we can distinguish a sacred and mysterious space inhabited by supernatural beings (*ǧinns* and *shayṭān*); this space and its occupants communicate with the visible world thanks to human and mediating figures (*kāhin*). The Qur'ān would come to modify profoundly this mode of perceiving reality. Jacqueline Chabbi very clearly understands this transposition based on an interpretation of Q al-'An'ām 22:6: *wa-ka-ḏālika ǧa'alnā li-kulli nabiyyin 'aduwwan shayāṭīna l-'insi wa-l-ǧinni yūḥī ba'ḍuhum 'ilā ba'ḍin zuḫrufa l-qawli ǧurūran wa-law shā'a rabbuka mā fa'alūhu fa-ḏarhum wa-mā yaftarūna* of which we give here the translation proposed by Droge: "In this way We have assigned to every prophet an enemy – satans of the humans and ǧinn- some of them inspiring others (with) decorative speech as a deception. If your Lord had (so) pleased, they would not have done it. So leave them and what they forge."[17] In a commentary on this verse Chabbi states:

> The Qur'ān, VI al-An'âm, 112, stipulates a particular transmission between the jinns and certain humans, *ins*; the former are supposed to make "revelations," *wahî*, to the latter; according to the verse, these revelations are "falsehood," *iftirâ'*, and "illusory and pernicious words," *zukhruf al-qawl, ghurûr*. Both the informant jinns and the human listeners are qualified as "satan," *shayâtîn* (plural of *shaytân*) by the Qur'ān; they are, moreover, globally

---

15 Esma Hind Tengour, "L'imaginaire dans l'Arabie du VIIe siècle, une topologie du surnaturel," in *Le Coran: De la Tribu à l'Empire: Autour de l'œuvre de Jacqueline Chabbi*, ed. Mehdi Azaiez (Louvain-la-Neuve: Presses Universitaires de Louvain, 2023): 47–8 (my translation from the French).
16 See Q *al-Ṣāffāt* 37:36. About this verse, Esma Hind Tengour argues: "When the Qur'ān claims that Muḥammad, the inspired one, received a *waḥy*, it is the pre- Qur'ānic imagery of 'inspiration' that is taken up. It is therefore understandable that the man Muḥammad was accused by his own people of being a poet and, at times, a poet possessed by the jinn." Tengour, "L'imaginaire dans l'Arabie," 50 (my translation from the French).
17 *The Qur'an*, trans. Arthur J. Droge, 85.

designated as "enemies of God," `aduww;` one can obviously suppose that, on the contrary, Muhammad's opponents considered the revelations transmitted in this way to be absolutely true as they were revealing the *Ghayb*; it should also be noted that the terminology used is particularly significant; it covers exactly the words that describe the relationship of the poet inspired (by *Waḥî*) to his inspiring jinn who was qualified as *shaytân*; it should not be forgotten that Mohammed was accused by his tribe of being a *madjnûn* poet himself, "possessed," i.e. inspired by an evil jinn (Sura XXXXVII, as-Saffât, 36), while other poets were obviously seen as being inspired by good jinns; see in the Sura XXVI, ash Shu`arâ' ("The Poets"), 210–212 and 221–226 (. . .) the charge both against the poets who lead astray and against the "demons," *shayâtîn*, inspirers, who are themselves astray.[18]

Chabbi highlights two central points that are essential to our investigation. First, the Qur'ān severely condemns the pre-Islamic representations of the world. With an unmistakable polemical tone, it denies the *ghayb/ǧinns*/humans triptych as possessing any formal relevance. Soothsayers, sorcerers and poets are in no way bearers of truth. As "enemies of God," they only receive false information inspired by demons. Secondly, this polemic and its accompanying condemnations redefine, by contrast, the nature of qur'ānic revelation and the modalities of inspiration.

Such a reconfiguration concerns these pre-Islamic communities and their conception of cosmic order and revelation. The qu'rānic novelty is undoubtedly the plenary place occupied by God, Allah, who is far more important in the Qur'ān than as He is presented in pre-Islamic poetry.[19] If this divinity is well attested before Islam, He becomes in the Qur'ān the unique God, Creator of the world, Author of the Qur'ān and Supreme Judge of the Last Day. In the qur'ānic discourse, Allah is the central subject where all genres converge, whether they are narrative, polemical, eschatological, normative or praise. He is the absolute master of the visible and invisible world and all creation is subordinate to Him. From a linguistic perspective, Mustapha Bentaibi masterfully underlines the role of this figure in the whole qur'ānic discourse:

> The voice of the speaker God manifests himself in his discourse as the author-narrator-creator, the recipient of prayers (promises of salvation) and the addressee of illocutionary acts (notably praise or prayer) (. . .) he speaks to qualify the Qur'ān, to give indications on its construction and on the way to interpret it, while challenging men and jinns to produce anything like it. In short, to command its reception, to admit the truth of its message and to institute a worldview.[20]

---

**18** Chabbi, *Le Seigneur des tribus*, 530 (my translation from the French).
**19** Izutsu, *God and Man in the Qur'an*, 100–11.
**20** Mustapha Bentaibi, *Quelques façons de lire le texte coranique* (Paris: Lambert & Lucas, 2009), 204 (my translation from the French).

Another figure, the prophet (*nabiyy*) or the apostle (*rasūl*) is central. His function is to ensure the faithful transmission of the revelation, the Qur'ān given by Allah. This complex mediating role is possible through a supernatural intermediary identified according to the Qur'ān and tradition by the Spirit (the angel Gabriel) or *"Amr"* of God. The integration of these three protagonists does not, as we have seen, remove the presence of other actors already attested to in the pre-Islamic era (*ghayb*, *ǧinns*, *kāhin*, *sāḥir*, *shāʿir* and *maǧnūn*). But it redefines both the nature of revelation and consequently the character of inspiration according to the Qur'ān.

## 2 A biblical oral tradition as "revelation"?

Remarkably, a qur'ānic verse whose source is derived from Jewish oral tradition acquires the status of divine revelation through the Qur'ān.[21] The provenance of this text makes the Qur'ān's departure from the Jewish understanding of the oral tradition in the Talmud all the more clear. In the Talmud, revelation does not have a divine nature; it is a human achievement derived from rabbinic wisdom.

The text bearing out this complex transmission is brief. It concerns a single qur'ānic "ethical" verse, namely Q al-Māʾida 5:32. Michel Cuypers has already analyzed the passage.[22] I shall introduce the text, then present a synoptic table highlighting relations between the Qur'ān and the Sanhedrin tractate (Table 1). Finally, we underline the importance conferred by the Qur'ān on Jewish oral authority.

The verse in question consists of 40 words and is divided into three propositions: the first introduces (a. *min ʿaǧli ḏālika katabnā ʿalā banī ʾisrāʾīla/* That is why *We decreed* for the Children of Israel that) a sentence (b. *ʾannahū man qatala nafsan bi ghayri nafsin ʾaw fasādin fī l-ʾarḍi fa-ka-ʾannamā qatala n-nāsa ǧamīʿan wa- man ʾaḥyāhā fa-ka-ʾannamā ʾaḥyā n-nāsa ǧamīʿan/* whoever kills a soul, without [its being guilty of] manslaughter or corruption on the earth, is as though he had killed all mankind, and whoever saves a life is as though he had saved all mankind.) which is followed by an anti-Judaic polemical condemnation (c. *wa-la-qad ǧāʾathum*

---

**21** This idea clarifies and extends the following comment by Gabriel Said Reynolds: "It is noteworthy that the Qur'ān refers to God's decreeing (in Arabic *katabnā ʿalā*) something for Israel, which is found not in the Bible but in the Mishnah." Gabriel Said Reynolds, "al-Māʾida," in *Le Coran des Historiens*, vol. 2a, eds. Amir-Moezzi and Dye (Paris: Cerf, 2019): 217. See also Gabriel Said Reynolds, *The Qur'ān and the Bible: Text and Commentary* (New Haven: Yale University Press, 2018), 199. For similar arguments, read also Geneviève Gobillot, "Qur'an and Torah: The Foundations of Intertextuality," in *A History of Jewish-Muslim Relations: From the origins to the Present Day*, eds. Abdelwahab Meddeb & Benjamin Stora (Princeton: Princeton University Press, 2013): 611–7.
**22** Michel Cuypers, *Le Festin: Une lecture de la sourate al-Mâ'ida* (Paris: Lethielleux, 2007), 154–5.

*rusulunā bi-l-bayyināti ṯumma 'inna kaṯīran minhum ba'da ḏālika fī l-'arḍi la-musrifūna*/Our apostles certainly brought them manifest signs, yet even after that, many of them commit excesses on the earth.). The first proposition emphasizes the divine action that prescribes (*katabnā*) a norm of universal character in favor of the Sons of Israel. The second proposition, which is central, enacts and formulates an ethical norm. The third proposition resolutely places the whole in an eminently polemical context. Beyond the strict delimitation of the verse, a rhetorical analysis places it at the center of a sequence between verses 27–40. The verse is thus preceded by a narrative pericope around the biblical figures of Abel and Cain and followed by a polemic against unbelievers in general.

**Table 1:** Qur'ānic text and biblical and parabiblical subtexts.

| Sanhedrin (tractate) 4:5 (trans. Danby)[23] | Sanhedrin (tractate) 4:5 (Hebrew)[24] | Q al-Mā'ida 5:32 (Arabic) | Q al-Mā'ida (The Banquet) 5:32 (Translation Ahmed Ali) |
|---|---|---|---|
| For we have found concerning Cain that slew his brother, | מצינו בקין שהרג את אחיו | مِنْ أَجْلِ ذَٰلِكَ كَتَبْنَا عَلَىٰ بَنِي إِسْرَائِيلَ | [a.] That is why We decreed for the Children of Israel that |
| [for it is written]; the bloods of your brother cry. It says not the blood of your brother, "but the bloods of your brother– his blood and the blood of his posterity." | דמי אחיך צועקים. אינו אומר דם אחיך אלא דמי אחיך. דמו ודם זרעיותיו | | |
| [Another explanation]: bloods of your brother – because his blood was cast over the trees and stones. For this reason man was created one and alone in the world: to teach that | דמי אחיך, שהיה דמו משלך על העצים ועל האבנים. לפיכך נברא אדם יחידי, ללמדך, | | |

---

[23] Herbert Danby, *The Mishnah* (London: Oxford University Press, 1933), 389. Quoted by Cuypers, *Le Festin*, 155.

[24] The Hebrew text comes from the "Vilna edition Shas": משניות עם שבע ושלשים הוספות שנוספו על כל המפרשים וההגהות שנדפסו בו עד כה, 13 vols. (Vilna [Vilnius]: Romm Widow and Brothers, 1913), consulted online at https://www.sefaria.org/Mishnah_Sanhedrin.4.5.

**Table 1** (continued)

| Sanhedrin (tractate) 4:5 (trans. Danby) | Sanhedrin (tractate) 4:5 (Hebrew) | Q al-Māʾida 5:32 (Arabic) | Q al-Māʾida (The Banquet) 5:32 (Translation Ahmed Ali) |
|---|---|---|---|
| whosoever destroys a single soul (*of Israël*) is regarded as though he destroyed a complete world, and whosoever destroys a single soul is regarded as though he saved a complete world. | שכל המאבד נפש אחת מישראל, מעלה עליו הכתוב כאלו אבד עולם מלא. וכל המקים נפש אחת מישראל, מעלה עליו הכתוב כאלו קים עולם מלא | أنه من قتل نفسا بغير نفس أو فساد في الأرض فكأنما قتل الناس جميعا ومن أحياها فكأنما أحيا الناس جميعا | b. whoever kills a soul, without [its being guilty of] manslaughter or corruption on the earth, is as though he had killed all mankind, and whoever saves a life is as though he had saved all mankind. |
|  |  | ولقد جاءتهم رسلنا بالبينات ثم إن كثيرا منهم بعد ذلك في الأرض لمسرفون | ʿOur apostles certainly brought them manifest signs, yet even after that, many of them commit excesses on the earth. |

Source criticism has pointed out the obvious relationship between this qurʾānic verse and a remarkable passage in the Sanhedrin tractate.²⁵ As the table above indicates, the ethical sentence in the Sanhedrin is repeated almost *in extenso* (in bold) in the Qurʾān. Nevertheless, the context in which this rewriting occurs changes the scope of the original talmudic sentence. This modification consists of three fundamental changes. First, the ethical prescription limited to Israel is universalized. Secondly, the passage is not part of a legal reflection as in the Sanhedrin tractate but of a polemic. The Qurʾān criticizes those among the Jewish people who oppose the prophets (including Muḥammad) in order to broaden the scope to include those who "commit excesses." Finally, and this is the point that interests us, the Qurʾān gives this prescription the status of a law revealed by God himself. This is based on the use of the verb *kataba* ("to write" or "to prescribe") and the pronoun attached to it (a majestic "We"). Here, it is unambiguously God who writes or prescribes – both readings are possible – this ethical law. To put it plainly, the Qurʾān confers on the rabbinic discussion and interpretation the status and value of a divine revelation. The verb *katabnā* supports this conclusion and removes any ambiguity. This is, moreover, the only instance where *katabnā* refers to the Mishna. The other four qurʾānic occurrences of this verb (4:66; 5:45; 7:145; 21:105) refer exclusively to pas-

---

25 About Q 5 al-Māʾida 5:32, see Gabriel Said Reynolds, *The Qurʾān and the Bible*, 199.

sages from the Hebrew Bible. These include Exod 32:27–28 for Q 4:66; Lev 24:17–20 for Q 5:45; Exod 24:12 for Q 7:145; and Ps 37:29 for Q 21:105. This undiscriminating use of *katabnā* for both the Hebrew Bible and the Mishnah demonstrates that the Qur'ān gives them equal dignity and value.

The case study described above has significant theological consequences. If we refer to one of the central dogmas of Islam, namely that the human nature of Muḥammad has no participation in the qur'ānic word, then we must accept the idea that the God of the Qur'ān, and even more of Islamic tradition, gives a privileged status to Jewish (and Christian) oral traditions. This extends to the point that God appropriates, legitimizes, and "canonizes" that which the Jewish communities (or later, the churches)[26] refused to acknowledge (as the word of God).

## 3 A participatory activity of Muḥammad in divine revelation?

In order to define further qur'ānic revelation, I analyze the stimulating text of Q 26:192–227. It underlines the nature of "revelation" as the Qur'ān conceives of it and clarifies at the same time its break with the pre-Islamic conception of inspiration. To justify these two points, I shall proceed as follow: I present the selected pericope (a.), then I comment on it (b.) and finally I determine the possible meanings and implications of this text for understanding the originality of qur'ānic inspiration and the possible role of the Prophet in its manifestation (c.).

### 3.1 Pericope 26, 192–227: A presentation

Following a set of narrative units (vv. 10–191), these twenty-six verses (192–227) form the last part of *sūra* 26. In addition to its largely polemical tone, this passage is characterized by its short verses that are morphologically and syntactically linked

---

[26] In this contribution, I have decided not to repeat the analysis of the pericope Q Maryam 19:16–32 (presented orally at the colloquium) which shows how the qur'ānic text rewrites Christian apocryphal traditions to narrate the nativity of Christ. The parabiblical subtext is presented by the Qur'ān as a *ḏikr* (a reminder) whose author is none other than God. Thus, the Qur'ān "canonizes" this narrative, giving it the status of a revelation. For a recent detailed analysis, see Guillaume Dye, "Lieux saints communs, partagés ou confisqués, aux sources de quelques péricopes coraniques (Q19 : 16-33)," in *Partage du sacré: Transferts, dévotions mixtes, rivalités interconfessionnelles*, eds. Isabelle Depret and Guillaume Dye (Brussels: EME Editions, 2012): 55-121.

to each other.[27] The presence of metatextual elements[28] is also striking, as can be seen from the repeated use of the root *n-z-l*, in vv. 192 (*tanzīl*), 198 (*nazzalnāhu*), 210 (*tanazzalat*) and 221 (*tanazzalū*). These last four verses, like compositional markers, indicate the structure of the whole in four parts (Table 2). The first part positively defines the revelation and its believing recipients (vv. 192–197), the second part evokes the opposition to the revelation (vv. 198–209), the third part supports the non-satanic nature (vv. 210–220) of the revelation. Finally, the fourth part condemns the individuals who carry false revelations: impostors and poets (vv. 221–227).

**Table 2:** The Qur'ān's quadripartite definition of revelation.

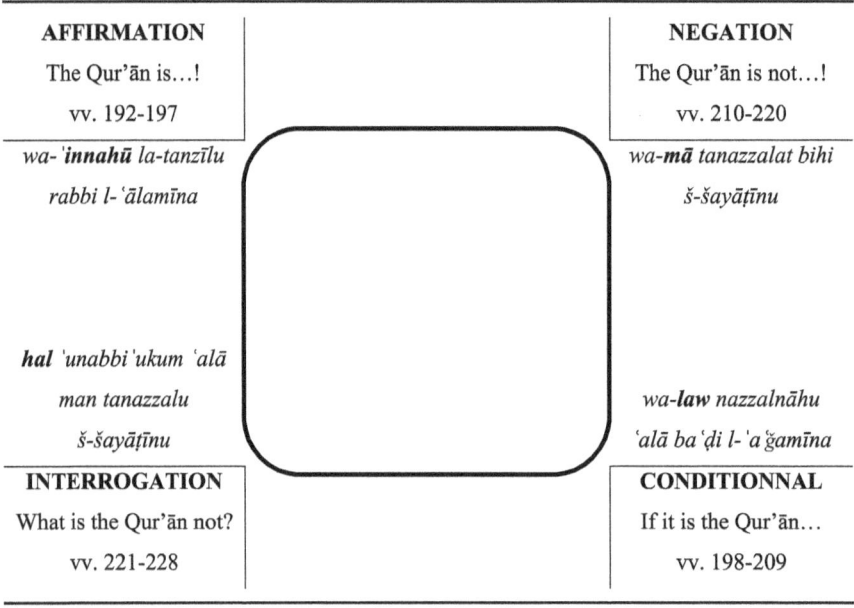

## 3.2 Pericope 26, 192–197: A presentation

Verses 192–197:[29] these six verses are a set of metatextual statements describing the nature of the qur'ānic revelation process. In v. 192, the pronoun "he/it" (*hu*) at

---

27 Angelika Neuwirth, *Studien zur Komposition* (Berlin: Walter de Gruyter, 1981), 276–7.
28 Jacques Berque, *Le Coran. Essai de traduction* (Paris: Albin Michel, 1995), 399.
29 For the original text in French, see: Mehdi Azaiez, "Sourate 26 al-shuʿarāʾ (les poètes)," in *Le Coran des historiens*, vol. 2a, eds. Amir-Ali Moezzi and Dye (Paris: Cerf, 2019): 990.

the beginning of the verse "And it is certainly a revelation" (*wa-innahū la-tanzīl*) refers to the Qur'ān. Blachère agrees but also points out that it can be a neutral formula equivalent to: 'this or that' marking a clear caesura from the verses that precede it. The term *tanzīl* here refers to the qur'ānic "revelation." It indicates the action of "descending" contained in the root *n-z-l*, expressed in words like *nazzala* and *anzala*. This is the notion most frequently associated with the revelation of the Qur'ān (Q 20:4; 32:2). It implies that the latter proceeds from God according to the qur'ānic verses where the divine speaker expresses himself, either in the first person ("I sent down the Qur'ān;" Q 2:41) or in a majestic "We" ("We sent down," Q 44:3; 76:23; 97:1).

V. 193 seems to indicate that qur'ānic revelation does not come directly to the Prophet but through a mediation, here evoked by the mention of "the faithful Spirit" (*rūḥ al-amīn*), the only attestation of this formula in the Qur'ān. The expression is to be compared with "the Holy Spirit" (*rūḥ al-qudus*, Q 16:2, 102) and "the Spirit of His Command" (*rūḥ min amrihī*, Q 40:15; 42:52). Most Muslim commentators identify this "Spirit" with the angel Gabriel (*ǧibrīl*) as indicated, for example, by Ibn Kathīr. As Droge reminds us,[30] this figure is also an agent of revelation in the Jewish and Christian Scriptures (Dan 8:15–26; 9:20–27; Luke 1:10–20, 26–37). Nevertheless, Jacqueline Chabbi points out that the angel Gabriel remains a minor figure in the Qur'ān compared to the importance he will have in Muslim tradition.[31]

In v. 195, the expression *lisān 'arabiyy mubīn* (cf. Q 12:2; 13:37; 16:103; 20:113; 39:28 and ff. with *qur'ānan 'arabiyyan* 41:3; 42:7; 43:3; and *lisānan 'arabiyyan* 46:12) is usually translated as "in clear Arabic." Claude Gilliot suggests that the qualifier *mubīn* should be read as "making [things] clear," suggesting that the Qur'ān "translates" or, better, "transposes" into Arabic (...) passages from a foreign language lectionary...". Federico Corriente, quoted by Kropp,[32] relates *lisān 'arabiyy mubīn* to the Hebrew *lāshon rā'uy* meaning the "appropriate language" or "chosen language" and quoted in the pseudepigraphic writing the book of Jubilees (12:25). This Hebrew expression (reconstructed from the surviving Ethiopian and Greek versions) is part of a narrative in which God asks these angels to open Abraham's mouth so that they can directly "converse with him in Hebrew, the language of creation." Corriente suggests that the Arabic language plays a similar role. It is the unique and direct medium used towards the Arab Nation so that it can no longer claim to be ignorant of the contents of earlier Jewish and Christian revelations.

---

**30** *The Qur'ān*, trans. Arthur J. Droge, 11.
**31** Jacqueline Chabbi, *Le Coran décrypté* (Paris: Fayard, 2008), 99–105.
**32** Manfred Kropp, "lisān 'arabiyy mubīn – 'Klares Arabisch'?," in *Books and Written Culture of the Islamic World*, eds. Andrew Rippin and Roberto Tottoli (Leiden: Brill, 2015): 280–1.

In v. 196, the plural term *zubur* (Q 41:84; 16:44; 23:53; 35:25; 54:43; 54:52), would generally mean "Scriptures" or "books."[33] In the singular (*zabūr*), the word means "psalms" (Q 4:163; 21:105) and thus reflects a long Jewish (Avot 6:9) and Christian (Mark 12:36–37) tradition that associates the psalms with David.[34] The term is probably borrowed from the Syriac *mazmūrā* or the Hebrew *mizmōwr* for "psalm."[35] Still others point out that *zubur* is attested in South Arabian inscriptions[36] or from pre-Islamic Yemen, where it denotes "a special South Semitic cursive script for letters and economic documents."[37]

## 3.3 Three arguments advocating a participatory revelation?

Concerning verses 192–196, the Qur'ān defines the nature of its revelation and the phenomenon of its coming into the world. The metatextual elements are particularly significant. The Qur'ān indicates its author (*rabb*), its process of revelation (*tanzīl*), its message (*hū*), its mediator (*rūḥ al-'amīn*), its first addressee (*ka*) and its language (*lisān 'arabiyy*). The whole enunciative spectrum from beginning to end is thus evoked. In counterpoint, and less systematically, the verses that follow describe what is a false revelation. It indicates the protagonists: the demons (who are powerless to hear snippets of the Qur'ān), the poets (under the sway of these demons), and the "foreigner" ("he who does not speak Arabic"). Thus the Qur'ān defines what it is and what it is not.

Crucially, this description envisions the way the Prophet receives revelation. In v. 194, the expression "on your heart" (*'alā qalbika*)[38] refers to the qur'ānic addressee who is the recipient of this revelation. Based on this verse, Fazlur Rahman argues that the revelatory phenomenon has a personal and internal character to Muḥammad. He writes: "(. . .) there is no doubt that while the Revelation emanated from God on the one hand, it was also intimately linked to his innermost personality.

---

[33] Reynolds, *The Qur'ān and the Bible*, 441; *The Qur'ān*, trans. Arthur J. Droge, 244; *Le Coran*, trans. Régis Blachère (Paris: Maisonneuve, 1949), 402.
[34] Reynolds, *The Qur'ān and the Bible*, 441.
[35] Arthur Jeffery, *The Foreign Vocabulary of the Qur'ān* (Leiden: Brill, 1987), 149.
[36] Arne Amadeus Ambros and Stephan Procházka, *A Concise Dictionary of Koranic Arabic* (Wiesbaden: Reichert Verlag, 2004), 120.
[37] Jan Retsö, *The Arabs in Antiquity: Their History from the Assyrians to the Umayyads* (London: Routledge, 2003), 289.
[38] *'alā qalbika* occurs only three times in the Qur'ān: Q 2:97; Q 26:194; Q 42:24.

Thus, the popular traditional accounts of the total externality of the agent of revelation cannot be accepted as correct."[39]

In his dissertation, Khalil Andani argues convincingly that "in the Revelatory Process, the qur'ānic idea of *waḥy* is a non-verbal spiritual inspiration as opposed to an auditory divine dictation, by which the Prophet 'reads' the Transcendent *kitāb* through the medium of the Holy Spirit and thereby produces the Arabic Qur'ān."[40] He adds: "the early Muslim community in the Prophet's lifetime and in the first several generations perceived Qur'ānic Revelation as part of a unitary 'prophetic-revelatory event' involving the active role of the Prophet in the production of both the Arabic qur'āns and extraqur'ānic prophetic guidance."[41]

The argument based on a semantic analysis that the qur'ānic *waḥy* is a non-verbal communication that requires a reading or, appropriately enough, a "translation"[42] of the heavenly *kitāb* is reinforced by exegetical analysis which shows how early communities of believers readily accepted the idea of participatory revelation. This can be extended by yet another grammatical argument based on the use of prepositions in the Qur'ān. Key here is *'alā*, for what descends on the Prophet does not come "in" (the expression *fī qalbika* does not exist in the Qur'ān) but "on" him. This distinction is not trivial. The preposition "in" (*fī*) would imply a fusional process. But the preposition "on" (*'alā*) implies the preservation of two distinct realities: the divine message and the prophetic being. They do not merge. This space of non-confusion between the person of the Prophet and the message transmitted suggests, as does Fazlur Rahman, a partial externality of revelation that goes against a classic Islamic interpretation. Therefore, and against the common understanding of Islamic doxa, Muḥammad is not the one repeating a divine dictation. The preposition "on" contains within it three characteristics that define the very process of inspiration. It indicates and preserves the idea of a hierarchy, an externality, and finally a human dimension to the very process of reception.

Without calling into question the central idea of the fully divine origin of the qur'ānic discourse, these semantic, exegetical, and grammatical arguments could

---

**39** Fazlur Rahman, *Major themes of the Qur'ān* , 2nd edition (Chicago: The University of Chicago, 2009), 100.
**40** Andani, *Revelation in Islam*, 107.
**41** Andani, *Revelation in Islam*, 107.
**42** Khalil Andani rightly refers to Benjamin Sommer who argues that the Pentateuch and prophetic literature "are best conceived as prophetic "translations" of divine speech, as opposed to dictated divine speech." Andani, *Revelation in Islam*, 97. Cf. Benjamin D. Sommer, "Prophecy as Translation: Ancient Israelite Conceptions of the Human Factor in Prophecy," in *From Bringing the Hidden to Light: The Process of Interpretation*, eds. Diane Sharon and Kathryn Kravitz (New York: Jewish Theological Seminary, Winona Lake, IN: Eisenbrauns, 2007): 271–90 (287).

therefore reopen a central question and suggest the possibility of an active participation of the Prophet in the process of revelation.

# 4 Conclusion

The qur'ānic notion of inspiration could be defined according to three striking ruptures: with the pre-Islamic world, the biblical tradition, and the traditional interpretations of "inspiration" in Islam.

Firstly, the qur'ānic *w-ḥ-y* breaks with a pre-Islamic historical context and radically modifies its sacred topography. While reusing key terms from pre-Islamic Arab society, the Qur'ān reconfigures this sacredness and redefines the nature, key actors and modalities of prophetic inspiration. Secondly, the model of prophetic inspiration is obviously based on the biblical model, but it departs from it by the very fact that it confers upon an oral tradition (cf. the example of the Sanhedrin tractate 4:5) the status of a divine revelation. It reminds us that the Qur'ān's engagement with biblical tradition is broad and involves various Jewish (and Christian) traditions. Third, a semantic, exegetical, and grammatical analysis would justify (or at least pose the question of) the possibility of an active role for Muḥammad in the process of revelation.

# Bibliography

Al-Bayḍāwī, ʿAbd Allah b.ʿUmar (d. 685/1286). *Anwār al-tanzīl wa-asrār al-ta'wīl*, vol. 2. Beyrouth: Dār al-kutub al-ʿilmiyya, 2003.

Ambros, Arne Amadeus and Stephan Procházka. *A Concise Dictionary of Koranic Arabic*. Wiesbaden: Reichert Verlag, 2004.

Andani, Khalil. *Revelation in Islam: Qur'ānic, Sunni, and Shi'i Ismaili Perspectives*. Harvard: Harvard University, Graduate School of Arts & Sciences, 2020.

Moezzi, Mohammad Amir-Ali and Guillaume Dye, eds. *Le Coran des historiens*. 2 Vols (1; 2A; 2B). Paris: Cerf, 2019.

Bentaibi, Mustapha. *Quelques façons de lire le texte coranique*. Paris: Lambert & Lucas, 2009.

Chabbi, Jacqueline. *Le Coran décrypté*. Paris: Fayard, 2008.

Chabbi, Jacqueline. *Le Seigneur des tribus: L'islam de Mahomet*. Paris: Noêsis, 1997.

Cuypers, Michel. *Le Festin: Une lecture de la sourate al-Mâ'ida*. Paris: Lethielleux, 2007.

Danby, Herbert. *The Mishnah*. London: Oxford University Press, 1933.

Dye, Guillaume. "Lieux saints communs, partagés ou confisqués, aux sources de quelques péricopes coraniques (Q19 : 16-33)." In *Partage du sacré: Transferts, dévotions mixtes, rivalités interconfessionnelles*, edited by Isabelle Depret and Guillaume Dye, 55-121. Brussels: EME Editions, 2012.

Fitzgerald, Michaël. "Islam and Revelation." *Islamochristiana* 4 (1978): 113-25.
Gobillot, Geneviève. "Qur'an and Torah: The Foundations of Intertextuality." In *A History of Jewish-Muslim Relations: From the Origins to the Present Day*, edited by Abdelwahab Meddeb & Bejamin Stora, 611–7. Princeton: Princeton University Press, 2013.
Gril, Denis. "Révélation et inspiration." In *Dictionnaire du Coran*, edited by Mohammad Ali Amir-Moezzi, 749–51. Paris: Robert Laffont, 2007.
Izutsu, Toshihiko. *God and Man in the Qur'ān: Semantics of the Qur'anic Weltanschauung*. 2nd reprint. Kuala Lumpur: Islamic Book Trust, 2008.
Jeffery, Arthur. *The Foreign Vocabulary of the Qur'ān*. Leiden: Brill, 1987.
Kropp, Manfred. "lisān ,arabiyy mubīn – ,Klares Arabisch'?" In *Books and Written Culture of the Islamic World*, edited by Andrew Rippin and Roberto Tottoli, 280–1. Leiden: Brill, 2015.
*Le Coran. Essai de traduction*. Translated by Jacques Berque. Paris: Albin Michel, 1995.
Loynes, Simon P. *Revelation in the Qur'ān: A Semantic Study of the Roots n-z-l and w-ḥ-y*. Leiden: Brill, 2019.
Madigan, Daniel. "Revelation and Inspiration." In *Encyclopedia of the Qur'ān*, vol. 4. Edited by Jane Dammen MacAuliffe, 437–448. Leiden: Brill, 2003.
Masson, Denise. *Monothéisme coranique et monothéisme biblique*. 2nd edition. Paris: Desclée de Brouwer, 1976.
Neuwirth, Angelika. *Studien zur Komposition*. Berlin: Walter de Gruyter, 1981.
Rahman, Fazlur. *Major themes of the Qur'ān*. 2nd edition. Chicago, IL: The University of Chicago, 2009.
Retsö, Jan. *The Arabs in Antiquity: Their History from the Assyrians to the Umayyads*. London: Routledge, 2003.
Reynolds, Gabriel Said. *The Qur'ān and the Bible: Text and Commentary*. New Haven, CT: Yale University Press, 2018.
Sommer, Benjamin David. "Prophecy as Translation: Ancient Israelite Conceptions of the Human Factor in Prophecy," In *From Bringing the Hidden to Light: The Process of Interpretation*, edited by Diane Sharon and Kathryn Kravitz, 271–90. New York: Jewish Theological Seminary, Winona Lake: Eisenbrauns, 2007.
Tengour, Esma Hind. "L'imaginaire dans l'Arabie du VIIe siècle, une topologie du surnaturel." In *Le Coran: De la Tribu à l'Empire: Autour de l'œuvre de Jacqueline Chabbi*, edited by Mehdi Azaiez, 37–54. Louvain-la-Neuve: Presses Universitaires de Louvain, 2023.
*The Qur'ān: A new Annotated Translation*. Translated by Arthur J. Droge. Sheffield: Equinox, 2014.
*The Qur'ān: With a Phrase-by-Phrase English Translation*. Translated by Ali Quli Qarai. Clarksville, MD: Khatoons, 2006.
משניות עם שבע ושלשים הוספות שנוספו על כל המפרשים וההגהות שנדפסו בו עד כה, 13 vols. Consulted online at https://www.sefaria.org/. Vilna [Vilnius]: Romm Widow and Brothers, 1913.

Alain Martial, Florence Draguet, Louis de Brouwer, Pedro Valinho Gomes

# 9 The Respiration of Scripture – Can there be Inspiration without Expiration?

## 1 Introduction

There is a theological problem with the traditional concept of the inspiration of Scripture. It is twofold: on one hand, the traditional concept of inspiration may lead to an inadequate sense of human possession of the truth; on the other hand, paradoxically, inspiration emphasizes an idea of the presence of God that tends to erase the presence of the human witness. In an attempt to address this twofold problem, this paper seeks to incorporate the notion of inspiration into the larger structure of the process of God's revelation. We intend to show that the traditional concept of inspiration is one-sided, and that therefore it must be conceived of alongside the complementary concept of *expiration*. Both concepts together form what we believe to be a more accurate and complete understanding of the process of revelation. This process is what we would like to call the respiration of Scriptures.

Inspiration has often been used as a concept through which communities claimed to know God's truth directly from God's action objectified in the text, with little to no awareness of mediations and their corollary: interpretations. However, (1) epistemologically there is a radical difference between owning the truth, as if we directly possessed God's point of view, and believing in God's truth, from the point of view of the knowledge of faith; and (2) the Scriptures can hardly be defined as God's directly accessible truth, without mediations and human interpretations. As we will see, that is what the incarnation of the Word as well as the history of the churches show us.

In this paper, we shall therefore define as follows the proposed set of concepts:
*Inspiration*: a collective reception of that which the community believes to be God's word, through the fragility and plurality of given testimonies;
*Expiration*: the collective and finite testimony of that which the community believes to have received as God's word;
*Respiration*: the *inseparable dynamic* of inspirations and expirations of these testimonies, inwards and outwards, through which God's self-giving takes place.

To display this structure, in what follows we shall first question, with Karl Barth, the identification of the Scriptures with the word of God, thereby recalling an important warning about any temptation to see inspiration as a confirmation of our own mastery of the truth. Then, once the political aspects of the redaction of the biblical text and the correlative claim of its inspiration have been illustrated through the brief presentation of two examples (1 Tim 2:11–13 and John 21), we will present the biological metaphor of respiration (inspiration and expiration) from which we will draw the elements of a critique of any theological attempt to possess the truth, and we will present the structure of the process of a mediated revelation.

## 2 The canon and the claim of the truth

Who said the Scriptures were inspired? And who can claim it? The simple statement of these questions demonstrates that any talk about inspiration can quickly become a very political question. The history of faith communities has also been one of many divisions and disagreements about what ought or ought not to be considered as inspired in the Scriptures.

Behind this, the real matter at hand concerns the relationship between the Scriptures and the word of God. It is God's word that is ultimately sought by the communities, and the significance of inspiration is to understand in what respect the Scriptures can or cannot be identified with or related to it. We argue here that it would certainly be an undue theological *reductio* to directly identify God with the text. We therefore start by presenting a precise distinction between God's word and the biblical text, before drawing consequences from this initial distinction.

In his *Dogmatics* (§4), Karl Barth proposes the necessary distinction by explaining how, just like the *prophets* or the *apostles*, the Bible is essentially a *witness* of God's revelation. Briefly put, as God is not reduceable or containable, the Bible must not therefore be seen in itself as the pure word of God, but only inasmuch as it orients readers towards God's revelation.[1] Barth conceived of the word of God in three interrelated forms: preached, written, and revealed. Although these forms cannot be separated, they cannot be confused either. Specifically, the insistence of Barth on the distinction between God's revelation ("in the Son," Heb 1:2) and the Scriptures, strongly underlines the aspect of *human and community* interpretation of the Scriptures. And this, along with the refusal of the *reductio* argument about God, is the central point for us. When one comes to scrutinize the Scriptures

---

[1] In the words of Barth: "The Bible [. . .] is not in itself and as such God's past revelation [. . .]. The Bible, speaking to us and heard by us as God's word, bears *witness* to past revelation". Karl Barth, *Church Dogmatics*, vol. I, 1: *The Doctrine of the Word of God*, transl. Geoffrey W. Bromiley, eds. Geoffrey W. Bromiley and Thomas F. Torrance (Edinburgh: T&T Clark, 1975), §4, 117.

closely in their materiality and in the history of their constitution, it can be seen clearly that matters of context, the history of communities, are determinative for the very construction of the texts. The writers are *witnesses*, they are entirely human and work according to their faculties.[2]

Once we accept this starting point of the relationship between Scripture and the word of God, the question of authority over the truth then becomes much clearer. Barth sets himself in direct opposition to past attempts to transform the witnesses into a new sort of hero by giving them undue possession over the divine initiative. On the contrary, if the Bible is to be related to revelation, it is only under God's authority, and not in any way because of a kind of heroic human conquest of the truth. In theology there can be no real, ultimate authority other than God, from whom all other authority is derived.[3] The acceptance of Barth's distinction must therefore change our view of the criteria necessary for claiming the truth. The point is precisely this: we are not the judges of the truth; he who reveals himself is. Indeed, to know God is always first and foremost to be known and loved by him. Hence, according to Barth, this is to be conceived of within the category of an action by God on man: "The Word of God in all its three forms is God's speech to man. For this reason, it occurs, applies and works in *God's act on man*. But as such it occurs in God's way which differs from all other occurrence, i.e., in the mystery of God."[4] To conceive of God's word is to reflect on God's initiative, his sovereign act. And that precludes any position that would forget that God's way is also God's mystery. There is a mystery in the relationship between the interpretation given by the witnesses and God's revelation, a mystery *in the hands of God*.

Now, if we accept that the Scriptures are essentially an interpretation and a witness of revelation, over which God has all authority, we still need a criterion for recognizing their specific status of "word of God," unlike other writings. Can we not count on the fact that the Holy Spirit guides the biblical writers? Certainly. But just as with the distinction made above, this must be understood according to the essential principle that the Holy Spirit is not in our possession. Again, Barth has an interesting way of picturing the action of the Spirit in this context. Rather than providing a justification of the validity of our own assertions about God, his understanding of the Spirit serves instead to affirm just one thing: the Holy Spirit is the one who makes God the true master of the appropriate reception of his word.

---

[2] Moreover, this is also how the gospels picture the fallible action of the disciples around Christ.
[3] As Barth puts it: "Why and in what respect does the biblical witness have authority? Because and in the fact that he claims no authority for himself, that his witness amounts to letting that other itself be its own authority. We thus do the Bible poor and unwelcome honour if we equate it directly with this other, with revelation itself." Barth, *Church Dogmatics*, vol. I, 1, §4, 117.
[4] Barth, *Church Dogmatics*, vol. I, 1, §5, 130, our emphasis.

For Barth, indeed, following the distinctions we have shown, the concurrence of the Bible and revelation can only be an *event*, entirely in the hands of God. This does not at all imply that man is entirely passive in the face of God's action, quite the contrary. But what is at stake is that there is above all a prohibition on claiming to possess the word and the ultimate criteria of its truth and divine origin.

> For what would it imply if we had made, or were in the process of making, that delimitation of the divine from the human? If we could do this, we should have said, or should be saying, what the Word of God is. The goal of all yearning in theology is to be able to do this, but this is the goal of an illegitimate yearning.[5]

Being able to draw the line here would imply placing oneself above God. But this is indeed illegitimate and unnecessary. We have nothing except *confidence* in the testimony of the witnesses and hope in the action of the Holy Spirit. It is never a question of our own certitude.

Why should we then still define a canon and what status can we attribute to the Scriptures? Far from disqualifying them, our reasoning allows us to affirm their essential character for us, but for a different reason that has now been made clear, also highlighted by Barth: the use of the Bible bears witness to the fact that we are not able to obtain the word of God from and by ourselves. There is an essential exteriority to be considered: Holy Scripture is not a kind of deep human reflection, a "Platonic anamnesis,"[6] but a call from the outside, a recollection of God's past revelation, reminding us of God's initiative "simply by the fact that it is the *Canon*."[7] And the canon owes its status precisely to the fact that it presents itself as the *favored memory* of the revelation that has occurred in Christ. A favored memory here means simply a memory that has been favored by the tradition of the communities, not only in the sense that they chose certain narratives instead of others, but also, and mostly, in the sense that they recognized in those narratives a *valuable and reliable testimony of the christological event of revelation*. The canon is therefore in itself already a reference to an exteriority. And it is because the canon is this valuable *testimony* historically recognized by the communities, that these same texts may continue to be received as a rule (i.e., a canon) in new community contexts throughout history, without having to make appeal to a concept of inspiration understood as a quasi-direct discourse from God. Ultimately, the fact that these texts are received as a canon means that the communities have access to something that is not construed by them but rather received and that both recalls and promises God's presence without ever objectifying it. If we accept this favored

---

5 Barth, *Church Dogmatics*, vol. I, 1, §5, 169.
6 Barth, *Church Dogmatics*, vol. I, 1, §4, 106.
7 Barth, *Church Dogmatics*, vol. I, 1, §4, 106, our emphasis.

position, the canon will then first serve as the recognition of an exteriority and a reference for the church, just as Christ is the exteriority and the reference for the canon. It constitutes an instance facing the church as a free authority[8] capable of both challenging the community, and not letting it be left to its own devices.

To summarize the path taken so far, we have shown that the relationship between the Bible and the word of God is simply that of a favored human testimony of Christ's revelation, always in need of placing itself with confidence under the authority of God. Hence, God's action on the human person according to this perspective is no longer that of a special inspiration of heroic women and men who directly (somehow miraculously) possess the truth, but his action lies now solely in the *event*, entirely in his hands, in which his word is "in the becoming,"[9] in that which the community recognizes and believes to be God's word. In the fourth part of our paper, we will further develop our answer to the risk of possessing the truth in the traditional concept of inspiration.

## 3 When the biblical communities claim the truth: The examples of 1 Tim 2 and John 21

Our view of the real and full role of human testimony in revelation permits us now to better understand and accept the political aspects of the Scriptures that we are going to illustrate with two biblical examples. These examples show how difficult the view of a very literal and quasi-unmediated truth of the texts can be, confronted with the concrete political games that presided over the redaction of the Scriptures. Human as they are, the biblical communities were obviously marked by all sorts of limitations and fragilities involved in the life of a community. The writing of the gospels, and indeed of the Bible, is then inescapably impacted by relations of influence and community interests characterised by the temptation to possess the truth.

The first example is from 1 Tim 2. Feminist theologians in recent decades have exposed the patriarchal environment in which texts of the Bible may have been written and/or read. In the book of Genesis, the creation of the woman narrated as occurring after that of the man justified the dominance of the latter over

---

**8** Barth, *Church Dogmatics*, vol. I, 1, §4, 112.
**9** We paraphrase the category used by Eberhard Jüngel in his essential work on Karl Barth: Eberhard Jüngel, *God's Being is in Becoming: The Trinitarian Being of God in the Theology of Karl Barth: A Paraphrase*, trans. John Webster (Grand Rapids, MI: Eerdmans, 2001).

the former.[10] This is how the author of the first letter to Timothy understands it: "A woman must quietly receive instruction with entire submissiveness. But I do not allow a woman to teach or exercise authority over a man, but to remain quiet. For it was Adam who was first created, and then Eve" (1 Tim 2:11–13). And the author insists: "It was not Adam who was deceived by the serpent, but the woman being deceived, fell into transgression" (v. 14). The text totally exonerates Adam, i.e., the man. Now, exegesis has shown that this letter is from a disciple of Paul, written in a social context where the freedom of women could have discredited the early church,[11] and we can see how this socio-political context impacts the author's interpretation of Gen 2. But this vision of the guilty woman has lasted for centuries, therefore shaping tenacious and discriminatory social attitudes, justified by reference to a text seen as inspired, without room for discussion. It thus becomes fairly evident that the theological interpretation of the text cannot dismiss this social context and power games in the name of an uncritical appeal to a divine saying.

A second significant example is chapter 21 of John's gospel. It is now commonly accepted that chapter 21 is primarily ecclesiological.[12] But chapter 20 already offered a conclusion to the book.[13] Why this ecclesiological addition then? The Johannine community pursued a twofold objective: on the one hand, the recognition of the ecclesial function of Peter in order to open the door to the universal church for the Johannine believers; on the other hand, the demonstration of the legitimacy of the fourth gospel within the church.[14] Benoît Standaert offers an interesting insight when he emphasizes that "the ecclesiological question concerns the *inter*-ecclesial dialogue between the Johannine community and the others, those who have the apostle Peter as a reference figure and the three synoptic gospels as

---

10 Gen 2:21–23: "So the LORD God caused a deep sleep to fall upon the man, and he slept; then He took one of his ribs and closed up the flesh at that place. The LORD God fashioned into a woman the rib which He had taken from the man, and brought her to the man. The man said, 'This is now bone of my bones, and flesh of my flesh; She shall be called Woman, Because she was taken out of Man'." All Bible translations come from the NASB 1995 version.

11 For instance: Chantal Reynier, *Les femmes de saint Paul: Collaboratrices de l'apôtre des nations* (Paris: Cerf, 2020).

12 Cf. inter alia Raymond E. Brown, *The Gospel According to John: XIII–XXI*, AB 29A (New York: Doubleday, 1970), 1082; Jean Zumstein, "La rédaction finale de l'évangile selon Jean (à l'exemple du chapitre 21)," in *La communauté johannique et son histoire: La trajectoire de l'évangile de Jean aux deux premiers siècles*, eds. Jean-Daniel Kaestli, Jean Michel Poffet, and Jean Zumstein (Geneva: Labor et Fides, 1990): 222, n. 34.

13 "Jesus performed many other signs in the presence of his disciples, which are not recorded in this book. But these are written that you may believe that Jesus is the Messiah, the Son of God, and that by believing you may have life in his name" (John 20:30–31).

14 Cf. inter alia Jean Zumstein, *L'évangile selon saint-Jean (13–21)*, CNT 4b (Geneva: Labor et Fides, 2007), 301-2.

a scriptural authority."[15] Indeed, according to this author, chapter 21 consists of an *apologia pro vita sua* of the Johannine community which is addressed to other Christian communities with the true aim of being welcomed by them. However, this apology does not only concern the last chapter of the gospel; it is to be found throughout the whole gospel. Consistently, the author insists, for example, on the desire for unity: "that all may be one" is repeated insistently in Jesus' great prayer in chapter 17 (vv. 11, 21, 22, 23); in chapter 10, Jesus mentions the desire that "there will be one flock with one shepherd" (10:16); the net drawn by Peter alone will not be torn (21:11b) and "the seamless tunic, woven in one piece" should not be torn (19:23–24).

Furthermore, according to Standaert, the synoptic data is reworked throughout the whole gospel and the text is written to show that the Johannine community has an authentic witness as its founder, who knew Jesus personally and before Peter. Therefore, it has its own privileged access to the origin, precisely through their witness who was there from the beginning and until the end.[16] To give just one illustration, in chapter 21, John recognizes Jesus directly on the shore: "It is the Lord!" (John 21:7). This contrasts with Peter's hesitation in Matt 14: "Lord, if it is you..." (Matt 14:28). Peter doubts, while the beloved disciple does not.[17] Once again, a valid reception of this chapter cannot claim to interpret it only with reference to God's action in the text, without referring to the social context and inter-community power games that are essential for understanding it.

Both these examples, from Genesis read by the author of the first letter to Timothy and from the fourth gospel, show first and foremost that the biblical texts cannot be read naively as a direct inspiration from God, and that their own interpretations of revelation can be criticized. When considering the canon as a whole (with each book and even each redacting trend in a particular book able to complement and correct another), a theological reading of the text can easily recognize that no single community can contain and possess the whole truth about God and human life.[18] The political games within the canon prevent us in fact from using the

---

**15** "La problématique ecclésiologique concerne le dialogue inter-ecclésial entre la communauté johannique et les autres, celles qui ont l'apôtre Pierre comme figure de référence et les trois évangiles synoptiques comme autorité scripturaire." Benoît Standaert, *Nouvelle approche du quatrième évangile: L'enjeu inter-ecclésial de son édition et les implications pour tout dialogue* (Rome: Studia Anselmiana, 2020), 29.
**16** Cf. the four main principles summarising the position of the so-called Johannine community: Standaert, *Nouvelle approche du quatrième évangile*, 19.
**17** Cf. Standaert, *Nouvelle approche du quatrième évangile*, 32.
**18** As Benoît Standaert points out: "C'est en tendant la seule corde johannique sur la harpe de tous ces écrits [de la Bible], eux-mêmes relus et commentés par la grande Tradition, qu'on réussira à tempérer le caractère absolu de certains dires contenus dans ce récit évangélique," in Standaert,

concept of inspiration as a general argument to claim the truth for one community or another. On the other hand, these political games at work in the biblical text allow us also to enlarge our understanding of the structure of revelation through such fragile and even contradictory "expirations" that make up these very human testimonies, as we will develop below.

Finally, all this forces us in fact to accept that the churches simply have the task of recognizing what they believe to be God's word, as per our definition of inspiration, under God's sole authority. This is the first part of our argument, and the first protective barrier we see against undue possession of the truth. But a further step is needed. Indeed, so far our view could still remain trapped in a form of static acceptance of a past favored testimony, repeating therefore in a different way the risks of political possession of the truth, and denying again to women and men of all time their role of participating in the reception of God's revelation in Christ. In order to show the living character of revelation and the dynamic movement of the testimonies, in order to definitively recognize God's mastery of the truth, we need to describe now the whole structure of the *respiration of the Scriptures*, and in particular the concept of expiration.

## 4 The expiration of the witnesses and the respiration of the word

Practical experience teaches that never-ending inspiration surely leads to suffocation. As we have shown before, the theological equivalent to such suffocation could be seen in a certain doctrine of divine inspiration that colonizes the whole process of God's communication to humankind, leaving little to no space for the concrete reality of interpretation, processing, and translation into human words of the very event that is experienced as revelation. And such a doctrine leads to the risk of an undue assertion of possession of the truth.

As such, the concept is, we argue, theologically and historically incorrect, because it is incomplete. There is indeed a difference between the event of revelation and what the biblical author is able to take in from it; there is also a difference between what the biblical author was able to take in (inspiration) from the event of revelation and what he is able to give out (expiration) from this event; there is a difference between what the biblical author is able to give out and what, from this, the reader is

---

*Nouvelle approche du quatrième évangile*, 340. What Standaert says about the Gospel of John can of course be said of all the books of the biblical corpus.

able to take in. The cycle then goes on, in and out, inspiring and expiring, in a dynamic that sets the scene for revelation to occur in communities throughout history. We will now explore further elements concerning the notion of the respiration of the Scriptures that should help us to avoid any undue claim to possession of the truth, namely the dialogical movement of revelation and interpretation in the act of reading and writing the biblical text.

There is certainly a theological specificity to the biblical text as a language event. The Bible is a text like any other, and at the same time a text like no other. The claim that God offers himself to language marks its specificity. But what does it mean to say that God offers himself to language? Saying that God speaks to the human person precisely through the words by which the human person speaks of God and to God represents a hermeneutical crux calling for interpretation. The fact that this hermeneutical crux has always been a cause of theological embarrassment can be traced in the long process of the definition of the biblical canon. As mentioned above, the idea of a verbal inspiration of the Bible does not stand up to exegetical work on the text and the theological categories it allows. Clearly, the biblical author is not a stenographer. The exegesis of the text forces us to admit that the idea of a literal inspiration "was a childish projection."[19] But even a subtler concept of inspiration applied to the Bible at large must be received with caution: one should identify the truth neither with the biblical formulations about the truth nor with the Bible itself as a whole.

This does not mean, however, a denial of the specificity of the biblical canon. The value of the canon does not depend on a supposed divine origin but on the fact that the text, as a language event, mediates God's revelation. For biblical theology, the author of the text is less relevant than the mediation of the text. Far more than the definition of the author and successive editors of a biblical text, establishing the text as a platform of mediation represents a priority task for a critical theological hermeneutic.

*Expiration* is therefore key: the biblical text is the type of language event that can be defined as a *witness* to revelation. The temptation of objectifying the word of God in the text and justifying this option with a particular idea of divine inspiration, only contributed ironically to a mythologization[20] of the very concept of revelation,

---

[19] Hans-Cristoph Askani, "Les enjeux du canon: Réponse à Pierre Gisel," *ETR* 95 (2020): 199. Denying the specificity of the canon because of the absence of a supernatural origin would however be as childish an argument as claiming to justify its value on the basis of such an origin.

[20] We argue that a certain traditional conceptualisation of inspiration contributes to a confusion of the word of God with the biblical text. On this, Bultmann's project of demythologization could be helpful to the understanding of our proposal. Following Bultmann, we could say that the primary goal of the encounter with the text is not a historical discernment of the truth of the events narrat-

as if God's self-communication was something ethereal, without historical grounding. A theology of the mediations of the word – capable, therefore, of working with the text as a mediation of something that is always beyond the objectifications of the text, but which can only be conceived of on the basis of these mediations – is preferable to a doctrine of revelation without mediations. In fact, the biblical text, as a witness to revelation, points to a certain irreducibility of the origin of the text.

What this implies is that the word of God is always offered through the mediation of a finite word of a finite witness. And it is only in the process of this mediation (i.e., an expiration) that the text may ultimately become the word of God. The *Deus dixit* is always truly a *testis dixit Deum dicere* (i.e., a "a witness said that God says"); and ultimately this *testis dixit Deum dicere* may open the space for a *Deus dixit*. It is the respiration of the Scriptures: inspiration and expiration.

In this approach, the text remains a means that God uses for his self-communication. And it can be said to be *inspired*, in the sense that the reading communities recognize in it what they believe to be God's word, expressed by the writing communities in their finitude. But this recognition is to be expressed and *expired* anew by these same reading communities, who are themselves called to be witnesses (ethically and kerygmatically, by their life and preaching). This whole process is therefore characterized by the finitude of all these communities, which prevents them from claiming possession of the word. By accepting this formulation, it will thus be possible to overcome a certain theological distrust of the category of testimony, as if human witnesses were completely incapable of becoming a word that signifies God. Even without appealing to a supposed divine authorship of the text, even taking a view of the Bible as an entirely human witness and admitting that the canonization of the texts is a historical decision that could ultimately have led to a very different conclusion, it is still possible to look at the biblical text as the

---

ed, but the existential orientation of the one who is confronted with the kerygma announced in the text. Through the text, God speaks, in the present, to the reader of the text. The word of God inhabits human words, even if it cannot be identified with them. But that the word inhabits the words is what can be understood by faith and should not be taken as a presupposition for hermeneutical work. This is how Bultmann explains it in a letter to Karl Barth: "It is misleading to equate the NT and the Word of God when discussing the methodological problem of NT hermeneutics. The Word of God is spoken in the human word and the NT stands before us as a literary record of history. Can it be interpreted otherwise than according to general hermeneutical rules? That it is God's Word cannot be made a presupposition from which to deduce hermeneutical rules of a different kind. It can show itself to be God's Word, and therefore validate itself, only in the event of believing understanding" – letter of Rudolf Bultmann to Karl Barth (Marburg, 11–15 November 1952), Bernd Jaspert, ed. *Karl Barth/Rudolph Bultmann Letters 1922–1966*, transl. and re-ed. Geoffrey William Bromiley (Grand Rapids, MI: Eerdmans, 1982), 153–4. This is actually not foreign to Barth's thought, even if there are nuances in their approaches that account for their differences.

place where the witness to God's word gives way to a *Deus dixit* (which, more than a statement on the content of God's saying is really the affirmation of the presence of God's revelatory event).[21]

This approach to the word of God through the witness leads us to be critical about any supposed mastery of the truth by the author and the reader of the biblical text, even beyond the already justified critique of a supposed literal truth of any of the texts of the Bible. The text, even as a whole, is not the word, but a witness to the word, i.e., in itself a process of reception, translation and offering. It is an expiration of something inspired and, in a sense, that inspires others, who then in turn may become the place of mediation of revelation through a new expiration. Neither the biblical author, as the witness of revelation, nor his reader, as the witness of the witness (and therefore witness of revelation as well), have words to contain the word, which is in "the becoming" in this process. Containing would mean inspiring until suffocation. Respiration is needed.

On what grounds do we suggest such a conceptualization? Is there any good reason to complement the so widely used concept of inspiration this way? We argue that, if we take seriously the starting point of Christian theology, our proposition is largely warranted in Christology itself. This is so not only because the process of revelation that we have described is entirely oriented from and towards the word of God revealed *in Christ*, as we showed before; what we describe as the respiration of the Scriptures is indeed more generally the respiration of *revelation*, rooted in the event of the incarnation of Christ, not only the master of the truth, but the truth himself (John 14:6). Even more relevant for our development, we argue that Christology shows *the* model of respiration and the true reality of God's revelation through the *in-carnation* of the word and its *ex-piration* on the cross, leading to resurrection, the gift of the Spirit and thereafter the life of the churches.

By understanding revelation through the lens of the cross, we may confirm that the process of God's self-communication occurs in particular through the expiration of the very word of God. The passion of Christ precisely highlights the conflicting politics at the heart of the revelatory process, and the dangers of possessing the truth (leading for example to the violent death of Christ himself). And it shows at its climax the true witness of God, expiring on the cross: καὶ κλίνας τὴν κεφαλὴν παρέδωκεν τὸ πνεῦμα (John 19:30b). The verb παραδίδωμι has here the meaning both of expiring and of giving, transmitting. So, the Word of God in flesh, receiving himself from the Father gives himself on the cross, as the true testimony of God. This was already visible in Christ's teaching: "I declare what I have seen in the Father's presence" (John 8:38), but this radical expiration on the cross takes us a

---

[21] Cf. Askani, "Les enjeux du canon," 205.

step further in the understanding of what it means to mediate the truth. In this conception, the witness par excellence (who is nothing less than the truth) is the one who lives a radical dispossession, until the final expiration that opens the future and leads to something new. The process is not one of sacralization as a traditional notion of inspiration would suggest; on the contrary, the process is one of dispossession, as Christology teaches, a process of making oneself available while being unavailable (that is, radically unobjectifiable) and opening the way to interpretation.

A theological phenomenology of revelation needs to recognize that revelation occurs for us in the process of its mediations. It accepts the contradictory politics around Christ, preserving God's action through the whole process of respiration by not taking as an absolute the human mediations, but by being absolutely centered in Christ's mastery of the truth. God is then mysteriously present in the inspirations and the expirations of the testimonies but only in the way described in John's gospel with the simultaneous distinction of the Son and the Father ("The Father is greater than I" [John 14:28]) and their paradoxical unity ("The Father and I are one" [John 10:30]).[22]

This process that we have described christologically is also at work in the words and actions of the primary witnesses of Christ, whose testimonies precede logically the writing of the Scriptures. All their testimonies take the form of a "receiving-transmitting" respiration: "I handed on to you [. . .] what I in turn had received" (1 Cor 15:3); "We declare to you what was from the beginning, what we have heard, what we have seen with our eyes, what we have looked at and touched with our hands, concerning the word of life" (1 John 1:1). No-one has the final word, whatever their importance may have been in the communities.

We are certainly aware that some references from the Scriptures were formulated in a way that easily led to the traditional interpretation of the concept of inspiration that we criticize here (cf. 2 Tim 3:15–17; 1 Thess 2:13; Gal 1:11–12; 1 Cor 14:36–38). The discussion of these examples is outside the scope of our work, but we argue nonetheless that they can be interpreted in a broader sense than that of a literal inspiration, because (1) they take on their full meaning in reference to the Word of God who is Christ, the real gospel, and (2), precisely following our own conception (that is no less based on the biblical Scriptures), these examples should not be interpreted as literal objectifications of eternal truths.

---

[22] We can note that this paradoxical unity is also the source of the distinction made above between the word of God revealed in Christ and written in the Scriptures.

## 5 The concept of respiration vis-a-vis contemporary theological reinterpretations of inspiration

Contemporary theology has proposed reinterpretations of the traditional concept of inspiration (and *Dei Verbum* actually both assembles and promotes some of these interpretations). We would like now to justify in what sense our proposal offers a relevant conceptual gain, by referring to one of these significant attempts proposed by Christoph Theobald, who suggests a conceptual shift in the notion of inspiration. Theobald observes a contemporary indifference toward the idea of inspiration among biblical scholars, as well as a change in the status of the Bible, now seen as a cultural object, a "classic" like any other, with a "democratized" access, to which therefore a plural methodology of reading and analysis is applied as to any other classic. He situates his reflection in the contemporary context, but the implications of what he sees can be generalized to any different historical context because it is theologically rooted in the very process of the reception of revelation, which is essential to the mediations that we have highlighted before.

Theobald, concerned with accounting for a theological understanding that takes seriously this multiplicity of contemporary receptions of the biblical text, essentially suggests that the concept of inspiration should no longer be related to the text in its cultural materiality, but rather to the effects of meaning that it produces in and among its readers.[23] Seen in the context of the reception of that which Jesus delivered to his people and in such a way as to make the effect of that reception possible, the concept of inspiration for Theobald becomes a way of pronouncing "*the relationship between a certain type of writing and the reading that is immediately linked to it*, a relationship that is itself totally informed by Jesus' *way* of making reception possible."[24]

In a way that is not far from our own reconceptualization of the notion, Theobald therefore sees inspiration as a dynamic movement, which is centered in these effects of meaning produced by the reading, and which leads it to be experienced as "inspiring" according to the situation of the various readers. As Theobald puts it: "it is not the book itself that is inspired, but the *relationship of reception* that we

---

[23] Cf. Christoph Theobald, « *Dans les traces...* » *de la constitution « Dei Verbum » du concile Vatican II: Bible, théologie et pratiques de lecture*, Cogitatio Fidei 270 (Paris : Cerf, 2009), 64.
[24] Theobald, « *Dans les traces...* », 72. Thus, for Theobald, the concept of inspiration would ultimately suggest a set of sufficiently strict conditions governing a specific type of writing and reading. We will not develop this aspect of his thought here.

can engage with; it is inspired insofar as it never ceases to inspire us."[25] This movement applies even when approaching the biblical text as a work like any other. Whatever the case, it is only in a process of appropriating the effects produced by the text (which implies the transformation of one's way of perceiving) that one may come to recognize the revelation mediated in the text. As a consequence, the fact that such a recognition results from a process of appropriation that allows anyone who has become a reader of the Bible to arrive at its acclamation as the word of God (1) precludes an understanding of inspiration confined to the letter of the text or identified directly with the divinely enlightened intention of the author or the text's canonising agents; (2) it also underlines the fact that every path of access to the Scripture as *verbum Dei* is inhabited by a hermeneutical moment. This means taking seriously the creative potential that runs through any process of reception of the text, a process that is never reducible to a passive act of conservation.

We could also add that, just as in our conceptualisation, Theobald maintains in this itinerary of reading the question of an opening up to an exteriority, i.e., God's self-communication. And this exteriority is mediated by what we have called a *favored memory* that becomes the mark demonstrating that the communities are not a law unto themselves, for "the Scripture and the early church which established it already exist, and [...] any subsequent birth of the church in any country is already preceded by them."[26]

In our view, the reconceptualization of inspiration by Theobald highlights in its own way one essential feature of the process of revelation that we described: by displacing the focus from the materiality of the text and by refocusing on the effects on the reader, it avoids any attempt at objectifying the truth, understanding God's self-communication as something that is never possessable. However, it seems to us that the full extent of the understanding of God should in fact take us well beyond what the concept of inspiration, historically charged, is able to contain. To deploy all the consequences of this necessary conceptual shift would mean going beyond a mere reinterpretation of the concept of inspiration (limited also by the history of its meaning). In particular, this shift must conceptualize to its full extent the dynamic of active *testimonies* that we have characterized as expirations.

---

[25] Christoph Theobald, *Le christianisme comme style*, vol. 2: *Une manière de faire la théologie en postmodernité*, Cogitatio Fidei 261 (Paris: Cerf, 2008), 643.
[26] Theobald, *Le christianisme comme style*, vol. 2, 72.

## 6 Conclusion

The concept of respiration represents a conceptual device that accounts for the divine initiative of revelation without evaporating all the space that the witnesses have in the process as mediators (and by witnesses we mean both writers and readers), introducing a fragility and a plurality in the very process of affirming God's word. Rooting our argument in Christology, we have shown that the respiration of Scriptures (and of revelation) is a conceptual scheme able to respond to the limitations and ambiguities found around the traditional concept of inspiration. If *inspiration* is taken as a collective reception of that which, through the fragility and plurality of given testimonies, the community believes to be God's word; if *expiration* refers to the collective and finite testimony of that which the community believes to have received as God's word; and if *respiration* is understood as the *inseparable dynamic* of the inspirations and expirations of these testimonies through which God's self-communication takes place; then we have a more complete conceptual referent, also capable of accounting for Theobald's reinterpretation of the concept of inspiration (and others in contemporary theology, even in their differences).

Specifically, this conceptual referent addresses the twofold problem we highlighted in our introduction: on one hand, it ensures that the truth (which, from a Christian believer's point of view, is ultimately Christ, the revealed Word of God) is never objectifiable nor possessable (neither in parts of the Bible, nor in the Bible as a whole) and is only in the hands of God, who alone is in control of his self-communication even when his self-communication is mediated; on the other hand, the conceptual referent of the respiration of the Scriptures recognizes that God's self-communication is mediated by the presence of the human witnesses (in their fragilities, amidst their social tensions and political games, etc.) without indulging in mythological schemes to account for such a complex dialogue between God and human beings. This is ensured by the essential addition of the *expiration* of the *witnesses*, rooted in the theology of the cross. Radical dispossession opens the way to resurrection. There cannot be inspiration without expiration. God's self-communication through and in human testimonies may better be described as the *respiration of the Scriptures*.

## Bibliography

Askani, Hans-Cristoph. "Les enjeux du canon. Réponse à Pierre Gisel." *ETR* 95 (2020): 197–206.
Barth, Karl. *Church Dogmatics*, vol. I, 1: *The Doctrine of the Word of God*. Translated by Geoffrey W. Bromiley, edited by Geoffrey W. Bromiley and Thomas F. Torrance. Edinburgh: T&T Clark, 1975.
Brown, Raymond E. *The Gospel According to John: XIII–XXI*. AB 29A. New York: Doubleday, 1970.
Jaspert, Bernt, ed. *Karl Barth/Rudolph Bultmann Letters 1922–1966*. Translated and re-edited by Geoffrey William Bromiley. Grand Rapids, MI: Eerdmans, 1982.
Jüngel, Eberhard. *God's Being is in Becoming: The Trinitarian Being of God in the Theology of Karl Barth: A Paraphrase*. Translated by John Webster. Grand Rapids, MI: Eerdmans, 2001.
Reynier, Chantal. *Les femmes de saint Paul: Collaboratrices de l'apôtre des nations*. Paris: Cerf, 2020.
Standaert, Benoît. *Nouvelle approche du quatrième évangile: L'enjeu inter-ecclésial de son édition et les implications pour tout dialogue*. Rome: Studia Anselmiana, 2020.
Theobald, Christoph. *Le christianisme comme style*, vol. 2: *Une manière de faire la théologie en postmodernité*. Cogitatio Fidei 261. Paris: Cerf, 2008.
Theobald, Christoph. *« Dans les traces... » de la constitution « Dei Verbum » du concile Vatican II: Bible, théologie et pratiques de lecture*. Cogitatio Fidei 270. Paris: Cerf, 2009.
Zumstein, Jean. "La rédaction finale de l'évangile selon Jean (à l'exemple du chapitre 21)." In *La communauté johannique et son histoire: La trajectoire de l'évangile de Jean aux deux premiers siècles*, edited by Jean-Daniel Kaestli, Jean Michel Poffet, and Jean Zumstein, 207–30. Geneva: Labor et Fides, 1990.
Zumstein, Jean. *L'évangile selon saint-Jean (13–21)*. CNT 4b. Geneva: Labor et Fides, 2007.

# List of Abbreviations

## Bible translations

| | |
|---|---|
| KJV | King James Version |
| NASB | New American Standard Bible |
| NEB | New English Bible |
| NJPS | Tanakh: The Holy Scriptures: The New JPS Translation according to the Traditional Hebrew Text |
| NRSV | New Revised Standard Version |
| RSV | Revised Standard Version |

## Collections and journals

| | |
|---|---|
| AARTTS | American Academy of Religion Texts and Translations Series |
| AB | Anchor Bible |
| ACCS | Ancient Christian Commentary on Scripture |
| ANTC | Abingdon New Testament Commentaries |
| AYBRL | Anchor Yale Bible Reference Library |
| BETL | Bibliotheca Ephemeridum Theologicarum Lovaniensium |
| BJS | Brown Judaic Studies |
| BZAW | Beihefte zur Zeitschrift für die alttestamentliche Wissenschaft |
| CahRB | Cahiers De La Revue Biblique |
| *CBQ* | *Catholic Biblical Quarterly* |
| CCSL | Corpus Christianorum Series Latina |
| CNT | Commentaire du Nouveau Testament |
| ConBOT | Coniectanea Biblica: Old Testament Series |
| CRINT | Compendia rerum Iudaicarum ad Novum Testamentum |
| CSHJ | Chicago Studies in the History of Judaism |
| *ETR* | *Études théologiques et religieuses* |
| *EvT* | *Evangelische Theologie* |
| FAT | Forschungen zum Alten Testament |
| GNT | Grundrisse zum Neuen Testament |
| *HTR* | *Harvard Theological Review* |
| ICC | International Critical Commentary |
| ISBL | Indiana Studies in Biblical Literature |
| IVS | International Voices in Biblical Studies |
| *JAJ* | *Journal of Ancient Judaism* |
| JBC | Jerome Biblical Commentary |
| *JJS* | *Journal of Jewish Studies* |
| *JR* | *Journal of Religion* |
| JSNTsup | Journal for the study of the New Testament Supplement Series |
| JSOTSup | Journal for the Study of the Old Testament Supplement Series |
| *JSP* | *Journal for the Study of the Pseudepigrapha* |

| | |
|---|---|
| *JSJ* | *Journal for the Study of Judaism* |
| *JTS* | *Journal of Theological Studies* |
| KEK | Kritisch-exegetischer Kommentar über das Neue Testament |
| LCL | Loeb Classical Library |
| NCBC | New Cambridge Bible Commentary |
| NICNT | New International Commentary on the New Testament |
| NJBC | The New Jerome Biblical Commentary |
| NSKAT | Neuer Stuttgarter Kommentar, Altes Testament |
| NTG | New Testament Guides |
| NTL | New Testament Library |
| *NTS* | *New Testament Studies* |
| OBO | Orbis Biblicus et Orientalis |
| OSHT | Oxford Studies in Historical Theology |
| OTL | Old Testament Library |
| QD | Quaestiones Disputatae |
| RBS | Resources for Biblical Study |
| *RelSoc* | *Religion and Society* |
| *RSPT* | *Revue des Sciences philosophiques et théologiques* |
| *RSR* | *Recherches de Science Religieuse* |
| SAA | State Archives of Assyria |
| SB | Sources bibliques |
| SBL | Society of Biblical Literature |
| SBLSP | Society of Biblical Literature Seminar Papers |
| SBL.SCS | Society of Biblical Literature, Septuagint and Cognate Studies |
| SBS | Stuttgarter Bibelstudien |
| SP | Sacra Pagina |
| TBN | Themes in Biblical Narrative |
| *TC* | *Textual Criticism* |
| TThSt | *Trierer theologische Studien* |
| TUGAL | Texte und Untersuchungen zur Geschichte der altchristlichen Literatur |
| *VT* | *Vetus Testamentum* |
| VTSup | Supplements to Vetus Testamentum |
| WBC | Word Biblical Commentary |
| *ZAW* | *Zeitschrift für die alttestamentliche Wissenschaft* |
| ZBK | Zürcher Bibelkommentare |
| *ZTK* | *Zeitschrift für Theologie und Kirche* |

## List of Contributors

**Emmanuel Durand**, o.p., Professor of Systematic Theology at the University of Fribourg (Switzerland)

**Konrad Schmid**, Professor of Hebrew Bible and Ancient Judaism at the University of Zürich

**Matthieu Richelle**, Professor of Old Testament at the UCLouvain

**Benoît Bourgine**, Professor of Systematic Theology at the UCLouvain

**Mark W. Elliott**, Professor of Biblical and Historical Theology and Head of Research, University of the Highlands and Islands, and Professorial Fellow, Wycliffe College, Toronto

**Benjamin D. Sommer**, Professor of Bible and Ancient Semitic Languages at the The Jewish Theological Seminary, New York

**Régis Burnet**, Professor of New Testament at the UCLouvain

**Mehdi Azaiez**, Professor of Islamic Studies at the UCLouvain

**Alain Martial, Florence Draguet, Louis de Brouwer, Pedro Valinho Gomes:** doctoral students at the UCLouvain.

# Index of Ancient and Modern Authors

Abraham, William 97
Albrektson, Bertil 104
Alexander, Philip 154
Alter, Robert 111, 117
Ambros, Arne 178
Ambrosius Catherinus, Aurelius (Lancelotto Politi) 160
Amir, Yehoyada 107, 108
Andani, Khalil 167, 179
Anderson, Gary 108, 134
Aquinas, Thomas 19, 25, 85, 88, 91–94, 96
Aratos 159
Aristotle 25, 87, 137
Askani, Hans-Christoph 191, 193
Assel, Heinrich 89
Assmann, Jan 27
Athenagoras 151
Auerbach, Erich 77
Augustine 43, 157, 158
Azaiez, Mehdi 1, 6, 167, 176

Baden, Joel 122, 124, 135
Balthasar, Hans Urs von 19, 86, 87, 96
Baras, Dan 121
Bardaisan 151
Barnabas 151, 152
Barry, Gerald 103
Barth, Karl 4, 6, 54, 68, 69, 105, 183–187, 192
Bartor, Assnat 116
Batnitzky, Leora 110
Bauckham, Richard 148, 149
Bauer, Thomas 33
Baumgartner, Walter 116
Bede the Venerable 157–159
Bengel, Johann 160
Benjamin, Walter 57
Ben-Sasson, Hillel 127
Bentaibi, Mustapha 171
Berlejung, Angelika 27
Berque, Jacques 176
Beyerle, Stefan 84
Bigman, David 107
Birmelé, André 42
Blachère, Régis 177, 178

Blake, William 102
Blanchard, Yves-Marie 19
Bland, Kalman 108
Blondel, Maurice 93
Blum, Erhard 122
Bogaert, Pierre-Maurice 66
Bourgine, Benoît 1, 4, 54, 56, 74, 75, 88
Braulik, George 84
Breed, Brennan 51
Brettler, Marc 138
Breuer, Mordechai 112
Briggs, Charles 111, 116, 118
Brosend, William 149
Brown, David 103, 137
Brown, Francis 111, 116, 118
Brown, Raymond 162, 163, 188
Buber, Martin 106–108, 111, 113
Bührer, Walter 32
Bullinger, Heinrich 159, 160
Bultmann, Rudolph 191, 192
Burnet, Régis 1, 6, 157
Burrus, Virginia 156

Calmet, Augustin 160, 161
Calvin, John 93, 159, 160
Caputo, John 23
Carasik, Michael 116, 117, 126
Carpenter, Joseph 122
Carr, David 122
Carroll, John 147
Cassuto, Umberto 117
Chabbi, Jacqueline 169–171, 177
Childs, Brevard 86, 90, 91, 113, 128
Clement of Alexandria 151, 152
Cohen, Hermann 102, 104, 110, 125, 130
Cohon, Samuel 26
Collins, John 84
Commodian 151
Congar, Yves 93, 137
Corriente, Federico 177
Crüsemann, Frank 128
Cuypers, Michel 172, 173
Cyprian 152

Davids, Peter 150
Davies, Brian 85
De Brouwer, Louis 6
De La Potterie, Ignace 21
De Lubac, Henri 20
De Lugo, Juan 95
De Vio, Thomas (Cajetan) 158–160
DeSilva, David 150
Dillmann, August 116, 122
Donelson, Lewis 150
Dorff, Elliot 106, 120
Dozeman, Thomas 122
Draguet, Florence 6
Drey, Johann 86
Driver, Samuel 103, 111, 116, 118, 122, 124, 130
Droge, Arthur 168, 170, 177, 178
Dulles, Avery 94, 103, 104
Duns Scotus 85
Durand, Emmanuel 2, 3, 13, 16, 17, 42, 46–48, 54, 56
Dye, Guillaume 175

Ebeling, Gerhard 42
Eichhorn, Johann 161
Eisen, Arnold 110, 120
Elliott, Mark 2, 4, 5
Enns, Peter 103, 138
Epimenides 159
Erasmus, Desiderius 158
Erlewine, Robert 102, 104, 125
Eskola, Timo 84
Eusebius of Caesarea 155, 156
Even-Chen, Alexander 106–109, 120

Fabry, Heinz-Josef 134
Fackenheim, Emil 104
Farkasfalvy, Denis 21
Fehr, Wayne 86
Fischer, Georg 27
Fishbane, Michael 26, 27, 74
Fitzgerald, Michaël 168
Fitzmyer, Joseph 162, 163
Fowl, Stephen 97
Fox, Michael 34
Frankel, Zacheriah 110
Franzelin, Johannes 94, 95

Freedman, David 151
Fuller, Reginald 162

Gadamer, Hans-Georg 5
Garrigou-Lagrange, Réginald 95
Geldhof, Joris 90
Geller, Stephen 103, 124, 126
Gerstenberger, Erhard 27
Gertz, Jan 122
Gesundheit, Shimon 26, 115
Giangreco, Rosalia 36
Gilliot, Claude 177
Gillman, Neil 105, 106, 120
Glatzer, Nahum 106, 110
Gobillot, Geneviève 172
Goldingay, John 58
Goodman, Micah 108
Goshen-Gottstein, Alon 137
Gottlieb, Michah 101
Gourgues, Michel 13, 14
Green, Joel 147
Greenberg, Moshe 130
Greenstein, Edward 135
Gril, Denis 167, 168
Grünstäudl, Wolfgang 151, 155
Guardini, Romano 91, 93
Günther, Anton 93

Hakohen, Ẓadok 107
Haran, Menahem 122
Harford-Battersby, George 122
Harrington, Daniel 138, 161
Ḥazzequni 114
Heinemann, Isaac 110
Held, Shai 104, 108, 121
Hendel, Ronald 112, 125
Henry, Michel 15
Heschel, Abraham 5, 102–110, 117, 119–121, 136, 148
Hirsch, Eric Jr., 137
Hirsch, Samson 113, 117
Hodge, Archibald 93
Hofius, Otfried 84
Homer 76, 77
Hultin, Jeremy 150
Hutner, Isaac 107

Ibn Ezra  116, 117, 126, 129, 130
Ibn Kathīr  177
Idel, Moshe  105
Irenaeus of Lyon  151, 152
Izutsu, Toshihiko  169, 171

Jacobs, Andrew  156
Jacobs, Jonathan  87
Jacobs, Louis  106–107, 120
Japhet, Sara  134
Jeffery, Arthur  178
Jerome  21, 43, 156, 158, 162
Johnson, Luke  147, 162
Joosten, Jan  134
Joseph, Simon  151
Josephus, Flavius  32, 33, 152
Joüon, Paul  114
Jullien, François  58
Jüngel, Eberhard  187
Just, Arthur  147
Justin Martyr  151

Kalimi, Isaac  26
Kaplan, Lawrence  109
Kasher, Menahem  116, 117
Kasper, Walter  90
Kearns, Conleth  162
Kellner, Menachem  109
Kepnes, Steven  108, 110
Kieckhefer, Richard  124
Kilby, Karen  23
Kimelman, Reuven  105
Klawans, Jonathan  85
Klein, Hans  147
Kleutgen, Joseph  93
Knohl, Israel  134
Koehler, Ludwig  27, 116
Kook, Abraham  107
Kornfeld, Walter  134
Kraftchick, Steven  149
Kropp, Manfred  177
Krüger, Thomas  111, 129, 130
Kugel, James  86
Kurzweil, Zvi  110

Lacoste, Jean-Yves  92
Lactantius  152

Landsberger, Benno  34
Langstaff, Beth  159
Lee, William  103
Legaspi, Michael  1
Lenzi, Alan  129
Lessing, Gotthold  93
Levenson, Jon  26
Levering, Matthew  90, 97, 98
Levin, Christoph  28
Levinson, Bernard  72–75
Lim, Timothy  85
Loewenstamm, Samuel  124, 129
Lohfink, Norbert  28, 74, 84
Lorberbaum, Yair  136
Loynes, Simon  167
Lucifer of Cagliari  155
Luther, Martin  25, 92, 113, 159

Madigan, Daniel  168
Mahnke, Allan  128
Maimonides  102, 108, 109, 112, 115, 121, 130, 131
Mäkipelto, Ville  45
Marion, Jean-Luc  92
Martial, Alain  6
Masson, Denise  168
McCord Adams, Marilyn  85
McDonald, Hugh  102–104
Meinhold, Arndt  34
Meir, Ephraim  107
Menander  159
Mendelssohn, Moses  101, 113, 135
Merleau-Ponty, Maurice  15
Mettinger, Tryggve  124
Milgrom, Jacob  85
Miller, Patrick  128
Mirsky, Yehudah  136
Montag, John  91, 92, 94
Moore, Nicholas  156
Mroczek, Eva  4, 59–61
Muraoka, Takamitsu  114
Murphy, Mark  85
Murphy, Roland  162, 163

Naḥmanides  114, 128
Najman, Hindy  4, 57, 58, 115
Neuwirth, Angelika  176
Neyrey, Jerome  149, 151, 161

Nicholls, Aidan 87
Nicholson, Ernest 128
Nickelsburg, George 150, 151, 154
Nicklas, Tobias 151, 155
Nienhuis, David 154
Noth, Martin 117

O'Collins, Gerald 93–96
O'Meara, Thomas 91
Oeming, Manfred 32
Orchard, Bernard 162
Origen 69, 96, 152
Orr, James 103
Ovid 29

Pannenberg, Wolfhart 42, 104
Paulsen, Henning 150, 151
Perlman, Lawrence 109
Perrone, Giovanni 94
Philo of Alexandria 152
Plato 25, 76, 186
Preston, Patrick 160
Priscillian 156
Procházka, Stephan 178
Propp, William 115, 117, 118

Quli Qarai, Ali 167

Rabad, the (Rabbi Abraham ben David) 131, 133
Rabbi Akiva 116
Rabbi Shimon bar Yoḥai 116, 154
Rabbi Yishmael 116, 117, 127
Rahman, Fazlur 178, 179
Rashbam 128, 129
Rashi 116, 129
Ratzinger, Joseph 93, 98, 103, 138
Reeves, John 151
Regev, Eyal 134
Reines, Alvin 108
Rendtorff, Rolf 122
Retsö, Jan 178
Reynier, Chantal 188
Reynolds, Gabriel Said 172, 174, 178
Riaudel, Olivier 47
Richardson, Ernest 156
Richelle, Matthieu 1, 3, 4, 44, 51, 52, 62
Ricoeur, Paul 87, 88

Ringgren, Helmer 134
Rofé, Alexander 129
Rom-Shiloni, Dalit 26, 27
Rosenblum, Henry 112
Rosenzweig, Franz 5, 87, 88, 104–108, 110, 111, 113, 120, 136, 148
Rosett, Arthur 106, 120
Ross, Tamar 107, 110
Rowland, Tracey 92, 93, 95
Rowley, Harold 103, 104
Ryssel, Victor 116, 122

Samuelson, Norbert 88, 107, 109, 110
Sarna, Nahum 117
Sauvage, Baptiste 23
Savran, George 126
Schechter, Solomon 138
Scheeben, Matthias 94
Schelling, Friedriech 89, 90, 91
Schenker, Adrian 16, 53
Schleiermacher, Friedrich 102, 103
Schmid, Konrad 2, 3, 19, 20, 25, 30, 31, 34, 35, 74, 122
Scholem, Gershom 115
Schwartz, Baruch 122, 128, 132–135
Seeligmann, Isac 116, 126
Seeskin, Kenneth 102, 125
Senior, Donald 161
Silman, Yochanan 109
Simon, Ernst 108
Simon, Uriel 108
Ska, Jean-Louis 29
Smend, Rudolf 28
Smith, Mark 125
Smith, Wilfred 137
Söding, Thomas 97
Solomon, Norman 42
Sommer, Benjamin 2, 5, 13, 26, 27, 90, 91, 101, 110, 115, 122–124, 126, 127, 134–136, 148, 152, 161, 167, 179
Sonnet, Jean-Pierre 132
Spinoza, Baruch 102
Stackert, Jeffrey 122
Standaert, Benoît 188–190
Steck, Odil 74
Stoellger, Philipp 84
Stone, Michael 150

Suarez, Francisco  92, 93, 95
Sweeney, Marvin  26, 27

Tatian  151
Tekoniemi, Timo  45
Tengour, Esma Hind  169, 170
Tertullian  151–154, 157
Theobald, Christoph  195, 196
Thomas, William  103
Thurén, Lauri  149, 161
Tillich, Paul  101, 104, 105, 107, 121, 124
Toeg, Aryeh  115, 119
Tov, Emanuel  44
Tucker, Miika  45
Tupper, Richard  115
Turner, Denys  23

Ulrich, Eugene  44

Valinho Gomes, Pedro  6
Van der Toorn, Karel  125
VanBeek, Lawrence  154
VanderKam, James  151, 152, 155
Venard, Olivier-Thomas  47, 50, 51

Viezel, Eran  109, 110
Von Kühn, Johannes  91
Von Rad, Gerhard  27, 35, 103, 124
Voorwinde, Stephen  16

Wagner, Andreas  35
Waldenfels, Hans  93
Ward, Keith  103, 105, 134, 135
Watson, Francis  84
Watson, Frederick  103
Webb, Robert  149
Webster, John  97
Weinfeld, Moshe  124, 130
Weiss Halivni, David  130
Wellhausen, Julius  122, 124
Wheeler Robinson, Henri  103
Wicks, Jared  95
Wolfson, Elliott  108

Yoshiko-Reed, Annette  151, 152, 154

Zahn, Molly  49, 53
Zielinski, Agata  15
Zumstein, Jean  188

www.ingramcontent.com/pod-product-compliance
Lightning Source LLC
Chambersburg PA
CBHW020231170426
43201CB00007B/394